ON THE EDGES OF HISTORY
A Memoir of Law, Books and Politics

About the Author

Michael Sexton has degrees in law from the universities of Melbourne and Virginia. After some years as an academic lawyer and writer, he commenced practice as a barrister in the mid-1980s, taking silk in 1998. He currently holds the position of Solicitor-General for New South Wales. He has been chairman of the NSW State Rail Authority and a board member of the NSW Public Transport Authority, the NSW State Library, the Sydney Writers' Festival and the University of Technology. He is the author of a number of legal texts and several books on politics and history, including:

Illusions of Power: The fate of a reform government (reissued as *The Great Crash: The short life and sudden death of the Whitlam government*)

War for the Asking: Australia's Vietnam Secrets (reissued as *War for the Asking: How Australia invited itself to Vietnam*)

The Regulation of Foreign Investment in Australia (with Alexander Adamovich)

The Legal Mystique: The role of lawyers in Australian society (with Laurence W Maher)

Australian Eyes Only

Australian Defamation Law and Practice (with T K Tobin QC)

Uncertain Justice: Inside Australia's Legal System

ON THE EDGES OF HISTORY

A Memoir of Law, Books and Politics

Michael Sexton

Connor Court Publishing

Connor Court Publishing Pty Ltd

Copyright © Michael Sexton 2015

ALL RIGHTS RESERVED. This book contains material protected under International and Federal Copyright Laws and Treaties. Any unauthorised reprint or use of this material is prohibited. No part of this book may be reproduced or transmitted in any form or by any means, electronic or mechanical, including photocopying, recording, or by any information storage and retrieval system without express written permission from the publisher.

PO Box 224W
Ballarat VIC 3350
sales@connorcourt.com
www.connorcourt.com

ISBN: 978-1-925138-64-1

Cover design by Ian James, cover photo by Peter Jones

Inside photos: Page 118 (Besford/Fairfax Syndication), Page 132 (Fairfax Syndication) Page 230 (Rice/Fairfax Syndication)

Printed in Australia

CONTENTS

1 Solicitor-General: Centre Stage in the Law	1
2 The Way We Lived Then: A Child of the 1950s	27
3 Crime and Punishment: Counsel for the Prosecution	56
4 Outward Bound: Melbourne to Washington	73
5 The Great Crash: Inside the Whitlam Government	98
6 Publish and Be Damned: Re-writing History	124
7 Man and Machine: The World of Politics	153
8 Meet the Mystique: Taking on the Bar	183
9 The Human Factor: Victims of Law and Medicine	207
10 Free Speech: Theory and Practice	231
Endnotes	251
Acknowledgements	259
Index	261

1

SOLICITOR-GENERAL
Centre Stage in the Law

"It's the best job going in the law". This was Mary Gaudron on being Solicitor-General for New South Wales. She did not hesitate, nevertheless, to leave the job in 1986 to become the first woman to be a justice of the High Court. But the High Court was a position that no lawyer would refuse. It always seemed to me that Mary was right about the post of Solicitor-General. So, when it was offered to me towards the end of 1998, I jumped at the opportunity, aware, however, that not everyone in the legal world would welcome my appointment. I had been at the Bar for fourteen years but I had also been an academic and a writer – not a traditional path to this post.

The job does not carry the same financial rewards as the private Bar. But it means dealing with all the big issues in law and government. The title does not, however, say much about the role. Indeed, it is inherently confusing because the Solicitor-General is always a barrister. The office has its origins in England of the 15th century where, as still today in New South Wales, the Solicitor-General was the Second Law Officer of the Crown, with the Attorney-General being the First Law Officer. In Australia, there is a Commonwealth Solicitor-General, one for each State and each of the two Territories. There is a Solicitor-General in Britain (where, however, he or she is a member of the House of Commons), New Zealand and the United States, although their roles vary somewhat from each other and from the Australian model.

In all these cases, the Solicitor-General is basically the government's chief legal adviser. In theory, this is the role of the Attorney-General but in recent years it has become unusual for members of parliament to have any other real career before politics. So it is much less likely today for the Attorney-General to be someone who has practised the law for any length of time. In any case, the electoral and parliamentary duties of the Attorney-General leave little real time for attending to court or working on legal advices.

As it happened, the Attorney-General who took my appointment to the Cabinet – Jeff Shaw – had practised as a successful silk at the Bar before entering politics. I did not work with Shaw for long. He stood down as Attorney-General in 2000 and, after a brief return to the Bar, was appointed as a judge of the Supreme Court of New South Wales in 2003. This was in the face of gossip in the legal world that he had a serious drinking problem. I had never seen it personally but I had certainly heard some dramatic eyewitness accounts of Shaw being carried out of social functions. In 2004 he was involved in a motor vehicle accident near his home and was taken to a nearby hospital. Blood samples were taken – one for the police and one for Shaw – but both left the hospital with Shaw. Ultimately the police sample was returned and disclosed a very high blood alcohol level. Shortly afterwards Shaw resigned from the Supreme Court. The NSW Police Integrity Commission held an inquiry to these events. The findings were inconclusive and the Director of Public Prosecutions decided not to bring any charges against him. But all this took a huge toll and Shaw died in 2010 at the age of 60. It is hard to imagine that some of the people involved in his appointment to the Supreme Court were not aware of the risks involved in making him a judge but, as with so many aspects of the law, these risks were never mentioned in the accounts of Shaw's career and its sad conclusion.

In New South Wales the Solicitor-General usually appears for the State in all cases before the High Court involving questions of constitutional law and in many other cases – civil or criminal – where the State is a party and has a significant interest at stake. These kinds of cases can also be found in the NSW Court of Appeal as well as in the Federal Court. In my early years as Solicitor-General there were, on the civil side, for example, cases about the liability of the State for sexual assaults on students by teachers and for the conduct of prison escapees who committed crimes after breaking out of gaol.[1] On the criminal side, there were cases about what reference can be made in a trial to the accused's failure to go into the witness box and others about the way DNA evidence can be put to a jury.[2]

For many of the years after the Second World War, the major constitutional cases before the High Court were disputes between the States and the Commonwealth about the allocation of powers in the Constitution between these two spheres. In recent times, however, there have been very few of these kinds of disputes. The only major confrontation between the States and the Commonwealth during the last decade was the challenge to the Howard government's industrial relations legislation, Work Choices, in 2006. I thought that the challenge was hopeless because the legislation was based on the Commonwealth's power to regulate the affairs of corporations and there were a number of decisions of the court that strongly indicated an expansive reading of this power. But all the States had Labor governments and they were determined to go ahead, largely at the insistence of their union allies who thought –

probably wrongly – that they would be disadvantaged by the new legislation. My view was not an especially acute legal judgment as many law students could have given the same opinion. So I found myself putting arguments to the High Court that I thought were a waste of time. This only happened very occasionally and there was no point in complaining – it was part of the job. The States lost but less than twelve months later the Howard government was voted out of office and the legislation was changed significantly.[3]

This was a one-off case. It is much more common in the High Court to see private litigants arguing that no government – State or Commonwealth – has the power to regulate, for example, political advertising on television, because of a guarantee of freedom of speech under the Constitution, or gambling across State borders, because of the Constitution's requirement of freedom of interstate trade. The Solicitors-General for the Commonwealth and the States, for their part, are likely to be there arguing that one or both levels of government does, indeed, have this power.

Such consensus at the Bar table does not, however, make the judges of the High Court any easier to confront. On major cases all seven judges sit, often interrupting each other to fire questions at the barrister standing below at the lectern in the centre of the long Bar table. That lectern is one of the loneliest spots in the legal world. It revives all the terrors of the classroom; experienced silks can be reduced to incoherence under this onslaught. The number of judges that normally sit in any other appeal court is three; the High Court can be by far the most intimidating forum in the country.

The other major part of a Solicitor-General's job is giving legal advice. Requests for advice can come from the Attorney-General or other ministers, and from departments and government agencies. Often the question might be one of statutory interpretation, particularly whether a government body has the power to do something that it wants to do under legislation, but almost any area of law might arise, such as contract, taxation, superannuation, charitable trusts or mining law.

Traditionally the Governor in New South Wales and in some of the other States has asked the Solicitor-General for independent advice if he or she is concerned about the legality of a government decision that has to be signed into law by the Governor. This could put the Solicitor-General in a difficult position. It would obviously be embarrassing if its own chief legal adviser suggested that the government's actions were illegal. The government might well take the view that the Governor was required under the Westminster system to accept the recommendation of the Cabinet. This was one of the hotly disputed questions arising in the dismissal of the Whitlam government in 1975 when the Governor-General consulted a number of lawyers outside the government, including the Chief Justice, Sir Garfield Barwick, without informing the Prime Minister or the Attorney-General. It has not, however, been a difficulty in New South Wales in recent years. If the Governor sought advice from the Solicitor-General, the government never raised any objection.

There was a political crisis – although not like 1975 – in New South Wales in 2009 when a second Premier, Nathan Rees, was deposed by his own party a little more than a year after Morris Iemma, Bob Carr's successor, had suffered the same fate. This led to public calls for the government to be dismissed by the Governor. The *Sydney Morning Herald* reported that the Governor, Professor Marie Bashir, had sought my advice on all this turmoil.[4] The press reports noted, however, that unless a government loses a vote of confidence on the floor of the Legislative Assembly, there is really no way an early election can be called.

When the Attorney-General is out of New South Wales, the Solicitor-General carries out almost all his or her functions.[5] This is an unusual arrangement. In other States and at Commonwealth level one of the other ministers is appointed to play this role. Even when the Attorney-General is in New South Wales, he or she usually delegates a range of functions to the Solicitor-General. The most controversial of these is deciding what contempt of court prosecutions are to proceed, either against the media for publishing material that has interfered with a criminal trial or against individuals who have, for example, tried to influence or intimidate members of a jury. It is not surprising that this task has been delegated. Any politician would wish to avoid being the person who decides if the kings and queens of talk-back radio should be prosecuted for their comments about current criminal proceedings.

It is not only politicians who can find themselves in trouble on the question of whether contempt prosecutions should be started. On occasions, judges had complained to the Attorney-General about the lack of prosecutions for contempt. This was a complaint about me in relation to media publications that had been referred to the Attorney-General by judicial officers. Normally these publications were referred by judges in criminal trials who thought that the position of the accused had been prejudiced by the publication. Sometimes the judge had aborted the trial on the basis that nothing he or she could say to the jury could undo the damage done to the accused's case. While I thought that the law of contempt should be modernised, in deciding whether a prosecution should take place, I had applied the law as it stood. Some judges were also sensitive about talkback radio presenters who criticised their decisions but I took the view that proceedings should not normally be instituted in these circumstances on the basis that judicial officers were paid to resist these pressures and it was reasonable to assume that they would resist them.

Shortly before I had taken the job of Solicitor-General, I was asked by one of the book publishers for whom I frequently provided legal advice whether I would consider a book based on some of the cases that I had been involved in the previous fifteen years. I chose a range of cases that seemed to say something about how the law worked but it was not until October 2000 that the book, *Uncertain Justice: Inside Australia's Legal System*[6], was published. Though aware that it was unusual for a Solicitor-General to write such a book, I was unprepared for the storm that broke when the book was released. Much of the publicity surrounded one short passage, not something that I had intended to highlight.

I had set out some cases involving the police, and then referred to the question of police corruption, largely a consequence of the huge funds available to drug traffickers. I then wrote:

> There is a multiplier effect here because, at the same time as the illegal drug industry has weakened police capacity, it has caused sharp rises in the occurrence of certain crimes, such as housebreaking and armed robbery. Housebreaking, for example, has been effectively decriminalised in Sydney, in the sense that it is frequently not reported, seldom investigated and hardly ever the occasion of conviction and imprisonment. Some of these increases in criminal activity are the result of long-term social changes, including the breakdown of traditional families and population pressures in some urban areas.
>
> This is particularly true in Sydney where the incidence of many crimes, including both armed robbery and unarmed robbery, are three and four times higher than in Melbourne and even further ahead of the other capital cities. But there can be little doubt that the financing of drug purchases is also a significant factor in all parts of the country. This raises the controversial question whether all drug use should be decriminalised. This would certainly destroy the industry's inflated price structure which is largely based upon the legal unavailability of the drugs.[7]

The day before the book's launch, Tony Stephens wrote a piece in the *Sydney Morning Herald* under the headline "Sexton, drugs and the courts' role." Stephens quoted these passages but set the stage at the very start of the article:

> A new book by the NSW Solicitor-General will startle his more conservative colleagues.
>
> Housebreaking has been decriminalised. People who have had their houses burgled had long suspected this, of course. Now Michael Sexton, NSW Solicitor-General, makes it semi-official.[8]

Naturally I wanted publicity for the book but not quite in this form. The level of crime in New South Wales and the way it is dealt with by the police are always contentious political issues. What I had said could embarrass the government if it was picked up by the Opposition. All this was made worse because the Premier, Bob Carr, was due to launch the book the next day.

When Carr rose to give his speech, I waited nervously to hear what he would say, especially as I knew that he had a very strong view that drug use should *not* be decriminalised. There was no mention of housebreaking or drugs. He spoke about litigation not being an answer to social problems, one of the themes of the book. I knew that our long friendship had led Carr to put aside his normal political reactions when a member of his staff later gave me a copy of the speech that had been written for him. It was not the speech that he had delivered. The one prepared for him did mention drugs and housebreaking and set out some figures designed to rebut my statements in the book.

I assumed that these figures had been provided by the NSW Bureau of Crime Statistics. When they were not used by Carr, the Bureau's director, Don Weatherburn, wrote an article published in the *Sydney Morning Herald* which appeared two days later. Under the heading, "There's more to fighting crime that filling jails", Weatherburn referred to the housebreaking issue:

> Views of this kind are so common they would be unremarkable were they not espoused by the State's second most senior law officer. In his case they betray a lamentable grasp of the facts on crime and sentencing.[9]

Weatherburn was clearly angry. He did, however, concede that the clear-up rate for the offence of housebreaking was only between five and six percent and that less than two percent of burglaries led to a prison sentence. It remains true that household break-ins are really only reported to police because this is necessary before making an insurance claim. There is no suggestion that most of these reports will ever be followed up by the police.

There was something of an irony in this exchange as the Bureau's own figures showed the levels of crime in New South Wales were very high in comparison to those of Western countries. As I had observed in *Uncertain Justice*, these figures are not the fault of particular governments – although some have done more than others to deal with the problem – but derive from social changes, particularly during the previous two decades. One social change, however, has probably reduced the incidence of housebreaking, given the flooding of the market with cheap consumer goods of all types, including computers, phones, televisions and stereo systems, over the last decade. Cash and jewellery hold their places as the most sought-after object of burglaries.

What I found striking, however, in the job of Solicitor-General, where I could not help being aware of the prevalence of crimes, like housebreaking and street assaults, that most affected ordinary members of the community, was that many – not all – members of the legal profession and law schools refused to admit these facts. It is certainly true that they generally live in the wealthiest suburbs where crime is a relatively rare occurrence. But this is a view that seems to ignore the evidence of official figures and many reports. It is also a view that is completely divorced from the experience of the general community.

A related matter that highlights this discrepancy of views is the sentencing of persons convicted of murder and other violent crimes. A good example is the offence of armed robbery. This is a particularly anti-social crime because of the lasting psychological effects on the victims – even assuming that they are not killed or seriously injured – who are often persons working alone in convenience stores or gas stations late at night. The Crimes Act provided for a sentence of up to 25 years for armed robbery, although the usual sentence was between four and five years (which meant perhaps three and a half years before eligibility for parole).

In 2002 the NSW government proposed changes to the existing sentencing legislation to set out standard non-parole periods for a range of offences, including murder and armed robbery. The trial judge would still have considerable discretion to move from the standard figure in any particular case.[10] This new legislation, which was ultimately passed, was opposed by every section of the legal establishment – the Bar Association, the Law Society, the NSW Young Lawyers, the Legal Aid Commission, even the Director of Public Prosecutions. The previous year the Bar Association had complained publicly that politicians on both sides in New South Wales were "engaged in a poll-driven scramble to propose increasingly vicious laws and sentencing regimes." The Bar's statement spoke about the "fate of the unpopular and oppressed in countries such as South Africa under apartheid, Chile and Argentina under military rule and Nazi Germany."

This was a revealing statement because it seemed to reflect a view – not only found in the legal profession – that the criminal justice system represents some kind of danger to ordinary members of the community who might at any time fall within its clutches. In fact, it is mostly concerned with a relatively small but still significant section of the community who are professional criminals from late childhood until the end of their lives. This does not mean that they should not have a fair trial or be treated humanely if imprisoned. But the problem for law enforcement bodies is how to protect society from this group. Those bodies do not pose any threat to ordinary members of the community. The problem of how to stop or reduce this cycle of criminality in the first place can often be the subject of social and economic policies by other areas of government.

This apparent incapacity to understand the need for law enforcement was illustrated by a statement issued by the NSW Council for Civil Liberties (CCL) in May 2004. This was an organisation that I had been deeply involved with at one time, serving on its governing committee in the late 1970s and early 1980s. But it now complained that the number of listening device warrants approved in 2002 was higher than the number in 2001. Under NSW legislation it is necessary for the police and other law enforcement bodies to apply to a judge of the Supreme Court for approval to install a listening device – usually in a house or car or on the body of a wired informer.[11] It is also necessary to obtain a warrant to intercept telephone calls but this is done under federal legislation.

The CCL had said:

> These figures prove that there is very little difference between *Big Brother* on TV and Big Brother in the community.
> It's an alarming increase in surveillance and people need to be aware that we are in danger of becoming a police state . . .

Invasion of innocent people's privacy should be done only as a last resort.

I knew these comments were nonsense because I was well aware of how applications for listening device warrants were dealt with. Under the NSW legislation details of the application have to be provided to the Attorney-General so that he or she could object to the warrant being granted.[12] This was another function of the Attorney-General that had been delegated to the Solicitor-General and, unless I was out of town, I would always see this material. The legislation provides that an application is only to be made if the police or other agency making it suspect that a criminal offence has been or is likely to be committed and that the use of a listening device is necessary to investigate that offence or obtain evidence of its being committed.[13] The warrant will not be granted unless the judge who hears the application is satisfied that there are reasonable grounds for that suspicion.

It is obvious that discussions of their plans by criminals are only likely to take place when they believe those conversations are private. That is why telephone interceptions and listening devices are an important part of investigations by law enforcement agencies. The safeguards set out in the legislation suggest that there is no real possibility of it being directed against law-abiding members of the community, although it is hard to imagine why the police or other bodies in this area would want to waste their time and resources on persons whom they do not suspect of being involved in a criminal offence.

Apart from their hostility to more effective means of crime investigation, like listening devices or DNA evidence, the most striking feature of many legal bodies is their indifference to the victims of crime. This is, indeed, a problem of the entire criminal justice system. Early in 2002 Sir John Stevens, Commissioner of the Metropolitan Police in London, made an emotional attack on this system:

> The fact is that, all too often, the criminal trial is simply an uneven game of tactics played out by lawyers in front of an uninformed jury with the disillusioned victims and a bemused defendant looking on . . . We let the very people for whom the whole system of criminal justice owes its existence, and upon whom it relies, to get treated with what most people would regard as utter contempt.[14]

Though an overstatement, it reflects the view of many victims – amongst those who survive – and their families of their own experiences. This is partly because in most criminal trials much material that would be very damaging to the accused, including his or her previous convictions, is kept from the jury, although everyone else – the judge and the lawyers on both sides – is aware of it. This is naturally very frustrating to victims and their families in, for example, cases where the accused is charged with rape or a serious assault and has a long history of similar conduct. In addition, the dynamic of a criminal trial tends to overlook the victim. The prosecution sets out its version of events but does not normally attack the character of the accused. The defence may not dispute what happened but might call a great deal of evidence designed to diminish the responsibility of the accused, for example, because of the influence of alcohol, drugs, depression or abuse as a child. It is a common reaction of victims and their families to feel that the accused is the chief object of sympathy in the courtroom. Chief Justice Phillips of the Victorian Supreme Court commented in 2003:

> ... apart from an objective description of the circumstances of the offence by the Crown Prosecutor, practically the whole of the sentencing proceedings was taken up by addressing the interests of the offender.

... I have detailed these matters, not in a spirit of personal criticism [of the sentencing judge], but to illustrate my belief that, currently, too many sentencing proceedings give the appearance that the interests of victims and their loved ones are not being sufficiently addressed.[15]

Some prosecutors make an extended effort to inform victims and their families about why a criminal trial takes the form that it does, but, from my own experiences in the NSW Court of Criminal Appeal, I know that it is not easy to explain the way the victim disappears from view.

The so-called "Green mango murder" was one such experience in the Court of Criminal Appeal. In February 1997 David Laxdale, who lived with his wife and two young children in western Sydney, heard a noise outside his home one night. When he went outside to look, he found four young men taking mangoes from a tree in the garden and chased them into the street. He was punched, kicked, then stabbed to death. One of the young men – who has to be called T because he was just under 18 at the time – was charged with his murder.

In March 1999 T was convicted of the murder of David Laxdale after evidence from the other three assailants. He denied at the trial that he knew that Laxdale had been stabbed at all. The prosecution was able to show, however, that he had gone into hiding almost immediately after the killing and had given a false name to the police on two occasions while on the run. The prosecution also called evidence that a green mango had been found near the scene of the killing and cut with a knife. T had said in evidence that he had been eating a green mango prior to these events but denied using a knife to cut it.

T appealed to the Court of Criminal Appeal against this conviction. I appeared for the Crown. The chief ground of appeal was that a record of interview given by T to the police – which contained damaging admissions by him – was wrongfully admitted into evidence at the trial. It was not surprising that it was admitted because the defence did not raise any objection to it at that time. In the Court of Criminal Appeal, however, it was argued that T was just over 17½ years old when the interview was given – although he had told the police that he was 18 – and, under NSW legislation, a statement by a person under 18 was not admissible, except when an adult effectively representing the under-age person was present at the interview (unless the court considered that there was a good reason for an adult not to be present).[16] The appeal was allowed and a new trial ordered on the basis that there was a significant possibility that, if this objection to the interview had been raised at the trial, it would have been excluded.[17] The victim's family were completely bewildered by this result. I could only say to them that it was open to the judges of the court to take this approach, although I had argued they should not do so. The Crown prosecutor who had appeared at the trial, Barry Newport QC, said in a report to the Director of Public Prosecutions that it was "sometime since I have seen an argument succeed with so little merit".

The retrial took place in November 2001. On this occasion, instead of saying – as he had at the first trial – that he did not know the victim had been stabbed when he was attacked, T now said that he had seen one of his companions stabbing Laxdale. The prosecutor wanted to cross-examine T on these different versions but the trial judge said that this would be unfair to T – even though one of the two versions must have been false.

Nevertheless T was convicted of murder again. There was another appeal to the Court of Criminal Appeal. The chief ground of appeal arose out of evidence at the second trial – given by one of the other attackers – that T had called a friend on his mobile phone shortly after the killing and said, "I stabbed somebody". The friend was not called as a witness by either side and it was argued for T that he should have been called by the prosecutor and that the trial judge wrongly directed the jury on this question. The three judges of the Court of Criminal Appeal accepted this argument, although the Chief Justice said that his mind had "fluctuated on this issue".[18] I did not argue the second appeal for the Crown. I certainly did not envy the task of the person who did and then had to try to explain to the Laxdale family what had happened.

So there was a third trial, in July 2004. On this occasion T did not give any version of what had happened. Some of the other young men, who had previously given evidence, were no longer in Australia or could not be found. The result was that T was found not guilty by the jury. So David Laxdale had been stabbed to death outside his home and no one – although one of the attackers must have been responsible – was ever convicted of any offence in relation to his death. His family had sat through three lengthy trials and two hearings in the Court of Criminal Appeal. It is hard to imagine that they had any faith left in the legal system.

The unreality of some areas of the criminal law was graphically illustrated by a case that I unsuccessfully argued for the Director of Public Prosecutions in the High Court in 2001. The accused had been convicted of bank robbery. A security camera was running during the robbery and showed the four intruders with varying degrees of clarity. Two police officers gave evidence at the trial that they knew the accused and recognised him as one of the persons caught by the security camera. One of the police officers had seen the accused half a dozen times in his local neighbourhood in the six months preceding the robbery and spoken to him on at least three of these occasions. The other police officer had often spoken to the accused in the street. He had also arrested him twice and spent several hours in his company.

After his conviction, the accused appealed to the NSW Court of Criminal Appeal on a number of grounds but these all failed. He was then granted special leave to appeal to the High Court. Soon after the case started in Canberra, I realised that our side was in trouble. A number of the judges suggested that the evidence of the police officers should not have been admitted to the trial because it was simply irrelevant to any of the issues. This had never occurred to the trial judge, to the three judges of the Court of Criminal Appeal nor to any of the lawyers on either side who had appeared before these courts below. Nevertheless four judges of the High Court took this view and the appeal was allowed and a new trial ordered.[19] One judge considered that the police officers' evidence was relevant to the question of whether the accused was one of the four bank robbers – a conclusion that seems obvious but was rejected by his four colleagues.

It may have been better at the trial if the prosecution had just let the jury compare the security photos with the person sitting in the dock. But the prosecution lawyers may have been worried about the quality of the photos and thought that it would be useful to have evidence from local police officers who were very familiar with what the accused looked like. At any rate, this was an example of the truism that the prosecution has to win on every point at every stage whereas the defence only has to succeed on one at the trial or on appeal. There was a retrial but the verdict was not guilty.

All these trials were conducted before a jury but the issues on appeal were about directions of law or decisions to admit evidence given by the trial judge. In 2004, by contrast, I was involved in a number of cases where the conduct of the jury itself was the issue. The first of these was something of a legal saga even before any question was raised about one of the jurors.

In 1991 Thomas Keir had been tried for the murder of his second wife who had been burnt to death in a fire at their house. He was acquitted. He was later charged with the murder of his first wife, who had disappeared, after a number of bones were discovered buried under the foundations of his house. He was tried on the second charge of murder in 1999 and convicted. The conviction was, however, quashed by the Court of Criminal Appeal and a retrial ordered on the ground that the trial judge had explained the DNA evidence about the bones incorrectly to the jury.[20] I appeared for the Crown in the Court of Criminal Appeal and so became familiar with the case.

The retrial took place in 2002. Keir was again convicted. There was another appeal to the Court of Criminal Appeal. The ground of appeal was that some members of the jury had looked up Keir on the internet and seen that he had been tried – and acquitted – on the charge of killing his second wife. This had come to light because a number of the jurors had a conversation at the end of the trial in the hotel opposite the court with the defence barrister. I appeared again for the Crown in the Court of Criminal Appeal, although I knew that the appeal would almost certainly be allowed. It was and a third trial on this charge – the accused's fourth murder trial in total – was ordered.[21]

Each of these trials had taken two to three months. The case raises a real question as to whether juries can be isolated from the internet, now that it is available in almost every household and on most mobile phones. In its judgment in this case, the Court of Criminal Appeal suggested that these kinds of inquiries by members of a jury should be made a criminal offence and this was done in 2004.[22] Other judges have suggested that jurors may have to be confined together as soon as a trial starts – as they were in earlier periods – and not be allowed to go home at the end of each day. Given that this particular trial went for some months and that major drug trials might last much longer, this last suggestion hardly seems practical.

The reality is that, if a jury cannot be relied on to follow the instructions of the trial judge to decide the case on the evidence before them, the present system cannot work. There has been some research done in the United States that supports the theory that, once a trial starts, jurors do focus on what they see and hear in the courtroom rather than on earlier media coverage of the case.[23] Because the United States has no law of contempt as it is known in Britain or Australia, juries there are often aware of much more apparently prejudicial material about the accused than in this country. It is possible for an American court to say that an accused cannot receive a fair trial because of the amount of adverse media publicity but it is a very rare occurrence.[24] Yet no one in the United States has suggested that this makes the criminal justice system unworkable. It seems unlikely that courts or governments in Australia will be able to stop the tide of information that is running over the whole of society, including members of juries, and, like King Canute, they may be unwise to try.

In 2004 Keir was tried for a third time – before a judge alone (to which he agreed). He was convicted yet again. He appealed to the Court of Criminal Appeal. I appeared again for the Crown. The appeal was dismissed and the saga finally ended.[25]

Another case at about the same time suggested that juries are no longer always prepared to accept the version of events given by the lawyers and the trial judge. This trial was one of a number in 2002 that had their origins in a wave of sexual assaults that took place in south-western Sydney a few years earlier. There was no doubt that a whole group of young women had been raped at different times by gangs of young Lebanese men and these events had received enormous publicity. But the question at the trials was still whether those who had been charged were the persons who carried out the sexual assaults.

In one of these cases the accused were two brothers. One was charged with bringing the victim to a park and the other being one of the men who arrived soon afterwards and raped her. There was no dispute that the first brother had driven the victim to the park but he denied that he had called the others and the second brother denied the sexual assault. The second brother had been identified by the victim, initially from a collection of photos and then later in person when he attended court. At one point in the trial the prosecution called evidence about the lighting in the park. It is hard to see why this evidence was introduced. It is true that the events took place at night but the victim was obviously at very close quarters with whoever assaulted her. But this evidence had far-reaching consequences. Both brothers were convicted and they appealed to the Court of Criminal Appeal.

A year and a half later, and after the appeal had been heard but before the judgment had been handed down, the foreman of the jury struck up a conversation with a country solicitor at a barbecue in Sydney. He talked about the trial and how he and another juror had visited the park one night to inspect the scene of the crime. The solicitor reported this conversation to the authorities and the brothers were allowed to add a new ground of appeal based on the conduct of the two jurors. It turned out that they wanted to see what the lighting at the park was like at night. One problem with their inspection, however, was that there was no guarantee that the lighting was the same as on the night of the assaults, even if the lighting had any relevance in the first place. Another problem was that neither side could put any arguments about what the jurors had seen at the park because they did not know of the visit.

Although the prosecution and defence were both represented by lawyers when the Court of Criminal Appeal reconvened to hear this ground of appeal, the court asked that the Solicitor-General appear as well. There was, however, little I could say in opposition to the argument that the convictions should be quashed and that there would have to be a new trial. There would have been no problem if the whole jury had asked to see the scene of the crime and been taken there by the trial judge and the lawyers for both sides. But they had to make the request during the trial and that had not happened.

The convictions were quashed and a new trial ordered.[26] The Court of Criminal Appeal suggested that the directions given to a jury by a trial judge should underline that the case had to be decided on the evidence heard at the trial and not on any external matters. I had said that they could be told that they should bring anything unusual about other members of the jury to the attention of the trial judge but that this direction had to be given carefully because otherwise some members might take this as an invitation to complain if their views about the case were rejected by their colleagues.

The court had previously expressed the view that it should be a criminal offence for a juror to make enquiries – over the internet or any other way – about the accused in a criminal trial. It now added that this offence should be expanded to include any private visits or inspections by members of a jury. Legislation in 2004 incorporated these additions. But making this kind of conduct a criminal offence ensures that it is much less likely that a juror will admit that it happened at all. This might mean that, although there has been a serious irregularity in the jury's verdict, it never comes to light. As suggested earlier, the criminal justice system operates on the assumption that the juries will follow the instructions of the trial judge and decide the case only on the evidence before them. If that assumption cannot be relied on, then the system itself needs to be changed. My own view was that it can normally be relied on and that the exceptional cases, such as the visit to the park, were not a reason to make juries subject to a range of criminal offences.

This case illustrates how juries are more questioning of the legal system than they were in the past. This poses a particular problem in criminal trials because members of the jury do often realise that everyone else in court is aware of information that has been kept from them. There are sometimes good legal reasons why this is so but it is easy to see how it can be frustrating for jurors. One particular piece of information that is currently kept from jurors is the record of any previous convictions of the person on trial. There has always been some limited scope for the prosecution to lead evidence of earlier convictions where, for example, the way in which a previous bank robbery was carried out by the accused is so strikingly similar to the one with which he is now charged. But in general a jury will not know that a person charged with, for example, sexual assault has a series of convictions for crimes of the same kind. In might be thought obvious that the question of whether the accused has a propensity to commit offences of the kind with which he is charged has at least some relevance to his guilt or innocence on the current charge. But most sections of the legal profession have always fiercely resisted this kind of evidence being available to a jury. It is, however, much more readily available to a jury in Britain under legislation in that country.[27] In March 2013, Paul de Jersey, then Chief Justice of the Supreme Court of Queensland, said that the British position should be adopted in Australia:

> Why, for example, should a jury be denied knowledge that an alleged rapist committed another rape six months earlier, subject to appropriate warning from the judge, or that an accused charged with fraud has a string of convictions for dishonesty ... I trust the intelligence and wisdom of my fellow citizens. I do not accept a claim that, made aware of prior misconduct, jurors would automatically say: "He did that so he must have done this."

It is hard to see what real objection there could be to this change in the existing Australian law.

Another problem confronting the criminal justice system in recent years is how to deal with organised crime, that is, organisations specifically established to engage in widespread criminal conduct, most particularly the so-called motorcycle gangs.

Legislation intended to deal with the role of organised crime was enacted in New South Wales in 2009.[28] This allowed the Commissioner of Police to apply to a judge of the Supreme Court for a declaration that an organisation represented a risk to public safety and order because its members associate for the purpose of engaging in serious criminal activity. If this kind of declaration was made, the Commissioner could then apply again to the Supreme Court for a control order in relation to the members of the organisation which would effectively prevent them from associating with one another. It was obvious from the start, however, that the legislation would be challenged because the organisations affected were well-financed with access to high-powered lawyers.

But the first challenge came not to the NSW laws but to a similar statute in South Australia.[29] The challenge was brought by the Finks Motorcycle Club and found its way to the High Court in mid-2010.[30] The South Australian legislation also allowed the court to make control orders against criminal organisations but the initial declaration of the organisation was made by the State Attorney-General. The South Australian Solicitor-General appeared to defend the legislation and, along with the Solicitors-General from all States and Territories, except Tasmania and the ACT, I went to Canberra to support the South Australians. We were not successful. A majority of the High Court struck down the legislation on the basis that it undermined the independent status of the court making the control orders by giving the appearance that it was simply putting into effect the decision already made by the Attorney-General.

Most of us were back in Canberra a few weeks later for the challenge to the NSW legislation. This challenge had been brought by the Hells Angels Motorcycle Club.[31] The NSW statute did not have the same problem as the South Australian legislation because the initial declaration was made by a judge and not by the Attorney-General. This time a majority of the High Court said that there was a different problem about the declaration – the legislation did not state that the judge had to give reasons for this decision and this was inconsistent with the role of a judge. I thought the legislation assumed that reasons would normally be given and I put this to the court but it was rejected.

We had lost but on something of a technical point and one that could be very easily fixed by the addition of a few words to the relevant part of the legislation. This was done early in 2012 but I assumed that at some stage there would be another challenge anyway. There were, however, a number of other candidates for a challenge as Queensland, Western Australia and the Northern Territory had by then enacted similar legislation concerning criminal organisations and South Australia had produced a new version of the statute that had been struck down by the High Court.

The challenge came in the High Court to the Queensland legislation late in 2012 by the Finks Motorcycle Club. The Club complained that under this legislation criminal intelligence material compiled by the police could be seen and relied on by a court but not by the members themselves. These provisions of the legislation were upheld by the court, although with strong suggestions that they could not be used in a way that was unfair to the members of the organisation.[32]

These decisions demonstrated the difficulties that law enforcement bodies often faced in the courts. When *The Legal Mystique*, a study of the Australian legal profession by Laurence Maher and myself, was published in 1981, one of the book's complaints was that judges were drawn from not just a narrow section of the community but from a very confined group within the legal profession. It is true that thirty years later there is more diversity on the bench, not least because there are much greater numbers of judges and appointments of women have become very common. Nevertheless, most judges have led relatively sheltered lives, growing up in comfortable families, attending good schools, making a lot of money in the law and settling in the best parts of town. So it would be unusual for them to have ever been the victims of crime. They do sometimes sit on criminal cases but these are often very technical exercises where, as already observed, the victim is far from centre stage. The problem is not that judges have any sympathy for criminal conduct but that the level of violence and brutality is often so far removed from their own experiences that they find it hard to imagine. This caste of mind is sometimes reflected in lenient sentences and sometimes in a suspicion of the activities of law enforcement bodies, including the police. As already suggested, law enforcement agencies pose little threat to most members of the community. Challenges to legislation dealing with criminal conduct are often framed in the language of civil liberties but more often reflect the interest of professional members of the criminal community.

2

THE WAY WE LIVED THEN
A Child of the 1950s

The path to the law – and to everything else – began on 24 September 1946 when I was born in the Mercy Hospital in East Melbourne. It marks me chronologically as one of the first of the post-war baby-boomers. But there was really nothing else about it typical of that generation.

My parents were not a young couple who had married towards the end or just after the war to start a family. My father, Cyril Francis Sexton, was a lawyer in the Commonwealth public service and 45 years of age. More significantly, my mother, born Eileen Dynan, was almost 44. They had been married for almost five and a half years when my mother was surprised, perhaps alarmed, to find herself pregnant for the first time. The possibility of some serious abnormality in the child increases sharply when women move into their forties. But at this time there were no tests in early pregnancy that would disclose this kind of problem. Not that the results of any tests were likely to have been acted on. Even apart from my parents' Catholic beliefs, abortion was a criminal offence. Few law-abiding members of the community would have known how to find a doctor who was prepared to terminate a pregnancy.

The families of both my mother and my father represented the story of Irish migration to Australia in the middle of the 19th century. The Sextons have their base, now as then, in County Clare on the west coast of Ireland. It was one of these, Patrick Sexton, who came to Melbourne in 1852 with his wife, born Ellen O'Connor. One of their six children was John O'Connor Sexton who married Ellen Mooney in 1899. They had two boys, my father and his brother, Gerald.

Ellen Mooney's uncle, Jim, a long-time official of the Australian Workers' Union, was one of the 238 settlers who set sail on 16 July 1893 from Sydney as part of William Lane's expedition to found the colony of New Australia in Paraguay. This utopian venture was the product of a grim period in Australian history. The early 1890s was

John O'Connor Sexton and Ellen Mooney on their wedding day – 19 July 1899

a time of economic depression with wide-spread unemployment and none of today's social welfare provisions. The response of the trade union movement to falls in real wages had been a series of strikes – all of them failures, most spectacularly the shearers' strike in Queensland in 1891 where 200 unionists were charged with conspiracy, intimidation and riot. Most were convicted and twelve of the leaders were sentenced to three years' gaol at hard labour.

The response of some in the union movement to these events was an effort to win seats in parliament with the ultimate aim of forming a government. This led in turn to formation of the Australian Labor Party. Others, however, had despaired of creating a just society in Australia and thought of starting afresh in some foreign land.

Lane, born in England in 1861, came to Australia in 1885. He worked as a journalist and by the end of that decade was editor of the union movement's newspaper in Queensland. In 1891 he obtained a grant of land – 187,000 hectares – from the government of Paraguay. James Mooney was one of Lane's organisers for the expedition. One of his tasks was to go to Tasmania and recruit young single women to join the voyage on *Royal Tar*. He spoke to the Launceston *Examiner* about the past and the future:

> We leave Australia for freedom. The circle of monopoly and usury is closing round this land. The whole conditions of labour are wrong. We believe it is possible to remedy this. We will have no debt or usury in New Australia, no unemployed, no parasites. From each according to his ability, to each according to his need. "Each for all, and all for each", is our motto.[1]

On 10 April 1893 the Sydney *Daily Telegraph* carried an editorial with a dire warning for the single women of Tasmania:

> The promoters of the New Australia scheme are now canvassing Tasmania to obtain single girls for their new

settlement in Paraguay. Whatever may be the intentions of the promoters – and we are quite willing to give them credit for good motives – we regard the proposal to take single girls on such a premature scheme as the very acme of absurdity, and likely to prove disastrous in the extreme to any girl who may be sufficiently foolish to be cajoled into joining the party. . . . to throw a lot of helpless girls on the mercy of the semi-savage world of Paraguay would be an event which for terrible results would have few parallels in the history of colonisation. Paraguay is one of the most unfortunate of the many unfortunate republics of South America. . . . The Paraguayans consist of a comparatively few whites, most of Spanish descent, native Indians and negroes, with a large proportion of a mixture of these three races – producing a people worthless for every purpose excepting plundering, murdering, and warfare of the most brutal character.[2]

James Mooney responded in a lengthy letter to the editor, which was printed by the newspaper. He defended the economic and social conditions of Paraguay and then wrote:

It is gratifying to know that the Tasmanian girls have somebody besides ourselves who take an interest in them. We thank you for giving the promoters of New Australia credit for good intentions. We also venture to submit, respectfully of course, that we not only think it practical as well as sensible to take single girls out to our settlement when we have homes prepared for them, but that they themselves think so, and are steadily joining us, for they know perfectly well that they will find happier homes and better husbands (when they wish to marry) in new Australia than they can ever hope to find in old Australia.[3]

A week before setting off, the settlers were farewelled at a Sunday afternoon meeting in the Sydney Domain. Chaired by John

Christian Watson, who was born in Chile but became Australia's first Labor Prime Minister in 1904, the chief speaker was William Holman, later Premier of New South Wales, whose younger brother was going on the expedition.

Although this was a period of severe economic hardship for many Australians, photos of the settlers on *Royal Tar* do not suggest a group that was down and out. This is not surprising as each male member was required to pay at least £60 – a considerable sum at that time – and those who had greater resources were expected to contribute all of them. Jim Mooney paid more than £200. Some had businesses that were sold; others put up their homes for sale.

The colony was formally established on 28 September 1893. There was no individual ownership of land or other property and no division between employers and employees. All members were to work for the common good. The difficulties of trying to establish a new society in a foreign land would have been formidable in any event but many of the settlers became disenchanted with Lane's autocratic regime, including an insistence on a complete absence of alcoholic drinks.

In mid-1894 Lane and a group of his supporters moved 70 kms south of the initial settlement and started a new colony with the name of Cosme. One of the early settlers at Cosme was the writer Mary Gilmore, then Mary Cameron, and 21 years old. She remained until 1900, marrying a fellow settler, having a child and editing the monthly newspaper. Lane himself resigned as head of the Cosme colony in mid-1899. He settled in New Zealand and became the editor of a conservative New Zealand newspaper until his death in 1917. During the first decade of the two colonies, more then 700 persons lived there at various times. Many ultimately returned to Australia, including Mary Gilmore and James Mooney, although some remained and their descendants are still to be found in that part of Paraguay.

It is easy to look back after more than a century and dismiss those who set off for Paraguay as utopians with no sense of the real world. But it was undeniably a tremendous adventure, and one that took considerable initiative and courage. Although it can be counted a conventional failure for those who left Australia and later returned, they took part in one of the most interesting experiments in modern Australian history and, it may be hoped, never came to regret doing so.

The names on my mother's side tell the same story of Irish migration. She was one of six children born to Michael Dynan and Hannah McCormack. Most of the men in these families had worked for the postal service, the railways or the tramways, all forms of modest but secure employment. The women did not work after marriage. My father was the first to break out of this world but it was not done easily. Although he later came to have many

Michael and Hannah Dynan with children Billy and my mother, Eileen, about 1904

associations outside the self-contained Irish Catholic community, his early life was entirely formed by it. Born in Carlton on the edge of Princess Park, he was educated by the Christian Brothers, first in North Melbourne and then in much more fashionable Toorak, where one school collected the relatively small groups of students who went on to matriculation. The Christian Brothers were noted for two things – their extreme brutality, even in the schools of that period, and their success with bright students. In his last year my father sat for the staff clerks' entrance examination for both the army and the navy and was placed in the first ten in the country in each. He took up a post in the Department of the Navy in 1917 and remained in this area for the next decade. Only the end of the Great War the following year stopped him being swept up into its killing fields when he turned eighteen. He had seen the AIF marching through the streets of Melbourne in 1914 on their way to the ships for Gallipoli or, later, the western front and knew how many had already perished. Casualty lists in small print covered whole pages of the newspapers during the four years of fighting.

Outside the office, there was no need to leave the Irish Catholic world of inner Melbourne. In 1928, for example, he was president of the North Fitzroy branch of the Catholic Young Men's Society, an organisation that filled weekends and evenings with highly-organised competitions in football, cricket and debating together with a range of social events. Two years later, after a mass for the old boys of the school attended by Melbourne's Irish Archbishop, Daniel Mannix, he proposed the toast to the "Hierarchy and Clergy". This was reported in Melbourne's Catholic newspaper, *The Advocate*:

> Mr C.F. Sexton said that the Hierarchy and clergy were worthy of the deepest gratitude of the Catholic people for their unceasing labours in furtherance of the work of the Church and the temporal welfare of the people. The

Catholic Church was making great progress in Australia. The bulwark of Christianity, the Catholic Church stood four-square against social and other evils, and was ever foremost in advocating the rights of the oppressed. The recent successful Eucharistic Congress in Sydney had focussed the attention of the whole Catholic world on Australia. To the Irish pioneers they owed much in Australia. He trusted that the bonds of affection and goodwill between clergy and people would never be broken. They were proud to welcome his Grace the Archbishop. Under the inspiring leadership of his Grace wonderful progress was being made in the Archdiocese of Melbourne. The Catholic education grievance had not been remedied, despite all the appeals made by his Grace and the clergy generally. Catholics should unite in demanding fair play, and should not be unmindful of the fact that the increasing cost of State education was adding to their burdens.[4]

I came to realise as a child that both my parents were sometimes less accepting of the Church's iron rule than most of their contemporaries. But this embarrassingly fulsome speech captures some of the mixed feelings of pride and persecution in the Celtic community of this time.

That same year my father transferred to the Commonwealth Attorney-General's Department with the goal of taking a law degree part-time at Melbourne University. He did this in the first half of the 1930s. It was the heart of the Depression years and he moonlighted on weekends at the Melbourne *Herald*, writing for the sport pages with some of his fellow law students. Until the end of his life he had a sharp eye for the stock phrases used by sport writers everywhere to avoid any semblance of fresh imagery.

Although the salaries of public servants were actually reduced during this period, they had a guarantee of continuing income in a time of widespread unemployment. Some pleasures could still be taken cheaply. Photographs from these years show my parents and their friends holidaying in Victoria's snowfields and formally dressed at dance halls and supper clubs around Melbourne. Because they did not marry until their late 30s, they lived at home until then. There were financial reasons for this but it was the normal way until the 1960s. Before her marriage there were five unmarried adult children in my mother's home – three of whom never married – and one still at school.

My first memories of the Dynan household in the early 1950s were the stuff of one of Eugene O'Neill's dramas. Its head was Hannah Dynan. Born in 1875, she was small and fine-boned but with a strong constitution. After six children between the ages of 25 and 45, she survived her husband by thirty years to live to 95 without any loss of mental faculties and very little physical deterioration until the last year. Although then in their forties and fifties, the three unmarried children still lived at home and each, in their own way, was a sharp source of sorrow to my grandmother. The oldest son, Billy, had worked in the tax office but had been pensioned out on health grounds – a code word in this case for a drinking problem. I never knew the reason for Billy's unhappiness and, like all important questions in the family, it was never spoken of. When he was sober, he was always friendly to me. When he came home drunk, he would pick a fight with the nearest person, reduce my grandmother to tears and slink off to his room at the back of the house. This familiar scene was played out almost every Christmas day during my childhood. The house itself was like a stage setting from the turn of the century. Whatever their original colour, all the rooms had faded into one blend of sepia. All the furnishing seemed to merge into this dark background.

The two daughters at home were Marguerite, known as Rita, and Mary, always called Molly. I had seen a lot of Rita from a very early age because she often looked after me if my parents were going out. But then she stopped coming to our home. I found out much later that she had become involved with one of the men with whom she worked in the head office of the Victorian Railways. He was married and this was a time when divorce was unusual. Their relationship lasted for decades but Rita could never bring him to her own house because of her mother's disapproval. And she felt that my mother had not supported her when she needed it. I met the man for the first and only time years later at my father's burial in the Melbourne General Cemetery. I noticed a figure standing somewhat apart from the gravesite and wearing, despite the heat,

My mother dressed for the 1920s and in her twenties as well

a dark three-piece suit and a felt hat. As everyone started to leave, he came up, shook my hand and told me who he was. He died soon afterwards. Victims of their era, he and Rita never had a chance to spend some of their lives together.

Molly's life had taken a different but equally destructive turn. Intelligent and amusing but without any guile or toughness, she had gone into the convent after school. She was broken by the harsh training in this religious army and returned to the world, although she never ventured very far into it. It was proof of her ability that she later became the personal assistant to a number of heads of Commonwealth departments at a time when there were few other

My father in the 1925 football season

jobs for women in the public or the private sector where they could use their talents. Even as a small child, I found her entertaining company, but her sensitivity to slights, real or imaginary – a trait shared to some extent by my mother – sometimes led to fierce clashes in the workplace. And there was always a feeling of failure about the convent, which, again, was never spoken of. Neither the Sextons nor the Dynans had the large number of priests, brothers and nuns that some Catholic families produced. Molly was the only person on either side of the family in a century who entered a religious order. But it was considered vaguely shameful in any Catholic family that a son or a daughter should leave the order, even if they did so before taking their final vows. As Maryanne Confoy, Morris West's biographer, wrote of his decision to leave the Christian Brothers close to the end of his training:

> The years from the 1940s to the 1960s were hard years for those few who chose to leave religious commitments, whether it was before or after perpetual vows. Most Catholics did not even distinguish between whether the vows taken were temporary or for life or simply for twelve months. Once the call had been received, one was expected to persevere, as married couples persevered. There was always a note of question, or judgement of the person leaving. . . .
>
> It was often more acceptable for a man or woman who left their religious order to be able to claim a breakdown as a reason for departure than to offer any other reason for leaving. Pity was easier to offer in that case. There had to be something wrong with the person who left an Order. People could not imagine any other reason for reneging on their commitment. There could be no weakness in the institutional system, so it had to be a flaw in the individual.[5]

My mother's other two brothers married but one of these unions was yet another source of bitter sadness to my grandmother. John Dynan, always known as Jack, was a lean and laconic sportsman, an Australian type common in the first half of the last century but seldom seen in its later years. The woman he wanted to marry had been divorced. Apart from the social stigma in the early 1950s, this meant that there could be no Catholic wedding. None of his family attended the wedding and he was effectively excluded from the Church, although I doubt that Jack considered the second of these consequences a great hardship.

All this suggests a world dominated by religious dogma and doctrine. So it was, in many ways, although less in my own home than many others. It was true that we went to mass on Sundays and did not eat meat on Fridays but there were no prayer sessions at home nor constant visits from the parish priest. I was never sent to be an altar boy like most of my contemporaries. I sensed that my parents did not want to be quite as close to the Church as many of their friends, although they never explained why.

None of this stopped me from being sent at the age of five to the local parish school, run by the Sisters of St Joseph. Many years later in Canberra I met Allan Behm, then a senior member of the Defence Department, who insisted that we had been at this school together. No doubt he is right but I have few sharp recollections of the three years that I spent there. My strongest memory is of drinking icy milk on winter mornings in the schoolyard. The milk was put out in crates, presumably as part of some government program to improve the nutrition of school children. I could never stand the taste of plain milk again.

One of the things that stopped my parents being closer to the heart of the Catholic community in Melbourne was that they had never been members or supporters of the Movement. This body – the Catholic Social Studies Movement, to give it its full title –

had been established by B A Santamaria just after the war with the strong support of Archbishop Daniel Mannix. Many years later, in *The Australian*, I wrote about my first sight of Santamaria:

> In the early 1950s I went with my father to a function after Sunday Mass at the local parish church in Mont Albert in Melbourne's eastern suburbs. The speaker at the function was B A Santamaria and he spoke about Vietnam.
>
> Not many people were talking about Vietnam in Australia at that time but he stressed the importance of the survival of the regime in South Vietnam and the qualities of its Catholic leader, Ngo Dinh Diem. I was struck by the speaker's intensity but, unlike most the audience, I retained some scepticism. This was because I was in the unusual position of growing up in a Catholic family but one that did not support the Democratic Labor Party. Many Catholics, of course, not only supported the DLP in an electoral sense but also were actively involved in its affairs and in those of the Church organisation effectively led by Santamaria – the Movement.[6]

But the real point of the article was that Mannix and Santamaria rejected the values on which Australia's political system was based:

> What is remarkable, however, is that, despite their impact on Australian political life, neither Santamaria nor Mannix ever accepted the notion of parliamentary democracy under the Westminster system.
>
> ... In an extraordinary letter, written to Mannix in 1952, Santamaria suggested that eventually the Movement would be able to "completely transform the leadership of the Labor movement and introduce into the federal and state spheres large numbers of members who possess a clear realisation of what Australia demands of them and the will to carry it out" ...

This had been the situation for many years in Mannix's own Ireland and also in Spain and Portugal. It had also been true, to a lesser degree, in Italy. In contrast to England and the US, these countries did not proceed on the assumption of a secular and pluralist society where questions of faith and morals were left to individuals. On the contrary, the dogmas of the church, in areas such as divorce, abortion and contraception, were imposed on the whole community by the government, including those members of the community who were not adherents of the church.

. . . Santamaria's attitude to so many of these issues was perhaps summed up in his statement in 1952 that one of the great evils of modern history was the birth of the "modern, liberal, democratic, secular state" in Europe in the years between 1750 and 1848. Think of the notions that are rejected in this statement: modern, liberal, democratic, secular.[7]

Until the mid-1950s the Movement operated as a highly secret organisation with its organisational base in the various parishes across the country. In terms of numbers and resources the Church was the largest organisation in Australia. It was not true in all the States, but in Victoria, under Mannix's administration, all these resources were at the disposal of the Movement. The meetings took place in parish halls and money was available from Church funds. As Patrick Morgan wrote about this exercise:

> Santamaria's unique strategic insight at this point . . . was to realise that the Australia-wide parish network was a superb vehicle on which to base a political operation. For this strategy he saw the parish in secular terms. Each parish priest had a list of parishioners with addresses – this could be used to do an audit of all those in the parish who belonged to a union. Catholics were then mainly working class or lower middle class and therefore likely to be union

members; in addition they were strongly anti-Communist and therefore likely to be willing workers in the anti-Communist cause. Each parish had its own organisations, like the Holy Name Society, from which ready-made leaders and organisational expertise could be recruited.[8]

I knew that my father had been asked to become involved with the Movement but had resisted. I could vaguely sense the feeling amongst some members of our parish that, as a reasonably senior government lawyer, he had talents that could be used but was not

My mother and father in the centre of Melbourne in the early 1950s

a loyal enough Catholic. Always gregarious and outgoing, he now belonged to range of non-Catholic organisations. This was a subject of suspicion in a tribal world. Even worse, he was not a member of the Knights of the Southern Cross, the Catholic alternative to the Masons as a social group and job network. Nor was my mother – more reserved, sometimes even aloof – interested in any of the Catholic women's organisations that operated as counterpart to the men's societies.

For many Catholics, however, the combination of a moral crusade and a secret society was a potent mixture. I saw the burning eyes of Movement activists at Sunday mass. Catholics who had stayed active in the Labor Party, including its deputy federal leader, Arthur Calwell, were often driven out of their local parishes and attended mass in other parts of town. As late as 1960, Bishop Arthur Fox said publicly that no Catholic could in good conscience vote for the ALP. If this view was accepted, it made voting Labor a mortal sin which, until absolved in confession, resulted in eternal consignment to the fires of hell. When the *Catholic Worker*, a periodical which Santamaria had helped to establish in the late 1930s, wrote in 1955 that Catholics could vote for any party except the Communists, Bishop Fox, at Mannix's direction, sent a lethal note to every parish priest in Melbourne:

> Reverend and Dear Father,
>
> The issue of April 1955 of the Catholic Worker has been sent to the distributors this week against the advice of the chaplain who also acts as censor of this newspaper.
>
> I myself am forbidding its sale at the Cathedral and at the churches in the Cathedral parish from next Sunday onwards. The parish priests, of course, are not bound to follow my example; but the Archbishop has asked me to let you know the above facts, and that he does not approve of certain matters appearing in this issue.[9]

Most parish priests did, in fact, feel bound to follow his example. Circulation fell at once from 35,000 to 15,000 and never recovered.

Did I believe in mortal sin, the fires of hell and all the other dogmas? It would be easy to say: certainly not. But I am not so sure. In his autobiography, Jim McClelland, sometime senator and minister in the Whitlam government, and not a man to be intimidated by anything in later life, wrote that "during an important part of my boyhood, roughly the period between the ages of 10 and 15, my faith was often a terrifying burden which drove almost all joy from my life".[10] This was the late 1920s when McClelland was growing up in a Catholic family in Melbourne. I could hardly make this grim claim but, in such a closed community, it would have taken an unusually strong adolescent personality simply to reject the world view held by everyone else. There was nothing especially spiritual about Australian Catholicism, nor its Protestant alternatives, being rather an intricate code of conduct and an elaborate series of rituals. But, until I left school and went to university, I hardly met anyone who did not subscribe, at least on the surface, to these beliefs.

Our home was in Surrey Hills in Melbourne's eastern suburbs. After the 1970s some of its curving tree-lined streets and large federation houses became part of a real estate boom. In the 1950s, however, it was comfortable but far from fashionable. Although we were only a few minutes walk from the main rail line running east from Melbourne, there was a farm at the bottom of our street occupying several hectares and with a creek running through it. Its owner, a woman who seemed terribly old but probably was not, would sometimes wave an ancient rifle at the neighbourhood children who tormented her. There was a municipal tip next to the farm where we used to play, leaping over burning piles of ash and rotting garbage. But the local council was in no danger of being sued if one of us had been injured. This was a time when injuries were your own fault.

It would be easy to portray these childhood years now as ones of deprivation. By the standards of half a century later, they were certainly more austere. But most people led much simpler lives. Few families had cars, although we had a large, slow, noisy Dodge from the 1930s. In the absence of neighbourhood restaurants evenings were usually spent at home. Before the arrival of television, there was a lot of reading, mostly history and the classics, and listening to the radio, especially serials and quiz shows. In addition, I was taken regularly to the local cinema and occasionally to stage plays in the city with supper afterwards at the Windsor Hotel in the theatre district. It is true that nothing was wasted and even small purchases were carefully considered, especially by those who lived through the Depression and the rationing of the war. But there was no real sense of hardship when there was so much less to buy.

Saturday afternoons at the football, a Melbourne institution, were part of this modest lifestyle. Most weeks my father and I stood, with his brother, in the "outer" – the section of the ground without seats and without cover – often being lashed by wind and rain. At the end of the game the crowd ran onto the oval and kicked their own footballs. It did not seem unusual to me then – it does now – that my father, a desk-bound lawyer in his fifties, could still hit me on the chest from 45 metres with a drop kick. We watched Essendon and whatever side they were playing because the two brothers had inherited this team from their father. I had decided, however, at an early age that I was a Geelong supporter. It is hard to know why because they were the only team outside Melbourne, based about seventy-five kilometres southwest of the city. When I was old enough I started to go to their matches with the boy next door. He was my age and a Geelong supporter, although the rest of his family were Hawthorn followers. Every second Saturday during the football season, when our team played at home, we would take the train from Melbourne to Kardinia Park in Geelong with a determination that puzzled both our families.

I was always surprised as a child that my father and his brother, as the only two children in that family, had so little in common. Gerald was six years younger and had a career in what was then called the CBC Bank. He was a senior bank manager when this was a position of considerable authority in the community. He was small, dapper and slightly pompous. There was not much love lost between my mother and my father's side of the family, although she much preferred Gerald to some of the others. When the football finals came around in September, we all went to the MCG. This was a big step up from the "outer" because my father had joined Gerald and himself up as members in the 1920s. We all sat together but, in a sharp demonstration of their different attitudes to spending money, my father took me into the members' dining room while Gerald sat outside with the sandwiches and thermos he had brought from home.

After the Essendon games my father would detour on the drive home to the Whitehorse Hotel in Hawthorn to meet some friends for a drink. These were the years of 6 o'clock closing for pubs so there was no danger of staying all night. I sat in the corner with a soft drink, reading the evening paper. The air was heavy with cigarette smoke and the smell of stale beer. The noise was enormous as the men in the bar – there were no women –shouted happily at each other. I was quite content in my corner but it was very much a scene from the life of an only child. The absence of siblings usually results in a very close relationship with one or both parents. There is no need to compete with anyone for affection – or for anything else. None of this provides much preparation for the fierce hatreds and jealousies that govern so much human behaviour in the rest of life.

Nor does it provide many of the social skills that are useful at school. At the end of year three I was sent off to the main Marist Brothers' School in Melbourne which was about three or four kilometres from home. I rode my bike there and back every day, head down, peddling furiously, somehow protected from the surrounding traffic. The school had been established only in 1950 when some classrooms had been tacked onto an old mansion in the solid middle class and now very expensive suburb of Camberwell. The house had some grounds but not enough for playing fields. Football and cricket before school and at lunch time were played on asphalt. I still have a hole in one knee where it skidded for more than a metre over this stony surface one winter's morning. In keeping with a much harsher era in schools, no one took the slightest notice as blood poured out of the wound.

The Marist Brothers and the Jesuits had a reputation for being marginally less violent than the Christian Brothers but not a day would go past at school without several members of the class – only eight years old when I started – being savagely and publicly beaten. Even in one of my later years, I can recall the headmaster hitting one of my friends across the face and sending his glasses flying across the room. As a rather studious child, I was largely, although not entirely, immune from these assaults. I had started reading my father's books at an early age and then started to acquire some of my own. If there was a question in class as to what was the capital of Bulgaria or who won the battle of Salamis, I could be relied on to provide the answer. This did not always endear me to my fellow pupils or even, I noticed with slight puzzlement, to all of the teachers. Some of them seemed to be irritated because I did not volunteer this information but could produce it when asked. After taking the first year to adjust to the new environment, I had found my way to the top of the class and no longer felt the need to impress anyone.

In something of a contrast to this apparently brutal regime, there was a strong emphasis on academic success, with special classes for those sitting external scholarship examinations. There was also a well-organised inter-school debating competition which took up quite a lot of my time in later years at school. But perhaps the biggest contrast could be found in the ballroom dancing classes conducted for senior students by the headmaster so that we would be able to put on a polished performance at the occasional dance held jointly with nearby convent schools.

As for sexual abuse, now revealed as common in many Catholic and government institutions for children, I did not notice any overtures by teachers to students. There were certainly none to me. This was not a boarding school so the opportunities for advances were much more limited, although if they were ever made to any of my classmates, I doubt that I would have noticed. No one had ever told me that such things happened.

There was not much in the way of travel during school holidays. My father sometimes took planes to the other capitals for work but even this was unusual for most people. I did not know anyone growing up who had travelled outside Australia. Over the long summer break we spent a month at Dromana, southeast of Melbourne on the Mornington Peninsula. Now an expensive and stylish seaside resort, it was then a sleepy village with a few old beach houses on the cliffs. We rented one of these from a Scottish widow called McGregor. Sometimes one of my mother's sisters would join us for these languid Januarys where every day seemed just like the one before.

Meanwhile, back in Melbourne, we had been transferred, without moving house, into a new parish. Like an electoral commissioner changing the boundaries of parliamentary electorates, the Church authorities had established the new parish of Wattle Park. The presiding priest at Surrey Hills parish had been an elderly Irishman with few thoughts of changing the world. The new pastor was an energetic and egocentric young man, John Kelly, who became a bishop in Melbourne. He was what was known in the Church as a builder. He first built a new church, then a school and then two tennis courts. These were my introduction to the game that was to occupy much of my time for more than forty years. In contrast with Surrey Hills, the new parish had quite a number of couples in their late twenties and early thirties with young children. Some of these, both men and women, played tennis and played it very well.

There was a very strong Catholic tennis competition in Melbourne and the new club fielded a number of teams. When I reached the top team, I was still a school boy amongst grown men, who collected me for the away matches because I had no driving licence, let alone a car. My doubles partner, Alan Stiles, was a down-to-earth builder, who taught me a great deal about tennis and something about life. One Saturday afternoon, chatting between matches, Alan told me a story that captured the darker side of the Church in those days. Alan and his wife had a number of children but the youngest of these was perhaps three or four. Although in our case the parish priest seemed to keep something of a distance, he obviously visited other homes, including Alan's, quite frequently. On one of these recent visits, Father Kelly had cross-examined the Styles on whether they were using some form of birth control. This seems, in retrospect, a breathtaking invasion of privacy and attempt at intimidation but I suspect there was nothing unusual about it then.

One constant concern at home over these years was the prospect of a move to Canberra. Many top jobs in some of the Commonwealth departments, including the Attorney-General's Department, had remained in Melbourne, where all the departments had originally had their head offices. These were gradually being relocated to Canberra. My father was now Assistant Crown Solicitor attached to the Department of Supply and responsible for large-scale defence contracts. If this job was transferred, we would go with it. I later came to know Canberra well but at the time it seemed the unknown. For my parents, Melbourne was where their family and friends had always lived. My father managed to last out until his retirement without the summons to Canberra. It would, naturally, have been better for his career to make the move because there were greater opportunities for advancement in head office. Even in Melbourne, his career was probably not helped by the fact that he had become president of the Council of Commonwealth Public Service Organizations. This reflected a long-standing interest in industrial relations but was no doubt puzzling to some of his colleagues in the senior levels of the bureaucracy. He was, however, appointed by the government to a number of statutory bodies that dealt with employment conditions in the public service and the superannuation entitlements of its employees.

Normally no account of these school days would be complete without a terrifying sermon from a monastic retreat – a scene most memorably portrayed by Joyce in *Portrait of the Artist as a Young Man*. In fact, the school retreats, which took place at the Jesuit seminary at Watsonia, were quite restful. The days were spent in silence, walking in the tree-lined grounds of the monastery and listening to lectures in the chapel. Some of these were thoughtful, with only sparing references to hell-fire and damnation. The meals were also taken in silence in the long dining room except that one of the novices – trainee priests – read aloud from spiritual works. Two of them would turn up in later life. Gerard Windsor left before taking his vows and became a well-known writer. When I moved house in Sydney in the early 1990s, I found myself living three doors from Windsor and his family. Another of the readers was Michael Finnane, whom I met when I first arrived in Sydney in the early 1970s. He had left the seminary to take up the law and later became a silk and District Court judge in New South Wales.

In my last two years the school moved from Camberwell to Bulleen in Melbourne's northeast where it had purchased a large tract of land some years before. From having no playing fields at all, we suddenly had ovals and training tracks that stretched for hectares. Despite these fine facilities, my own football career was lacklustre. Its highlight – or perhaps lowlight – occurred in a local junior competition when I played on Peter Crimmins, who later captained Hawthorn to an AFL premiership and died in 1976 in his late twenties. He was very fast and highly skilful. I was neither. I spent the game chasing, but seldom catching, him and trying to get in the way of his kicks for gaol – usually without stopping them. Tennis seemed a much better bet and football ended with my school days.

The precocious style of my high school debating years was reflected in a letter that I wrote for publication in *The Advocate*, Melbourne's weekly Catholic newspaper, shortly after finishing at school. This was the first of many publications over the coming years of my strong and, no doubt, often unwelcome opinions. The commitment of Australian troops to Vietnam was announced in April 1965 and was strongly supported by most sections of the Church. In the best debating traditions, I decided to provoke this broad group by using one of its own candidates for sainthood – an Austrian farmer, Franz Jaegerstaetter, who was executed by the Nazis in 1943 when he refused to serve in the German army. Jaegerstaetter was not a pacifist but objected to the particular war in which his country was then engaged – the same position taken by a number of Australian young men conscripted during the Vietnam period. He had been the subject of a number of books in the early 1960s and one of these had recently been reviewed in *The Advocate*. The letter, which was designed to be hugely offensive to most of the paper's Catholic readership, was short and sharp:

> In the light of recent statements made by members of the Church on the Vietnam war it was interesting to read

in *The Advocate* of the same week a review of a book just published and telling of the life and death of Franz Jaegerstaetter, the Austrian peasant who chose execution rather than serving in the German forces in World War II. Jaegerstaetter was urged by certain members of the clergy to abandon his stand, but he remained adamant. History, however, in giving its verdict, has recognised Jaegerstaetter as the one who adhered to true Christian principles. In judging our times, history will pass the same verdict and there will no praise for those who, like Bishop Fox and Mr B.A. Santamaria, advocate a holy war against communism which can justify any means of achieving its end. It is disappointing that it has been left to members of the Protestant clergy to stand up for the true precepts of Christ in this matter.[11]

It is hard to imagine such a letter being published at any other time in *The Advocate*'s history. It not only attacked a bishop but also the heroic layman, Santamaria. And it said the Protestant clergy had behaved better. But the editor at this time, Michael Costigan, was more liberal-minded than any of his predecessors – or successors. In next week's edition, there was a strong counter-attack from Eric D'Arcy, who had been the spiritual adviser to the Movement in the 1950s and was later Archbishop of Hobart. It was inexcusable for me to have written the letter but even worse for the editor to have published it:

I wish to protest against your publishing a letter which describes Bishop Fox as advocating a war "which can justify any means of achieving its end". His Lordship's name is quite a different thing to bracketed in the same sentence, *quasi ex aequo* [as if the same] with that of Mr B.A. Santamaria.

It is one thing to debate the correct application of general moral principle to a particular situation. It is quite a different thing to attribute to a Catholic a very wicked principle which he neither holds nor teaches. When that Catholic is a personal friend of mine, as is Mr Santamaria, I resent the misattribution very much. But when he is a Bishop, and indeed the Bishop at present administering our own archdiocese, I not only resent it as a serious case of false ascription: I also deplore it as a grave breach of that respect and courtesy which Catholic tradition requires us to show to our pastors.

It seems bad to me that a Catholic should write such a thing; but that a Catholic newspaper should publish it is insupportable. You will remember what Saint Paul said of those who accused him of teaching that one may do evil as a means to good. May we not expect, Sir, that you will publish an apology, at least to His Lordship?[12]

Some years later D'Arcy and myself were both on the teaching staff at Newman College, the Catholic residential hall at Melbourne University. We never spoke of this exchange, although no doubt it was not forgotten. D'Arcy also taught in the Philosophy Department at Melbourne University and the next letter in this saga was from one of his colleagues in that small department:

... Surely the demand made by my friend and colleague, Dr Eric D'Arcy that you should apologize to Bishop Fox for printing a letter about him ... is entirely misconceived?

... Finally, I think in his letter Dr D'Arcy treats Mr Santamaria very badly. Poor Mr Santamaria is faced with the spectacle of his Defence Counsel flatly stating that he is Not Guilty of espousing a very wicked principle, yet producing not one skerrick of evidence in support of the plea.[13]

This contribution to the debate was in relatively polite terms but the final instalment to these exchanges, by another colleague of D'Arcy's in the Department of Philosophy, was not so polite:

Father D'Arcy made serious charges against the editor of *The Advocate* and one of its correspondents. He claimed that it was "insupportable" that a Catholic newspaper should publish a letter in which it was stated that Bishop Fox and Mr Santamaria advocate a war "which can justify any means of achieving its end", and that it was a bad thing that a Catholic should write such a thing. . . .

Father D'Arcy implies that reference to the public statements of Bishop Fox and Mr B.A. Santamaria will disclose that they have not been prepared to support a war "which can justify any means of achieving its end". I think he is wrong. I believe that it can be demonstrated that the public utterances of Bishop Fox and Mr Santamaria on Vietnam are informed by the tacit acceptance of the view, "let the end justify the means". . . .

I do not believe that they are men who knowingly follow a wicked principle. Nor do I believe that Fr. D'Arcy is wicked in accusing your correspondent of attributing "to a Catholic a very wicked principle, which he neither holds nor teaches". But I think it is inexcusable that a professional philosopher should be so obtuse in construing your correspondent's letter.[14]

There was obviously no love lost between these two philosophers. The word "obtuse" is academic jargon for dull or stupid. I had begun a long career of publishing offensive opinions.

3

CRIME AND PUNISHMENT
Counsel for the Prosecution

When I took the post of Solicitor-General I did not imagine that criminal cases would absorb a great proportion of my time. The job is seen traditionally, and rightly, as having a particular focus on questions of constitutional law. But I became involved, in the appeal courts rather than at the original trial, in some of the most sensational criminal cases in New South Wales in recent decades.

In these cases I was appearing for what is called the Crown. This signifies Australian's inheritance of the British legal system where the Sovereign was the source of all legal power. In a practical sense, however, prosecutions are now instituted in this country by the Commonwealth or the relevant State or Territory on behalf of the general community. This position is perhaps more accurately reflected in the United States where prosecutions are undertaken in the name of "The People" against the person charged with the particular offence.

Much public debate about the criminal justice system has focused on whether the sentences handed down by judges are out of touch with the views of the general community. One response to these community concerns was legislation by the Greiner government in New South Wales in 1990 to ensure that life sentences could mean just that – life without any possibility of parole[1]. This legislation, however, sparked legal challenges for more than a decade after it was passed, moving finally to the High Court in 2004.

This was because, out of the group of prisoners who had been sentenced to life under the old system, there were twelve who had been the subject of a recommendation by the trial judge that they should never be released on account of the nature of the crime they had committed. Two of these prisoners were Allan Baker and Kevin Crump. They had abducted Virginia Morse from her family property in western New South Wales late in 1973. During the next few days she was raped, tortured and finally killed. When sentencing Baker and Crump, in the Supreme Court, Justice Taylor said:

> For sheer cruelty, for callous indifference to suffering, for a complete disregard of humanity, for the complete absence of a spark of human decency, what you have done to this woman and to her children and to her husband is without parallel in my experience, and I have sat here many times over the years. You have outraged all accepted standards of the behaviour of men ...
>
> I believe that you should spend the rest of your lives in gaol and there you should die. If ever there was a case where life imprisonment should mean what it says – imprisonment for the whole of your lives – this is it.
>
> If in the future application is made that you be released on the grounds of clemency or of mercy, then I would venture to suggest to those who are entrusted with the task of determining whether you are entitled to it or not that the measure of your entitlement to either should be the

clemency and mercy you extended to this woman when she begged you for her life.

The new system allowed anyone with a life sentence to apply to the Supreme Court to have that sentence reduced to a fixed term.[2] It was recognised that most people with old life sentences would have been released on parole at some stage. In 1997 Crump made an application and succeeded in obtaining an order that he would be eligible for parole after serving 30 years, that is, late in 2003. The NSW government's response to this decision was to alter the parole system so that, when considering someone in Crump's position, the Parole Board could only make a release order if the prisoner was in imminent danger of death or so incapacitated that he or she no longer had the physical ability to do harm to any person.[3]

Despite this unpromising legislative climate, Baker made an application to have his life sentence reduced in mid-2001. The basis on which this could be done had also been changed since Crump's successful application. It now was necessary to show "special reasons" why a new sentence should be fixed[4]. Baker's application was unsuccessful but he appealed to the Court of Criminal Appeal on the ground that the requirement of special reasons contravened the federal Constitution. I took the brief for the Crown in the Court of Criminal Appeal.

Baker's lawyers argued that the legislation was designed to impose a test that no one could ever meet and so the court was being forced to take part in a sham. There was a second argument, that the legislation singled out only those with a life sentence who had been the subject of a non-release recommendation by the trial judge – which had sometimes happened in those years but usually not. The husband of Virginia Morse was present for the hearing in the Court of Criminal Appeal. When I spoke with him during the case, I was conscious that, even after 30 years, he had never really recovered from the events of 1973.

Baker's arguments were rejected by the Court of Criminal Appeal[5] but the High Court granted special leave to appeal and this was heard in Canberra in February 2004.

Early in my argument, Justice Kirby took up the question of the original non-release recommendation:

> It is a very peculiar judicial function to require later judges to act on a statement which had no legal authority made 30 years earlier. It is a very peculiar judicial function indeed and I could very well understand the judges having to do this would regard it as deeply offensive because it is arbitrary and unequal in the way it falls upon prisoners and touches liberty.

I responded that, even if this was so, the New South Wales parliament could take the trial judge's recommendation into account. But I suggested that it did have some relevance:

> All those selections are, in one sense, arbitrary but it is not irrational in the sense that the recommendations were made by judges of the Supreme Court, many of whom, of course, have tried a great number of criminal cases. While it may be true to say that there were terrible cases about which no recommendation was made, it would, in our submission, be true to say that the cases about which the recommendations were made were terrible ones.

On the question of what would be "special reasons", Justice McHugh asked me to give some illustrations, to which I responded:

> One would be assistance, and it might be a particular striking form of assistance, to law enforcement authorities. One might be some kind of conduct or activities within the

prison system which had an enormously beneficial impact on a range of other prisoners, the setting up of some kind of system that benefited many others in the prison system.

Justice Kirby, however, was sceptical about these examples:

> But what if there are no opportunities? No one riots in the prison, a person did not happen to be a super grass, does not know anyone else, never had any contact with any other criminal, he just cannot qualify.

I stuck to my guns, saying that someone in this position might not be able to meet the test but that, as long as there were examples that qualified, it could not be said that the exercise was a sham.

In the final result, Justice Kirby dissented but the rest of the court found the legislation valid.[6]

Three years later, however, I was back in the High Court arguing about this legislation again. This time the challenge came from two of the killers of Janine Balding in 1988. Balding had been abducted from a railway station by five persons. After a series of brutal sexual assaults, she was drowned in a dam. Three of those persons were convicted of murder and, like Baker and Crump, were the subject of a recommendation by the trial judge that they should never be released. Two of the three were under 18 at the time of the killing. They said now that the non-release recommendation should never have been made in their case and should be quashed. I argued that there was nothing to quash as the recommendation was not a formal order of the court. In any event, even if it was quashed, the legislation governing their sentences now contained a clause – which I had drafted myself – saying that the recommendation was still effective to prevent their sentences being reduced to a fixed term.

The High Court rejected this second challenge to the legislation but it was still not the end of the saga.[7] In 2012 Kevin Crump challenged the parole legislation that prevented his release from prison on the basis that it nullified the court decision that had made him eligible for parole in 2003. So it was another argument in Canberra but the High Court found that the legislation had no legal effect on the earlier judgment and continued to be effective.[8]

Another long-running legal saga was the case of Kathleen Folbigg. She had been convicted of killing her four children in 2003. These cases of infant deaths are difficult because, in terms of the medical evidence, it is almost impossible to distinguish between the death of a small child through natural causes – a so-called cot death – and a death caused by suffocation. In the case of Mrs Folbigg, however, she had kept a diary and some of the entries contained what the Crown said were admissions that she had killed the children. Otherwise, the task for the prosecution would have been much more difficult.

Even so, it was a tortuous path. Before the trial Mrs Folbigg's lawyers tried to have each of the deaths considered separately. If that had happened, it would have been impossible to say beyond a reasonable doubt – the criminal standard of proof – what had happened in any of the individual deaths. When this argument was lost, she appealed to the Court of Criminal Appeal and I appeared for the Crown. The appeal was dismissed and the trial proceeded in relation to all four deaths.[9] After her conviction, she appealed again to the Court of Criminal Appeal and I appeared for the prosecution. That appeal was dismissed.[10]

Then, in 2007, her lawyers tried to reopen the earlier appeal to the Court of Criminal Appeal on the grounds that it had subsequently been discovered that one of the jurors at the trial had found out from the internet that her father had murdered her mother; and another juror had asked an acquaintance, who was a nurse, about one of the medical issues. I appeared once more for the Crown in the Court of Criminal Appeal and argued that neither piece of information would have influenced a juror to convict Mrs Folbigg and so the jury's verdict should stand. But I also complained about the fact that the attempt to reopen the original appeal was only possible because the paperwork had not been finalised at that time by the court's administrative staff. The courts do not like any criticism of their operations and my complaint was met by stony silence. This had been a problem in a number of cases, in one of which the court's papers had not been finalised fourteen years after the hearing of the appeal. Although the Court of Criminal Appeal did not relish being reminded of these facts, this was the end of the road for Mrs Folbigg. The judges accepted that the information obtained by the jurors had not affected the verdict of guilty.[12] It had been a very sad case from start to finish and concluded with Mrs Folbigg facing 25 years in prison. The case did, however, lead to a change in the Supreme Court's procedures for finalising judgments so that there could be no repetition of what had happened here.

In the aftermath of 9/11 the criminal justice system in all Western countries had to come to grips with the fact that there were small groups within their communities that were prepared to plant bombs in shopping malls as part of their political agenda. Late in 2005 the Commonwealth government proposed new anti-terrorism laws. All the States had referred some of their legislative powers in this area to the Commonwealth so that there would be no doubt as to the constitutional validity of the laws. But the Queensland Solicitor-General, Walter Sofronoff QC, advised the Queensland government there was still a problem – he thought that giving federal judges the power to make preventative detention orders in relation to suspected terrorists and control orders about their movements was contrary to the role of federal courts – where these orders would be made – and so unconstitutional.

I had already advised the NSW government that the proposed legislation was probably valid. The Queensland Premier, Peter Beattie, raised this disagreement publicly. He said he was concerned about a challenge to the proposed Commonwealth legislation and understood that there was a difference of opinion between the Queensland Solicitor-General, on one side, and the NSW Solicitor-General and the Commonwealth Solicitor-General, on the other side. Beattie said he had spoken to the Prime Minister, John Howard, and it had been agreed that the Solicitors-General from all the States would jointly look at the proposed legislation. During the next week there were numerous telephone hook-ups. The result was a legal opinion signed by all the State Solicitors-General – except myself – and the Northern Territory Solicitor-General.

All legal advices are matters of opinion. On this occasion I predicted the result but it was fairly close. The Commonwealth legislation was challenged in the High Court early in 2007. The challenge was to a control order that restricted the movements of a person who had trained with Al-Qaeda in Afghanistan but later returned to Australia. Five judges considered the making of this order was consistent with the role of a federal court under the Constitution.[13] Two of the judges thought it was inconsistent, underlining again how these questions were essentially matters of opinion on which members of the country's highest court could disagree.

To some extent this was a debate about the kind of legislation that could best deal with the threat of terrorist activities in Australia. In some parts of the world, however, the threat was much more immediate. In January 2004 I wrote in *The Australian* about terrorism in the Middle East, referring to some of the earlier models for this kind of warfare:

One of the chief reasons for pessimism about the future of this conflict is that the Palestinian militants have largely taken as their models the two classic urban terror campaigns of the post-war years – Algeria and Northern Ireland.

During the 1950s and the early 60s those groups in Algeria that wanted complete independence from France – usually referred to collectively as the FLN – declared as open targets not only French soldiers but also any European inhabitants or Algerians who had co-operated with the administration. The French responded with a brutal campaign of their own. One technique of the FLN that was particularly effective in destabilising civilian morale was the planting of bombs in cafes and hotels frequented by Europeans . . .

The tactics of the FLN were picked up and expanded by the IRA in the 70s and the 80s. Their real target was always the British government. The bombs left in pubs, clubs and shopping centres in Northern Ireland and England killed ordinary members of the community. But they were designed to convince the administration at Westminster that the price of keeping Northern Ireland as part of the UK was too high to pay. The IRA had picked its mark well.

Even Margaret Thatcher and Tony Blair – usually tough-minded realists in the area of foreign policy – lacked the stomach for the measures necessary to take on domestic terrorism. In an extraordinary performance for any government, they capitulated to a group that had killed one Conservative Party front-bencher, Airey Neave, at Westminster, fired rockets into Downing Street and narrowly missed killing Thatcher with a bomb that seriously injured several of her colleagues.[14]

Writing about history and international affairs often provokes hostile responses but, even so, the reaction to a book review published in the *Sydney Morning Herald* in July 2008 was extraordinary.[15] I had surveyed a number of books, including one about the destruction of the city of Smyrna on the Aegean coast by the Turkish army in 1922. In the course of the review, I had mentioned the killing of up to 1.5 million Armenians in Turkey in 1915. All Turkish governments, including the present administration, have denied that the Armenian killings ever took place.

The Turkish Consul-General wrote to the NSW Attorney-General protesting about my review:

> Last weekend I was dismayed and stunned to see that a review of the . . . book was published in the "Spectrum" supplement of the *Sydney Morning Herald* by Mr Michael Sexton in his capacity of the NSW Solicitor-General. I was further shocked to see that his review contained again biased and Turcophobe views of what transpired during those days.
>
> Mr Sexton of course has every right to write a review on a book if he so wishes. Yet we are of the belief that this is rather awkward and uncommon for an official, who functions within the administrative structure of the Attorney-General's Department and is under the direction of the Attorney-General . . .
>
> I would therefore sincerely appreciate if you could kindly look into the matter in your capacity as both the Minister of Justice and Attorney-General of NSW.

There seem to me to be two problems about the Consul-General's complaint. The first was that he assumed that I could be told what to do, and what not to do, by the Attorney-General. This may be the situation in Turkey but not in Australia. The Solicitor-General would normally provide advice and go to court, if the Attorney-General made that request. But this is very different from being directed what to write in a book review.

More importantly, however, the Consul-General's suggestion that I was somehow putting forward a view on behalf of the NSW government struck me as absurd. How could anyone imagine that the NSW government had an official position on events almost a century earlier in Asia Minor? It is hard to understand why the present Turkish government, which obviously can have no responsibility itself, does not acknowledge what happened to the Armenians and move on. But this seems not an option as far as it is concerned.

At this time I had been reviewing books, chiefly for the *Sydney Morning Herald*, but also for the *National Times* and *The Bulletin*, for almost thirty years. Most were much less controversial than the review of the Smyrna book. Most of these reviews dealt with works of history, biography or foreign affairs but sometimes with novels. Occasionally I would suggest that a book was simply not worth reading but generally I tried to look for a book's strong points. I had spent a lot of my life reading and writing books so the last thing I wanted to do was to deter other people from buying them. Nevertheless, I was always ready to express an opinion on political or social questions that were discussed in the book, sometimes in agreement with the author and sometimes in disagreement.

It seemed to me that, as long as the review made it clear what the author had said and what the reviewer thought about this, the reader could make up his or her own mind on the subject. There is a danger here of using a review to give a sermon by the reviewer on the questions of history or current affairs raised in the book. In some cases this temptation is harder to resist than in others. Most reviewers have strong views on some subjects and find it hard to stand back completely from them when they encounter a book on one of them. But it is always important to remember that it is the book that has to be at the heart of the review.

It is one thing to be sent a single book to review but quite another to get 150 books in boxes for assessment. This is what happened when I agreed to be one of the three judges for the non-fiction section of the NSW Premier's literary awards in 2009 and later one of the four judges for the history and non-fiction categories of the Prime Minister's literary awards in 2013. There was some good reading amongst all these works but a lot of bizarre subjects and bad writing. The book that stood out for me from those judging panels was the winner of the history prize in the Prime Minister's awards – Ross McMullin's *Farewell, Dear People* which told the stories of ten young Australian men whose promising lives were cut short by the Great War. This was an original and very moving contribution to the nation's history.

* * *

On occasions I have been asked by an Attorney-General for my view as to whether someone would be a good appointment as a judge. The question of how judges should be chosen has often given rise to fierce debate in the legal world. Appointments to the NSW Supreme Court are still formally the decision of the Attorney-General – actually the Cabinet but on the recommendation of the Attorney-General. In practice, however, the candidates for these positions are often supplied by the Chief Justice, the Bar Association or the Law Society. But the Attorney-General can still put forward a candidate of his or her own. In the case of many Australian courts, however, judicial positions are now publicly advertised but a list of recommended candidates is prepared by a committee of present judges, retired judges and, often, senior bureaucrats. This list of candidates is then presented to the Commonwealth or State Attorney-General for the final decision but it is politically very difficult to go outside the names on the list. Even appointments to the High Court are now made after a series of consultations with professional and community groups and the names thrown up by this process normally provide the shortlist for appointment.

I have always been doubtful about the utility of these kinds of appointments committees. It is true that there have been many bad judicial appointments over the years made by governments on the recommendation of the Attorney-General. But it is certainly arguable that these kinds of committees will narrow rather than broaden the range of persons appointed to the Bench. This was a point made by Justice Michael Kirby in 1999 when he said that committees that included current judges would be in danger of becoming "a further vehicle for judicial orthodoxy, each generation replicating itself in mirror image of its own esteemed qualities".[16] Defending the old system of appointment, Kirby said:

> The old ways could sometimes result in the appointment of controversial candidates who would never make it through a club-like atmosphere of a judicial commission or the political circus of a [US-style] legislative confirmation. There is a risk in judicial commissions and legislative confirmation proceedings that the appointment process will opt for the "safe" or "unknown" candidate rather than the intellectually vibrant, energetic and bold appointee.

One of the most tortious legal exercises that I encountered began with the disappearance of Kerry Whelan on 6 May 1997. She had arranged to meet her husband, Bernard Whelan, at his office in Western Sydney and then fly with him to Adelaide. When she did not arrive at his office, her husband drove to a hotel in Parramatta where he knew that she always parked her car. He found the car with the keys in the ignition but no sign of his wife. Neither he nor her children ever saw her again.

The last sighting of Kerry Whelan was made by the security camera in the hotel car park. She was shown walking up the exit ramp towards the street. She reaches the top of the ramp and appears to turn right. Then she moves outside the range of the camera. The following day Bernard Whelan received a letter demanding a ransom of $1,250,000 for the return of his wife. There was no further demand for a ransom and no return of Kerry Whelan.

Almost two years later, in April 1999, Bruce Burrell, at one time an employee of Bernard Whelan's and a friend of the Whelan family, was charged with the kidnapping and murder of Kerry Whelan. Burrell was committed for trial in relation to these charges later that year but an inquest into the presumed death of Kerry Whelan meant that the trial was delayed until late 2003. Then Burrell's lawyers asked the NSW Supreme Court to stop the trial going ahead. They had two arguments – that the Director of Public Prosecutions had at one stage said that Burrell would not be prosecuted; and that the jury at the trial would be aware of the unfavourable publicity that Burrell had received during the course of the inquest. Justice Wood refused to stop the trial proceeding[17] and Burrell appealed against this decision to the Court of Criminal Appeal, where I appeared for the Crown. This was the start of a long association with the Whelan kidnap and murder case. The Court of Criminal Appeal dismissed Burrell's appeal in June 2004[18] and in March 2005 the High Court rejected an application for special leave to appeal against that decision.[19]

So the trial proceeded. In the absence of a body or any witnesses to what had happened, the prosecution case was entirely circumstantial. But the Crown used security camera footage fromced the hotel to argue that a vehicle closely resembling Burrell's four-wheel drive had arrived and departed from the front of the hotel at the same time as Kerry Whelan disappeared. The prosecution also relied extensively on two sets of handwritten notes found at

Burrell's property – one which it said was a plan of the kidnapping and another which it said was a draft of the ransom note. Burrell did not go into the witness box to say what these notes meant. The trial lasted for three months and, after deliberating for ten days, the jury were unable to reach a verdict.

The second trial commenced in March 2006. In May Burrell was convicted of the kidnap and murder of Kerry Whelan. He was sentenced to life imprisonment. He appealed to the Court of Criminal Appeal and this case was heard in November 2006. I appeared for the Crown. Ian Barker QC and David Dalton SC appeared for Burrell. His lawyers had two main points. The first was that it was simply unreasonable for the jury to convict, given the wholly circumstantial nature of the evidence. The second argument was that the jury should have been discharged by the trial judge when, towards the end of the trial, he received a note from one juror suggesting that he or she was being intimidated by the other members of the jury.

The Court of Criminal Appeal rejected both these arguments but, in doing so, the judges referred to some evidence that had not been before the jury at the trial.[20] This mistake had occurred because the court had used a document – supplied by Burrell's lawyers – that was not part of the second trial. When this was pointed out by the Crown, the court delivered a second judgment, saying that the mistake had no influence on its ultimate decision.[21]

A little more than a year later we were all in the High Court where Burrell's lawyers argued that the Court of Criminal Appeal had no power to bring down a second decision when the first one had already been finalised. The High Court agreed and said that Burrell's appeal would have to be heard again by the Court of Criminal Appeal.[22] So in December 2008 – almost ten years after Burrell had first been charged – the appeal was reargued, with Ian Barker still for Burrell and myself still for the Crown. The appeal was rejected again in June 2009 and this was the end of a legal epic.[23] There was no appeal to the High Court on this occasion.

4

OUTWARD BOUND
Melbourne to Washington

Far from thinking about these kinds of cases in court, when I arrived at Melbourne University law school for the start of classes in March 1965 I had given very little thought to what the future might hold. Except for one thing. The following month the Prime Minister, Sir Robert Menzies, announced the commitment of Australian combat troops to Vietnam. More significantly, for young men of my age, the government had introduced a system of conscription towards the end of 1964. By means of a birthday ballot, some twenty year olds would be forced to spend two years in the army and perhaps in Vietnam. University students could defer induction until the end of their studies. This was something to think about because, although I was opposed to Australia's involvement in Vietnam, I was not a pacifist. Conscientious objectors could be exempted from service if they established their beliefs in court proceedings but this meant an objection to fighting in any war at any time.

I did not have to go to Vietnam but one of the myths of this period is that there was widespread opposition to the war in Australia in those days. In fact, opinion polls showed approximately two-thirds of the community in favour of the troop commitment and half in favour of conscription. Amongst Catholics, with the exception of a small minority which included my own family, there was overwhelming support for both. The following year, at the 1966 general election, the Liberal government, led by Harold Holt after Menzies' retirement, won a crushing victory over Labor. There were some other issues in the campaign but Labor's opposition to the war was a big factor in the result. Another myth from this time is that universities were hotbeds of revolutionary sentiment. Certainly not at Melbourne University, where most students had little interest in politics and few of my friends in the law school had the same view on Vietnam.

These friends were all new because almost all of my school contemporaries who went on to university had started courses in maths and science. None came to the law school. The composition of the student body there reflected the profession itself. There were

At the Melbourne University Law School ball in May 1968 with Ron Cahill, later chief magistrate in the ACT, and Jacinta Heffey, later a magistrate in Melbourne

three groups that were over-represented by the yardstick of the general community – Catholics, Jews and the products of nominally Protestant private schools – together with a miscellaneous group who did not fit in to any of those categories. There were some women students but nothing like the numbers in today's universities.

The law school buildings were more than a century old. Its cloisters looked like, and were intended to look like, a corner of Oxford or Cambridge. Many students fell into the role of their later lives. Future judges were cautious and earnest; trial lawyers were noisy and flamboyant; AFL footballers, some of whom went to university in the days before full-time professionalism took over, basked modestly in the glory that they enjoyed even in an academic world.

It was, however, a much more relaxed environment than the modern university. Almost all students were full-time. Because they did not have outside jobs, as so many students today have to, they spent a lot of time together and formed very close friendships, including with colleagues in other disciplines. There were three terms in the year and a single three-hour exam in each subject at the end of the third term. Some students never attended lectures and only bought the textbooks late in the year when they started work in earnest. I generally went to lectures because this seemed to save a lot of work. But there was plenty of time for sport. I played tennis with one of the university teams and squash for the Melbourne Cricket Club. And social events figured prominently in weekly activity. First term was the ball season and on many of these autumn nights we set off in groups – the men in black tie and the women in long dresses – to throw ourselves around the dance floor until the early hours of the morning. Often I was still driving home when dawn broke over the Melbourne skyline but there were no breathalyser squads in those days.

These years would certainly have been safer if there had been some deterrent to drinking and driving. I had a hair's breadth escape very late one night on a major but largely deserted road in Melbourne's eastern suburbs. I had spent the day on the tennis court under a fierce sun and the evening in a restaurant where red wine was enjoyed in generous quantity. I fell asleep over the wheel but the car continued to shoot along. Something made me lift my head. The car had drifted off the road and was about to collide head-on with a telegraph pole. I swung the wheel violently to the right. The left front hit the pole but the car bounced off and regained the road surface. After about 100 metres, I pulled up to see the damage. It was not as bad as I had thought but the gears had been jammed by the impact of the crash so there was no possibility of driving on. It seems amazing that I thought I could. I started walking. Eventually a lonely cab drove past and I climbed in. Next day I came back and had the car taken off for repairs. It would be easy to say that this was a stark lesson and that I never drove again after drinking heavily. But I did, although, I like to think, with a little more caution.

All law students had to take some courses in the Arts faculty and I chose the Classics Department for studies in Latin language and Roman history. Only a small group took classics even then, so staff and students knew each other well. In one burst of enthusiasm, a dozen of the students, including myself, took the train from Melbourne to Brisbane and then set off north to the subtropical Mount Tambourine for an Australian universities classics conference. For several days we listened to learned papers, and pretentiously conversed in Latin.

I had been elected secretary of the law students' society in my third year and devoted much effort to organising balls and dinners. Though not involved in any of the political parties on the campus, I wrote an article for the law students' annual magazine in 1967 that looked at Labor's chances of ending what was then eighteen years of coalition government in Australia under its new leader,

Gough Whitlam. Unaware of some unpleasant encounters that I would later have with Whitlam at close quarters, I was cautiously optimistic about the change, suggesting that it was not Labor's policies that were the problem:

> Labor's domestic policies have not been rejected because they are radical or socialist. Indeed, most of its plans for education, housing, social services, etc., have been eventually implemented by the Liberals, and there is certainly room for a more positive approach in some of these areas. Why Labor's policies have failed to carry conviction is because of their vagueness and lack of preparation ...
>
> When Mr Whitlam was elected to the leadership earlier this year, Labor took what could be the first step on the long road back. From the statements he has made since then, it is obvious that he is aware of the danger of retaining an exclusively trade union image in present-day society and of the need to broaden the party's membership and electoral appeal by embracing other sections of the community ... His position is one of great influence, but he can do little by direct action and the party is still the same one that suffered an inglorious defeat at the last election and has spent so many years in the wilderness. The process of rejuvenation will be a long and gradual one if it is to occur.[1]

This may seem too cautious in retrospect but it was still to take Whitlam another five and a half years to win government.

In next year's edition of the magazine, I complained about artistic censorship in Victoria under the government of Sir Henry Bolte, with a hint of literary criticism thrown in:

> The keynote of censorship in Victoria in recent years has been paternalism. The government seems determined to

treat the adult population as if they were the most innocent of children whose minds could be besmirched by the least trace of lurid writing. The result of this attitude is that books and magazines that are accepted without comment in other countries and in other states of the Commonwealth have been banned in Victoria ...

The high spot of Victoria's censorship activity came in 1964 with the banning of Mary McCarthy's novel, 'The Group'. Victoria had the distinction of being the only state in Australia and one of only two places in the world to prohibit the sale of the book. The result of this was that an essentially pedestrian novel that would have been a very average seller received tremendous publicity and, when the ban was later removed, large sales ...

The Melbourne police even went along on opening night to see the film 'Bonnie and Clyde' when it began here, lest the bloodthirsty scenes should prove too much for the fainthearted populace. Happily it was decided that the film could be viewed without any disastrous results. Who says our censorship laws are restrictive?[2]

Halfway through law school, I moved out of home and into Newman College, the Jesuit-run Catholic residential hall at the University. The various colleges occupied an attractive corner of the campus and their spires and quads reflected, like the law school, an attempt to capture some of the beauties of Oxford and Cambridge. Newman had been designed by Walter Burley Griffin and, although never fully completed to his original drawings, was still a striking piece of work, particularly the domed dining room and the tall gothic chapel. Dress for the evening meal was jacket and tie – or cravat – together with academic gown. I had never seen a cravat but I at once bought one. The early evening services in the chapel were attended by a handful of students from Newman and St Mary's, the Catholic women's college next door. I sometimes joined this small group, struck by the combination of architecture and ritual. This was, however, a very ethereal form of religious experience that had little application to everyday life.

After graduation I stayed in Newman as one of the resident tutors who gave classes in the evening to the students. At the same time I spent my days down town in the office of the Commonwealth Crown Solicitor. It was necessary to spend a year working in a legal practice before being admitted as a barrister or solicitor. The tutors came from a range of disciplines, including two doctors, a physicist, a biochemist and an engineer. The other two law tutors were Ken Hayne and Kevin O'Connor. They were something of a contrast. Hayne was a stern Presbyterian who already looked destined for the bench. Appointed to the Victorian Court of Appeal at a young age and then to the High Court in 1997, I saw him then from the Bar table. O'Connor had been born in London to Irish parents. He was another Geelong supporter and on Saturday afternoons could be seen, in a sky blue jacket with binoculars around his neck, crossing the quad on his way to the main race meeting of the weekend. In the late 1990s he was appointed the first president of the NSW Administrative Decisions Tribunal and we found ourselves in the same building in Sydney. He became a life-long friend, as did another of the tutors, Jeff Sellar, a physicist who studied in the United States and England before returning to an academic career in Australia.

Towards the end of 1970, shortly after I had been admitted to practice, the telephone rang in my small office as I was studying, without great enthusiasm, an airport leasing agreement. This call changed the course of my professional and personal life (for better or worse). I had assumed that I would soon take up practice at the Melbourne Bar. The caller was Robert Wright. I did not know him but he had spent the last year and a half as associate to Sir Edward McTiernan, one of the seven judges of the High Court. He was about to take a job with a Melbourne law firm and wanted to know if I would apply for his present post. The work ranged from making the tea to writing draft judgments. There was also the opportunity to see the country's best advocates arguing all the major cases before the court. Associates normally only stayed for one or two years in the job. McTiernan was based in Sydney but I thought that I could spend eighteen months at the top of the law and then return to my life in Melbourne. I was totally wrong about that.

A week later I flew to Sydney for an interview with McTiernan. He had been NSW Attorney-General in 1920 before he was 30 and then a member of the federal parliament in 1929. He was now 78 years old and had been on the court for four decades. Michael Kirby has written of McTiernan's appointment in 1930 at the age of 38:

> Still a bachelor, shy by nature with only a small circle of close friends, his retreat into the judicial monastery reinforced the introspection and other-worldliness which had been noted during his time in politics.[3]

I certainly saw this side of McTiernan but I came to realise that he had been quite ambitious as a young man and, like many shy people, was extremely determined when he wanted something.

The interview was conducted as we strolled through the large garden of McTiernan's house on Sydney's upper north shore. I obviously showed little enthusiasm for the carefully-maintained collection of plants and flowers. As we went back into the house, McTiernan remarked dryly, "I see botany is not one of your interests." There were, however, common interests in law, history, classics and religion. A few weeks later I moved to Sydney and started to adapt to the court's routine, which in those days, before the court established a permanent home in Canberra in 1980, meant spending about a third of the year on circuit in the other capitals. The associates were together much of the time on these expeditions and I made a couple more lifelong friends amongst my colleagues.

In *The Legal Mystique*, a book published in 1982 about the law in Australia with Laurence Maher, I was very critical about decision-making in the High Court. After suggesting that there needed to be less repetitive oral argument and more written submissions in the style of the United States Supreme Court, I complained about the way judgments were written:

> After tolerating and encouraging the maximum inefficiency in the presentation of a case, the High Court then compounds this by the way it goes about producing a decision. At this stage the US Supreme Court has a meeting of all judges who vote on the outcome of the case. One judge is then assigned the task of writing the opinion of the Court, if the judges are unanimous, or the majority, if they are not. Where a minority view exists this is written by one judge also. It is these opinions that are eventually published in the law reports together with the decision in each case.
>
> On no occasion do all judges of the High Court ever sit collectively except to actually hear a case in the courtroom. Instead each judge initially retreats to his own rooms to prepare an individual judgment in each case. In part this style of working is engendered by a life at the bar where solitary endeavour is the norm. Moreover the judges do not have substantial support staff. Apart from stenographic staff each judge has one legal assistant, usually a recent graduate, near the top of his or her law school class, who stays one or two years before going into practice.[4]

There is now a much greater reliance in the High Court on written submissions and the judges have no shortage of resources. There are still no formal conferences but joint judgments are more common. There is still, however, too much over-lengthy and repetitious oral argument by some barristers.

Outside the court, I lived in a series of group houses where late nights and seedy mornings were routine. I learnt about Sydney but it bore little resemblance to the Melbourne that I had grown up in. The differences in origin, geography and climate had produced a much tougher and more assertive city. Although some of the references were dated, I thought that John Douglas Pringle's impressions of Sydney in the late 1950s still rang true:

> Every nation reveals its character in the way it drives its cars, and the aggressive thrusting side of the Australian character rises to the surface as the drivers force their way through regardless of rules or common courtesy. You see it again in the dumps of rubbish which line the roads and the countless beer bottles flung casually into the bush or the creeks. You hear it at the races in the angry shouts of the crowd as the favourite fails and the jockey is jeered and hooted as he rides back to the paddock. You see it in the sight of drunks brawling on the footpath in William Street, while men stand round laughing and urging the winner to "put the boot in". You see it at Princes' and Romano's where smart, hard-faced, wealthy women lunch together and try to attract the attention of the photographers and "social reporters" sent there by the newspapers. For this is a rough, boisterous, greedy city, with little time for the grace of life and little respect for the shy and retiring. "Push" is a quality much admired. Parents push their children; children push themselves; and too often the young and strong and ambitious push the elder and weaker out of the way.[5]

Towards the end of 1971 I was ready to leave this brash environment and return to Melbourne but McTiernan asked me to stay for another six months and come to London with him. He was to sit as a judge on the Judicial Committee of the Privy Council, then the final court of appeal from many Commonwealth countries. It was usually composed of British judges from the House of

Lords but sometimes added a senior judge from somewhere in the Commonwealth. It was an oddity that appeals from the High Court to the Privy Council had effectively come to end in 1968 but continued from the Australian State Supreme Courts until 1986. The Privy Council was located in Downing Street, just a stone's throw from the Prime Minister's home and office. We took up residence, at great expense to the Australian taxpayer, in the Hyde Park Hotel, an old but opulent building in the heart of Knightsbridge and on the edge of the park itself. It was no coincidence that we had arrived at the height of the season for sporting and artistic events – cricket at Lord's, tennis at Wimbledon, opera at Covent Garden, Shakespeare at Stratford-upon-Avon.

Amongst the cases upon which McTiernan sat as a judge were a number of appeals from murder trials in the West Indies and Hong Kong.[6] Despite the abstruse legal arguments, conducted by members of the English Bar in Oxbridge accents, these were life and death decisions. A sentence of hanging had been imposed after the guilty verdict and would be carried out unless the appeal was successful. This was an early lesson that, even in the most important cases, a court can usually decide quite plausibly for either side and it is often a small point that tips the result in one direction or another.

When McTiernan and his wife went off travelling for some weeks in other parts of the British Isles, I did the same, but closer to the ground. In a small car owned by my English girlfriend, we drove through much of England, Wales and Ireland. The dark, soft greens of their woods and dales were a striking contrast to the light colours of the Australian bush, with its vast vegetation and shimmering heat hazes. There is little to rival a true English summer, although in some years the sun never emerges at all. This was a vintage summer. There were long days and velvet twilights. Many nights we slept in a field with no covering but a small tent, without ever being disturbed by the owner of the land.

This life was too good to last and in July the McTiernans were ready to return home. I had intended to join some friends from law school who were travelling in Europe but Sir Edward and Lady McTiernan were anxious to have an escort on most of the return journey. I decided to make the best of this change of plans and, after putting them on a plane in Hong Kong, flew to Japan and on to Kharbarosk in Russia's far east to take the Trans-Siberian railway back towards Europe. I call it Russia but this was still the Soviet Union. I was searched when I arrived and found to be carrying two passports – an official (green) one for my travels with the judge and an ordinary (blue) passport for other travel. This aroused deep suspicions and half a day passed while my baggage was minutely examined, with my toothpaste tube being squeezed out in front of me at one point. I should have had more sense but, finally, I was escorted to the railway station.

Over the following days the train pushed forward, day and night, into the vast expanse portrayed by Tolstoy and Dostoyevsky. Forest and lakes eventually gave way to steppes and wheat lands stretching to the horizon. This was the only time that I travelled alone and it was hard work dealing with the Soviet bureaucracy, especially when most tourists were in organised groups. But, after several weeks, I eventually arrived at Yalta on the Black Sea where I could travel by boat along the River Danube to Vienna. The night before the boat sailed I was having dinner by myself at one of the beachfront cafes when the couple at the next table asked me to join them. He was a Moscow lawyer, obviously wealthy; she was his girlfriend. His wife and family, he explained, were at home in Moscow. Not everything was different in the Soviet Union.

The day my boat docked in Vienna, I picked up my suitcase and set off for the general post office. Before I left London, my law school comrades said they would leave a letter there for me about their route across Europe. As I turned a corner in the old part of the town I saw one of them, Michael Serong in a gabardine overcoat that I recognised from London. With nowhere to stay and nowhere to go, I can say that I was never happier to see anybody. Serong's father had been the Australian Commander in Vietnam. The last Australian troops had left in 1971 but Ted Serong remained, working for the Americans. Two other residents of the van were John McArdle, later a silk and the Chief Crown Prosecutor in Victoria, and John Burns, who left the law for a highly successful career as a radio presenter in Melbourne. For the next four months home was our van and the tent that was usually pitched at night. This journey took us as far north as the fjords in Norway, south to the toe of Italy and west to Istanbul on the Bosphorus before turning back east to London. Unless it rained, which made outdoor life miserable, we spent most nights camping in woods or by streams. The mountains, lakes and valleys of the alpine regions provided a series of spectacular sites for picnic lunches. We sat on the ground,

Outside the van near Igoumenitsa in Greece in October 1972 with John Burns and Ian Campbell on the left and John McArdle and Michael Serong on the right

shirts off in the sun with some bread, cheese and wine from the nearest village.

In September, however, we were present at events that took centre-stage in world news. We were already in Germany so we decided to see if we could attend some of the events at the 1972 Olympic Games in Munich. The highly-organised ticketing and security at recent Games would make this a hopeless exercise. But in the main square of Munich tickets for all the major events were available on a black market that did not seem to be charging much more than the official price. We spent several days at the track and field stadium before the Games were abruptly halted. When Steven Spielberg's film *Munich* came out in 2006 I wrote about what happened in *The Australian*:

> On the night of 4 September 1972, when Black September personnel were preparing to attack the Israeli quarters in Munich's Olympic village, I was sitting at a crowded table in one of the city's noisiest beer halls.
>
> The table was an odd mixture. There was a small group of recent graduates from Melbourne University law school. We were on a long camping tour of Europe and had decided to take in the Games. The rest of the table was occupied by members of the chorus of Milan's La Scala opera company which was performing in Munich. Everyone joined in some singing, although it was no surprise that the chorus had much better voices.
>
> When the beer hall closed, we set off for our camping spot about 20 km outside the town. All the official camping grounds were full so we simply chose a wood near the site of the former Dachau concentration camp. Its proximity to Munich was a reminder that the existence of such places was hardly a secret in the German community of the 1930s.

Next morning we awoke late. The one-litre steins of strong beer had taken a heavy toll. We heard the news about the village and, along with a lot of the locals, drove to that part of town. The village was in a bowl and it was possible to look down on it from the surrounding heights. Although so close to the scene, we knew less about what was happening than if we had been watching television on the other side of the world. But it was only much later that anyone found out the full story of that day.

. . . The Munich police would not allow Israel to send a team to make an assault on the building occupied by Black September. We know – because all the captured athletes were ultimately killed – that no result of such an attack could have been any worse than the final outcome.

The Germans never launched an assault of their own either. At one point they made plans for an attack but called it off when it became clear that the preparations were being televised to the world at large, including the Black September invaders of the village. This was because the area around the occupied building had not even been sealed off from the media.

Later in the day the Germans agreed to a bizarre scheme under which the hostages and their captors would go by helicopter to a local airport where a plane would be provided by the authorities. This was to be a trap. The plane was occupied by armed police officers who would engage the terrorists. Shortly before the arrival at the airport of the helicopters carrying the hostages, the police on the plane decided that this was a dangerous mission and *voted* to call it off! Without consulting any of their superiors, they then left the plane standing empty.

When the terrorists and the hostages approached the plane, there were some uncoordinated shots fired by snipers. The snipers were not professional marksmen. They had no radio contact with each other. None of the rifles carried scopes or night-vision sighters. Some of the terrorists survived and killed all the remaining athletes.

... This astonishing record of German incompetence – or worse – is the real story of the Munich Games. It should be noted, however, that the conduct of the IOC was dreadful in its own way. It grudgingly suspended the Games for two days but then resumed them as if nothing had happened.

Before leaving Munich, we visited the Dachau site. It was one of the first of the concentration camps established after Hitler came to power in 1933. It was not set up at that time for Jews but for communists, social democrats and other political opponents of the new regime. It was fashionable in Germany of the post-war years to pretend that the country had somehow been captured by a small clique of Nazis who were quite separate from the rest of the population. Yet in the three months following Hitler's swearing in as Chancellor, 1.6 million Germans joined the Nazi party. We were usually a noisy group but there was complete silence as we walked between the barracks where the prisoners had been housed. They were a tangible reminder of the terrible life – and death – of millions at this and other camps in Germany and its occupied territories during the 1930s and 1940s.

By November the temperatures in Europe were falling sharply and there was no romance in sleeping under the stars. We crossed the Channel and headed for London, ready to return to Australia. But in London I found a letter waiting for me from the University of Virginia. The letter offered a place in the University's law school to do a master's degree and some scholarship funds as well. I had applied to the law school before leaving Australia but assumed that nothing had come of it. This was a big choice. I had always wanted to spend some time living in the United States but I sensed that this was my last chance to pick up the threads of life in Melbourne.

With University of Virginia roommate, John Mellyn, at the university's Kite Day on Brown's Mountain in May 1973

After some weeks of indecision over Christmas, I bought a plane ticket across the Atlantic and arrived in Charlottesville, about 190km south-west of Washington, where the university is located.

I was not at all prepared for the beauty of northern Virginia in general and the university in particular. Even in mid-winter, the colonial buildings and sweeping lawns were a striking combination. Later I would see it in full splendour in the fall when the long lines of trees turned golden. Thomas Jefferson wanted only two things on his tombstone – that he had written the Declaration of Independence and founded the University of Virginia. He did not mention that he had been president of the United States.

Initially there was nowhere to stay but I was taken into the family home of a New Zealander teaching at the law school that semester. His name was Geoffrey Palmer. Full of energy and enthusiasm, he had startled the students by walking around the classroom on the tops of the desks, while keeping up a barrage of questions to those below. One night after dinner we went for a walk around the town. I asked him what he planned to do at the end of the semester. He said that he was going to go back to New Zealand and get involved in politics. I asked him on what side. He said that his family had always been supporters of the National Party but he wanted to run for office with Labour. I remembered this conversation when, 16 years later, Palmer took over from David Lange as Prime Minister of New Zealand in 1989.

When I moved out of the Palmer household into one of the student dormitories, I found myself sharing rooms with a laconic New Englander from the law school, John Mellyn. This kind of proximity usually leads to one of two extremes – warm friendship or mutual incompatibility. We seemed to hit it off and Mellyn was a good guide to local customs. He had spent 18 months in Vietnam before coming to the law school. Although he did not often talk about those times, occasionally, over beer and pizza in one of the town restaurants, he described the grim realities of the war at ground level. Our next door neighbour was another law student, Mitchell Abbott, a Californian who also worked for Senator John Tunney. It was Tunney's successful 1970 campaign that provided the basis for Robert Redford's film, *The Candidate*. His room was piled high with cases of Californian wine that fuelled long discussions about American politics.

There had always been close connections between the law school and the Washington political world. Both Robert Kennedy and Ted Kennedy had been students in the 1950s. Robert Kennedy had set up a forum to bring prominent speakers to Charlottesville. By the time I arrived the forum was run by Charles Robb, who had married one of Lyndon Johnson's daughters and was later elected Governor of Virginia and then a United States Senator. Amongst the speakers he organised were Vice-President, Spiro Agnew; New

York Governor, Nelson Rockefeller; and – a bigger draw card than any politician – veteran newsman, Walter Cronkite. I could say that I had met the Vice-President, but not for long. A few months later Agnew was forced to resign. He was lucky to avoid going to gaol after pleading guilty to a bribery charge.

One of the courses I took was in labour relations law. The professor in charge organised a job for me during the summer in Washington with the Labourers' International Union of North America. This was the head office of the union. It had more than three quarters of a million members throughout the country, mainly located in the north-east and on the west coast, mostly in the construction industries. The union had its own building, a block from the White House, and a legal department with three in-house lawyers. During the summer period they were joined by two interns – myself and a young Italian-American woman who was a student at the University of Pennsylvania law school in Philadelphia.

When John Kennedy described Washington as a city of northern efficiency and southern charm, he did not intend it as a compliment. But it is a place of great beauty, with broad avenues leading through parks and trees to the familiar alabaster outlines of the Capitol, the White House and the Washington Monument. It is also a city where the chief business is government and very little happens without the involvement of lawyers. In the union's legal department even the interns worked on Supreme Court cases and lobbied members of Congress on legislation.

This was the summer of Watergate. Working so close to the White House, we half-expected to see palls of smoke rising from its rose garden as documents and tapes were destroyed. The hearings of the Senate committee investigating Watergate were broadcast in full late at night on the public television network. I have a sharp memory of the evening when, sitting with some friends after dinner, we watched John Dean, Nixon's in-house lawyer, give his evidence. We all thought that Dean was telling the truth when he described various forms of illegal conduct authorised by the President and some of his aides. There was something compelling about Dean's icy calm and boyish features. But we assumed that there could never be any corroboration of his allegations so that the committee would not be able to make any positive findings of illegality. Shortly afterwards, the committee discovered, largely by accident, that most White House meetings, including those described by Dean, had been taped. This was the beginning of the end for Nixon, although it took another year of congressional hearings and Supreme Court challenges before he resigned and climbed forlornly into a helicopter waiting on the White House lawns.

In late 1973 and early 1974 I was supposed to be back in Charlottesville. Some of the time I was. Quite often, however, I was in Philadelphia with my fellow intern from the union, Janice Bellace. She later became a professor in the business school at the University of Pennsylvania as well as president of the Singapore Management University and a member of the experts committee of the International Labour Organisation. Through her school and university friends I came to know the city well, from the Italian quarter of *Rocky* to the spacious Mainline estates of *The Philadelphia Story*. This was a place full of history. It had been the largest city in the British Empire towards the middle of the 18th century and then became the heartland of the American revolution.

We often visited New York City. If Paris is the most beautiful city in the world in traditional terms, New York is its more contemporary competitor. I sometimes walked 40 or 50 blocks, not because there were no buses or cabs, but simply to enjoy the towering skyline stretching ahead. Its localities were enormously familiar by name from the books, movies and songs of the previous hundred years

– Times Square, Wall Street, Central Park, Greenwich Village. Fifth Avenue in December, with snow on the sidewalks and the department stores crowded with winter-clad shoppers, was a Christmas scene I had imagined since childhood.

All this involved plenty of driving but it was done in some style. My physicist friend from Melbourne, Jeff Sellar, was now based at the University of Arizona. He went to Europe for several months during the summer and left his car with me – a Ford Mustang, pale lemon, with Arizona licence plates – a rare sight on the East Coast. It drove beautifully and made many trips up and down Interstate 95, the main artery of the north-east. I gave Sellar an abridged version of its travels when I finally returned the car but he was sceptical – especially after finding papers from a Canadian border post in the glove box!

The factories and refineries lining much of Interstate 95 were a constant reminder of the industrial might of the United States. But there was also a small town America, often surrounded by farming communities, whose life had little in common with Manhattan or Georgetown. I learnt about the spread of America's population when, with a Scottish student in the law school, I spent a month travelling the country on Greyhound buses. We swung through the south and south-west to California then came back through the mid-west and the Great Lakes. Notwithstanding contrasts in landscape, climate and culture between States like Alabama and Wyoming, there were many common threads between the hundreds of small towns that we passed through.

This was a big difference from Australia, where a large part of the continent remained uninhabited and most of the population lived in the suburbs of a few large cities. Beyond geography, however, the two nations had sharply different histories. The Americans fought a revolutionary war to obtain independence from Britain and then a civil war, with enormous loss of life, to preserve the union that had emerged from the first conflict. There were no comparable experiences in Australia's history. The result has been a relaxed, tolerant, even cynical, society in contrast to the more intense, more demanding, attitudes of Americans towards those providing either public or private services. The longer I spent in the United States, the more I was struck by the differences between the two societies, despite some superficial similarities. Americans were more passionate about everything, including America. And one consequence was a wider, and tougher, debate on public issues than occurs in Australia.

I thought about all this in mid-1974 when I had to decide whether to return home or not. If I settled down in Philadelphia and entered practice there, it seemed likely that I would remain in America for good. I was strongly attracted by its sheer energy and power. But I was also intensely curious about Australia under the Whitlam government elected in 1972. After growing up under more than two decades of Liberal rule in the 1950s and 1960s, I wanted to see this experiment at first hand and, if possible, to take part in it. This was simply the biggest decision of my life, although I did not understand that at the time. Nor did I realise until later – I certainly should have – how unfairly I had treated Janice. I made the decision alone, without talking to her or to my parents, who also deserved to know what was happening. This was partly because of my own uncertainties but it was confused at best and callous at worst. I still wonder sometimes what sort of family and career I would have found if I had stayed. But these were idle speculations once I had made the decision to return home.

Even then, the route to Australia took several months. I went first to London and then, with a woman friend from Melbourne University who had been living in England and was also returning home, to Cairo, to start an overland journey back to Australia. We each had our own – separate – romantic interests but made good travelling companions. The images of Egypt had been familiar since childhood but the beauty and mystery of the Pyramids at sunset still came as a shock, as did their close proximity to Cairo. To reach Luxor, however, with its tombs and temples, we took a train 1,000km along the Nile. As the train pulled into the main station at Cairo, it was obvious that the passengers packed on the platform vastly outnumbered the seats available. Spurred on by the prospect of having to stand for 24 hours or more, the crowd charged at the carriages long before they drew to a halt. Using such AFL skills as I had ever possessed, I crashed through a pack and fell onto two seats. The train departed with many passengers still clinging to the outside. On return to Cairo we made the much shorter trip to Alexandria on the coast. Although faded and down-at-heel in comparison with its colonial heyday, it was still recognisable as the exotic mixture of east and west that Lawrence Durrell had brought to life in the *Alexandria Quartet*.

From Egypt we headed east through a number of countries that became the scene of war and revolution in the next two decades. Travelling in Iraq was like entering a medieval kingdom. It was not that it seemed especially dangerous for visitors but I realised that, if some kind of accident occurred, we would just disappear and our families would never know what had happened. This was in the early years of the regime of Saddam Hussein but political discussion was not permitted. The bus from Jordan reached the Iraq border in the middle of the night. Everyone and everything on the bus was taken off and searched on the roadside for several hours. Some Palestinian passengers had a number of current affairs magazines. Naturally their contents were anti-Israeli and anti-American but this made no difference to the Iraqi border guards. They were confiscated anyway. When we reached Baghdad, we were taken home by a young soldier whom we met in one of the markets. He was only sixteen but was already married with a small child. I sometimes thought of him during the 1980s when Iraq and Iran fought a long war. He may have survived but hundreds of thousands of young men on each side lost their lives. The full extent of the casualties will never be known as both sides excluded Western observers and reporters from the war zone but have been estimated at one million dead for Iran and up to half a million for Iraq.

Iran itself seemed very different. This was the time of the Shah and Western customs were not only tolerated but encouraged. It would become obvious in a few years, however, that this was a very thin veneer. We had a hint of the militant Islamic world beneath the surface when we arrived in the city of Mashad during what are called the mourning days – a religious festival to mark the death of the prophet. The city was swelled by hundreds of thousands of pilgrims from other parts of the country. It was simply an accident on our part to arrive at that time but Mary was attacked in the street because of her t-shirt and jeans and we had to be hustled away by the local authorities. Within a few years the Shah was gone and women were savagely beaten if they appeared in public without being covered from head to toe.

Like Iraq and Iran, Afghanistan would also be closed to foreign travellers within a few years, in this case because of its occupation by Soviet troops. This must be one of the bleakest landscapes in the world, with hardly a tree or a blade of grass to be seen. There was also the sense of stepping back several centuries. On one occasion, as our ancient and creaking bus bumped through a mountain pass, I looked at the passenger in the next seat. Across his knees lay a musket and next to him on the seat was a cage enclosing a hawk. At regular intervals he, like most of the other passengers, spat into the aisle. After several hours there was a river of phlegm that changed direction every time the bus slewed into a curve on the winding road.

After Pakistan we crossed northern India to Calcutta and flew to Thailand. The train down the Malaysian peninsula brought us to Singapore where there was a flight to Australia. After several months of heat and dust I had lost quite a bit of weight but there seemed to be no other ill effects. While sitting in a café in Calcutta, I read an article in an English newspaper about the Whitlam government. Canberra sounded like a place of high excitement. And the government sounded like a complete shambles. Both turned out to be right.

5

THE GREAT CRASH:
Inside the Whitlam Government

Canberra in the winter of 1974 was an attractive sight. Mornings of sharp frost gave way to clear, dry days and finally brilliant sunsets as the light faded behind the surrounding Brindabella ranges. From the steps of the low-slung and white-washed Parliament House there was an uninterrupted view across Lake Burley Griffin to the dome of the War Memorial – a vista worthy of Paris or Washington.

My new working environment was less attractive. The federal Attorney-General's Department was located in a large grey stone blockhouse – blandly known as the Administrative Building – half a kilometre from Parliament House. I had been assigned to the Advisings Division, which provided advice to other departments and statutory bodies that had a legal problem – often whether they had the power to do something that they wanted to do. The lawyers in Advisings were considered the department's best and brightest and had been the source of most of its leaders up to that time. It was headed by Patrick Brazil, a very astute lawyer and bureaucrat, who became head of the department in 1983.

Advisings was, however, divided into sections and mine was led by a relatively young but, it seemed to me, humourless and pedantic lawyer. We did not hit it off. Not that I was an easy person to work with at that time. I was uncertain whether it had been a good idea to return to Australia. And, after my time in the United States many of the department's procedures appeared hopelessly old-fashioned and inefficient. I made no effort to disguise these views. Not surprisingly, lawyers who had spent decades in the department thought this was offensive from someone who had just arrived. No doubt I was brash and tactless but I was not the only person to be startled on first encountering this organisation. In the early 1980s Neil Brown QC, who was a minister in the Fraser government and had been for many years at the Melbourne Bar, acted as Attorney-General for three months when the Attorney-General, Senator Peter Durack, was ill. At the end of this time Brown wrote to the Prime Minister about his experiences:

> I thought it would be useful if I gave you some impressions of the Attorney-General's Department based on the experience of three months as Acting Attorney-General. In general I do not think that the Government is well-served by the Attorney-General's Department. There are some good lawyers in the Department who do some valuable work, but some of the work, I regret to say, is not well done . . .
>
> Further, management and administration skills in the department are rare and there seems to be no organisation of the work. My view is that there must be a substantial upgrading in this area before one *could* be confident that the department is properly run. Nor is there any co-ordination of work: some parts of the department are clearly not aware of the work being done in other areas.
>
> Further, a lot of the work is handled without an appreciation of the political implications. I do not mean party political; the point is that legal issues do not arise in a vacuum and they must be considered in their context which is a governmental and political one and this is not being done.[1]

Brown considered there was "a deep-seated malaise" in the department and I had very much the same reaction nearly a decade earlier. My impressions were not improved when I set off through the corridors on the first day to find my old friend from Melbourne Law School, Laurence Maher. He had been on the staff of the Attorney-General, Lionel Murphy, but had moved out of Parliament House and into the department some months earlier. As soon as I walked into his room, I knew that something was wrong. There was almost nothing in it. Most lawyers have so much paper in their offices that it is hard to get in the door. The department had been told by Murphy to organise a position so it did. But it seemed determined that Maher would not be given any real work to do, hoping that he would take the hint and move on. He had taken the hint and was busy finishing his thesis for a Master of Laws degree at the Australian National University and arranging to set up his own legal practice in Melbourne. It was, however, an utter waste of a highly-talented lawyer. It was also, although I did not realise it immediately, an ominous indication of how the department regarded those who worked in a Labor minister's office.

Even social occasions were stormy in my time at the department. In late 1974 the head of the US Environmental Protection Agency, William Ruckelshaus, visited Canberra to address a seminar on environmental law. Ruckelshaus was a keen tennis player and a game was organised for him at the American Embassy with the Ambassador and the Deputy Secretary of the department. They needed a fourth player to have a doubles match. I had started playing in the Canberra competition on weekends and was asked to fill in. I played with Ruckelshaus and, on the second point, smashed a backhand return that hit the Ambassador, Marshal Green, over the heart. He dropped his racquet and fell over. He got back on his feet and continued playing but I received no more invitations to the Embassy.

By early 1975 I had seen enough of the department and was thinking about the Bar in Melbourne. Then Lionel Murphy was appointed to the High Court. This decision had a large, if unintended, impact on my own life. The new Attorney-General, Kep Enderby, had been Minister for Manufacturing Industry and had no lawyers on his staff. Although we had never met, he asked if I would like to move into his office in Parliament House. This was the start of an exciting year but not a very smart career move.

Enderby was an interesting character. Bluff in manner, strongly built, a champion golfer in his twenties and the second-placed amateur in the British Open of 1951, he had been a legal academic and then a barrister in Canberra before winning the one ACT seat in the House of Representatives four years earlier. He did not have a factional or regional basis of support but owed his place in the ministry to the Prime Minister. In the late 1960s Enderby had been the ACT Member on Labor's national executive. He had supported Whitlam when the future Prime Minister was sometimes in danger of expulsion by his own party. Whitlam had not forgotten. This did not mean that Enderby avoided the Prime Minister's famous tirades but he was surprisingly phlegmatic about them. Soon after I arrived, he took a call from Whitlam when I was in his private office. I could hear the torrent of abuse from the other side of the room. When he put the phone down, Enderby was quite jovial: "Don't worry about Gough. He only says those kinds of things if he really likes you!" This seemed a far-fetched proposition to me. But I came to realise that there was some truth in it, at least as far as Enderby was concerned. Whitlam did not, however, like many of his other ministerial colleagues.

Enderby was intelligent and hardworking but, like many barristers, highly disorganised. I was happy to supply some organisation if I could. My chief colleagues in the office were John Iremonger, later one of Australia's leading publishers, and

Neal Swancott, who was the press secretary and went on to be the national secretary of the Australian Journalists Association. The three of us worked in an office not much larger than a telephone booth. If one person wanted to leave, the other two had to stand up so that he could get out. There is presumably now a law prohibiting these kinds of conditions for employees but none of us worried about that in 1975. In fact, Iremonger's infectious laughter and Swancott's mordant commentary provided a very congenial working environment.

This kind of accommodation reflected the general style of Old Parliament House. One of Labor's Victorian Senators, John Button, compared it at this time to being back at boarding school. The ministerial staff were mostly young and were constantly in each other's company. When they left the office it was usually to go to the Non-Members' Bar for a drink or to the staff dining room for a meal. The hours were long because of the parliamentary sitting times. Both politicians and staff frequently mingled with the various members of the press gallery who were upstairs. Most journalists were relatively young as well, even veterans like Max Walsh and Laurie Oakes. It was hardly surprising in this hot-house atmosphere that some people abandoned their existing families and others, like myself, met their future spouse.

One of the attractions of my new role was that the Attorney-General, as the government's chief legal adviser, is very close to the heart of the administration. There were certain to be plenty of interesting and sensitive matters coming across my desk in Enderby's office. One of the less attractive aspects of the job, however, was that I was now regarded by the department with suspicion bordering on hostility. This attitude has long changed in Canberra but the Whitlam government came to office after twenty-three years of one-party rule. Quite a number of ministerial staff did not come from traditional public service careers and clashed with senior bureaucrats, particularly some of the permanent heads, like Sir Arthur Tange at Defence and Sir Frederick Wheeler at Treasury, who had dominated this world in the post-war years.

The head of the Attorney-General's department was Clarrie Harders. He was small and softly spoken but a good all-round lawyer and a skilled bureaucrat. He liked to keep a very close eye on his minister and often arrived at the office in Parliament House in the mornings before Enderby so that no-one else could talk to the minister before he did.

On one of my first mornings in the office I followed Harders into Enderby's office and sat in a corner sorting some papers. After disposing of some routine matters, Harders said: "Attorney, this next issue is highly confidential." "Yes", said Enderby, "what is it?" Harders looked uneasy. "It's a very sensitive matter." Enderby looked puzzled. "Yes". Harders looked desperate. He glanced ostentatiously at me and had one more try. "It's extremely confidential." "Oh, you mean Michael!" exclaimed Enderby. "Don't worry about him. It's quite safe to talk." Harders gave up and started the story. I did not see a great future ahead if I returned to the department.

When, some years later, I wrote *Illusions of Power: The fate of a reform government*,[2] I was sometimes critical – Whitlam thought unfairly – of the administration's lack of direction:

> What was clearly lacking at the end of 1974 was any real notion of the government as an entity, with policies and priorities against which individual ministers and departments were required and, moreover, felt required, to test their own programs. In keeping with this seeming lack of appreciation that the government would be judged by the electorate as a unit, Cabinet conspicuously failed to discuss political tactics or the effect of its decisions in electoral terms.

Many of the government's failings were of its own making but rectification was well nigh impossible as it was trying to operate in a political climate that often verged on hysteria. Twenty-three years without a change of government had left many organisations, both public and private, badly equipped to deal with any kind of change. The policies of the Whitlam administration were far from radical but they often produced a violent reaction.

The government did not have the numbers to force legislation through the Senate and the Opposition recognised no mandate for any of its policies, despite the government's election in 1972 and re-election in 1974. Some sections of the bureaucracy, especially in the Treasury, were openly suspicious of the government and leaked information constantly to the Opposition. The media was largely unsympathetic and, in some cases, fiercely hostile. The governments of the major States – New South Wales, Victoria, Queensland and Western Australia – were Liberal Country Party coalitions and determined to inflict whatever damage they could on the federal administration. A range of private bodies, including the insurance industry and the bodies representing the medical and legal professions, were running virulent campaigns against government proposals that they saw as threats to their long-established interests.

The hostility of the organised medical profession to Medibank, for example, seems bewildering in retrospect. It was no more than a system of health insurance, still essentially in existence, under which the Commonwealth government would pay all or the major part of doctors' fees. In 1973, however, the Royal Society of General Practitioners urged doctors to send letters to their patients and suggested, in a guide to the contents, that the following be included:

> . . . the control of our country has fallen in the hands of socialists . . . socialism was the brain-child of Karl Marx, a bitter man and a strange mixture of semi-scientist and half-

baked philosopher. Lenin accepted the teachings of Marx, fomented a revolution in Russia, exterminated millions of ordinary decent people and enslaved the rest . . . the fight that the General Practitioners' Society in Australia is spearheading is basically a fight for freedom – not just freedom for doctors – but freedom for you, for your children, and for all people in the country.[3]

Much of the legal profession also appeared to be unhinged. The Australian Legal Aid Office was a modest proposal for a small group of salaried lawyers to provide legal assistance to persons of limited financial means in cases under federal law. In early 1975 the solicitor members of the Victorian Law Institute passed a motion by 1,396 votes to 548 in the following terms:

> The Council of the Law Institute be instructed to resist Governmental nationalisation of the profession at all costs, being destructive of an independent legal profession and as being likely to cause that profession to become no less than an arm of Government.[4]

The mood of the times was dramatically captured by Tasmanian Liberal Senator, Peter Rae, who said of this period in a newspaper article:

> Throughout 1974 and 1975, Australians saw a threat to their way of life. They demanded strong anti-socialist leadership. From Mt Isa to Bunbury I found small numbers of people talking about the prospect of armed rebellion.[5]

In its melodramatic, almost South American, flavour, this attitude reflected some of the hysteria that infected political debate. These external pressures exacerbated the government's internal problems. As I wrote in *Illusions of Power*:

> In retrospect the most effective feature of this opposition, which was always fierce and persistent, was the way in

which the familiar trilogy – Senate, State governments, private interest groups – meshed together to form a web from which few major initiatives emerged intact. There is no doubt that the Senate was the fulcrum of this campaign and that the attitude of the LCP Opposition in the Parliament – that Labor was not a valid or legitimate government – encouraged other groups in the community to adopt this view. When it found itself unable to implement its programs, the government became increasingly frustrated and desperate to find a way around the impasse. Moreover the Senate's ever-present ability to block supply led to regular periods of administrative paralysis and political neurosis inside the government. As the government began to disintegrate in 1975, in large measure due to this campaign of obstruction and destabilisation, it made it even easier to argue that Labor had had no right to hold office at any time.[6]

In the dramatic but isolated environment of Parliament House, there was little contact with the real world. Most of its inhabitants, whether politicians, staff or journalists, spent almost all their waking hours in the building, at least during sitting weeks. Late at night I sometimes walked across King's Hall with Malcolm Fraser who had taken over as Leader of the Opposition in March 1975. We did not know each other and Fraser had little in the way of small talk so our conversation was rather sparse. One thing I did notice, however, was that Fraser often turned off the lights in his own office because he was the last to leave. It was often said in government offices that Fraser was lazy but this seemed unlikely to me.

I still had two links with the outside world. One was the local tennis club where no one had any interest in talking politics. The other was the Australian National University where I went two evenings a week to give some classes in the law school on commercial law. Set by Lake Burley Griffin, with its 1950s buildings surrounded by trees, ANU seemed a very tranquil place after the feverish atmosphere of Parliament House.

By the middle of 1975 the government's position was parlous. The unemployment figure for the previous year was 5.2 per cent and for inflation 16.3 per cent – both post-war records. This level of unemployment is no longer unusual but it was a startling reading for inflation. There were some historical reasons for this figure but it also reflected the absence of central economic management. Most ministers came to Cabinet arguing their department's case for increased expenditure without any concern for the overall effect on the budget. These economic problems would have made it very difficult for any government to win the next election. But they were combined with a series of bizarre scandals that took the government to record lows in the opinion polls. One was the so-called Loans Affair, arising out of the efforts of Minerals and Energy Minister, Rex Connor, to borrow US$4000 million overseas through a Pakistani commodities trader, Tirath Khemlani. Another long-running saga involved loan documents coming out of the office of Deputy Prime Minister and Treasurer, Jim Cairns. There was also a lurid sideshow in the form of Cairns' apparent infatuation with his chief of staff, Junie Morosi.

On the evening of 2 July 1975 ministers and staff sat in their offices in Parliament House while the Prime Minister and the Deputy Prime Minister (now Minister for the Environment) took part in a stand-off. Whitlam had removed Cairns from his ministerial post but Cairns refused to go. Later in the evening Whitlam was driven out to Yarralumla and had the Governor-General, Sir John Kerr, terminate Cairns' commission as a minister. Never in a single week in Australian political history has a government had the kind of press coverage that took place in that first week of July. I later described the media reports in these terms:

> This was a week from which the government would

never recover. Beginning on 1 July, Cairns and Connor loan stories alternated on the front pages of the nation's press. The flood of material, true and false, was led by the Melbourne *Age* and its coverage for that week gave some indication of why opinion polls later recorded the government's support during this period at an all-time low of 33 per cent. On 1 July the *Age* headlined Phillip Cairns' [stepson of the Deputy Prime Minister] involvement in Arab loan negotiations to finance land development in Melbourne's western suburbs. The next day it led with telexes that referred to a US$600,000 commission for Phillip Cairns, and introduced an exotic cast of characters that included Eric Farnborough Sear Cowls, self-described bullfighter, CIA agent and management consultant, and 'Uncle Harry' Gilham who ran a one-man finance organisation out of Bulldog Drummond's London address. It was this material that had been the subject of a wild auction conducted in London between the representatives of *The Age* and *The Australian* to be finally knocked down to the *Age* for £5000. The crowded front page also carried a 'Please Explain' letter from Whitlam to Cairns concerning the 2.5 per cent Harris letter. On 3 July it was 'WHITLAM SACKS CAIRNS'. The admission of Sear Cowls that he had fabricated his account of Phillip Cairns' US$600,000 commission was lost in the welter of surrounding sensations.

On 4 July Connor's $4000 million loan took over in the headlines with allegations of a US$180 million commission, an early telex from Connor to Khemlani, and copies of five cheques, each made out to 'Bearer' for US$20 million and drawn on the London branch of the First National City Bank, which had been sent by Khemlani to a Zurich financier on the basis that they would be cashed when the loan came through. The front page of the following day carried a story from London of an offer of $A2 million from an undisclosed Australian source for other loan documents. There was also a report of alleged discussions – never substantiated – by Cairns in the Philippines in April relating to a US$9 million reclamation scheme for the city of Manila by a Sear Cowls company. By 8 July the Connor loan had taken over again . . .[7]

The new Treasurer was Bill Hayden. His chief of staff was an economist, Gae Raby, a graduate of the University of New England who had worked for the ANZ Bank in Melbourne. We later worked out that we must have been in the same bars on occasions after work in Melbourne without ever meeting. Instead we met in the Non-Members Bar in Parliament House – "that marvellous methylated hellhole" as Peter Blazey called it – and soon became good friends. Our relationship was to last a lot longer than the Whitlam government.

In an effort to arrest the avalanche of damaging publicity, Whitlam called a special sitting of the House of Representatives for 9 July 1975. Along with other government staffers, I watched from the gallery as Whitlam and Connor defended their loan-raising attempts and Fraser responded with allegations of illegality and impropriety. Cairns, speaking now from the backbenches, made a sad and almost incoherent protest at his dismissal. He was heard in silence by both sides, including those who had been his closest colleagues. Whitlam had lost none of his theatrical powers but not even the most optimistic person on the government side could believe that the Loans Affair had been put to rest. It was not raised again in the parliament until early October when it exploded with renewed force.

It was hard to imagine that there was anything else to go wrong but there was. Late in August there was a firestorm in the press about a document that Enderby had tabled in the House almost three months earlier. It was the report of a working party on criminal law legislation in the ACT. The report, the work of officers of the Attorney-General's Department together with an academic lawyer, called for submissions on its recommendations. But, buried amongst hundreds of other issues, were discussions of the law relating to abortion, incest and sexual assault in de facto relationships. These were portrayed in the tabloid press as proposals for abortion on demand, the legalisation of incest and the recognition of same sex marriages. The department should have alerted Enderby to the possibility of controversy when it gave him the report to table, without going through any of his staff, but this was exactly the kind of incompetence and political insensitivity that Neil Brown would later complain about.

When the storm broke, Enderby was abroad. The Acting Attorney-General, Senator Jim McClelland, was also Minister for Manufacturing Industry. I walked around to McClelland's office without much enthusiasm. He was known for his acid tongue and was entitled to be angry about this landing unexpectedly on his desk. "What idiots cooked this up?" he asked as I came in the door. I explained what the report really said and how it had not been and would not be adopted as government policy. It was agreed that McClelland would make these points in the Senate and that I would write a detailed letter to some of the newspapers that had taken up the issue.

One of these went to Sydney's *Catholic Weekly* which had given widespread coverage to statements condemning the government by the Catholic Archbishops of Sydney and Canberra. My letter was published but so was a response from Cardinal Freeman. He was not placated:

> The fact that these objectionable proposals were put into draft form shows that they were in somebody's mind.
> The fact that they were merely in draft form did not lessen

the chance that, unless checked by public opinion, they would find their way into the statutes.

If that was not in the mind of those responsible for the draft, why draw it up at all?

What Archbishop Cahill and I did was intervene before it was too late: intervene to frustrate an implied intent to do mischief.[8]

John Iremonger left the Cardinal's response on my desk with a note that said: "Dear Michael – In future please keep your mind to yourself!"

Early in September there was an opportunity to escape these dramas when Enderby went to Papua New Guinea, then a self-governing colony, to represent the Australian government at a number of official functions leading, imminently, to independence. In addition to the capital, Port Moresby, we spent time in

With John Iremonger on a visit with the Attorney General to Papua New Guinea in September 1975 to mark its independence

Lae, Madang and Wewak observing the transition from the old Australian administrators to their new indigenous equivalents. The Chief Minister, Michael Somare, was conspicuously impressive and became Prime Minister when independence was formally declared: several times Prime Minister and, once Foreign Minister, he struggled with the factionalism that came to dominate Papua New Guinea's parliamentary system and to make stable government in the new nation increasingly more difficult.

A less attractive interlude was the second meeting of the Constitutional Convention in Melbourne in the last week of September. The Convention had first met in 1973 to examine ways of adapting Australia's 1901 Constitution to the political and economic realities of a different era. In 1973 all of the parliaments – State and Commonwealth – sent delegations comprised of members from both government and Opposition parties. In the febrile atmosphere of 1975, however, this bipartisanship had been abandoned. Only the South Australian and Tasmanian delegations had members from all parties. In the other States and at the Commonwealth level, LCP members had withdrawn from the parliamentary delegations. The Convention had been scheduled to meet in Parliament House, Melbourne, but, a week beforehand, this arrangement was abruptly cancelled by the Victorian government. The meeting, instead, took place in the Windsor Hotel, directly across the street from the original location. The Premiers of the non-Labor States had come to Melbourne at the same time but they were meeting with Fraser and his Shadow Cabinet in the office of the Victorian Premier, also just around the corner from the Convention.

The Windsor was a Melbourne institution. Filled with dark panelling and deep carpets, it had long been the venue for society weddings and post-theatre suppers in Melbourne. This establishment bastion seemed an unlikely venue for an exercise in constitutional modernisation. The problems of the Convention had not improved Whitlam's mood. On the first day I was searching the hotel corridors in an effort to find Enderby. I entered an elevator to try another floor. The elevator stopped and the doors opened. Standing there, waiting to go down, were Whitlam and his press secretary, David Solomon. I spoke cheerily to Solomon: "I don't suppose you've seen Kep, have you? I can't seem to find him." Solomon seemed not to have heard me. Instead Whitlam responded in a half scream, glowering down at me and clenching his teeth: "Find him! He couldn't even find himself!" Before I could say a word, the doors closed and the elevator rushed upwards – and not a moment too soon. I knew that in some way the Attorney-General had displeased the Prime Minister.

I realised later in the day that the cause of these tensions was the removal of the Director-General of the Australian Security Intelligence Organisation, Peter Barbour. As the minister responsible for ASIO, Enderby was involved in the paperwork, which I found spread out on a bed in a hotel room. Enderby was usually quite open with me about events inside the government but he never made any reference to ASIO affairs. He did not, however, have an ASIO staff member in his office as Lionel Murphy had done. It was reported much later in the press that Barbour had been sacked after the CIA and MI6 expressed concerns about his private life, although he was appointed to a series of diplomatic posts over the next decade.

Meanwhile in Canberra the political temperature was still rising. On 16 October the Opposition used its numbers in the Senate – 29 votes to 28 – to defer passage of the budget bills until the government agreed to call a general election. There were some risks for Fraser and his colleagues in this strategy. There was, in the circumstances, no danger of losing any election that took place in the next few months, given the depths to which the government had sunk in the opinion polls. But neither were there precedents to suggest what might happen if the government refused to call an election. Why not wait eighteen months until there would be an election anyway? It seemed certain that the government would then suffer a massive defeat. But it was a measure of the feeling between the two sides that the Opposition was not prepared to wait.

Life in Parliament House now assumed an eerie quality as it became clear that neither side would give in. Whitlam used the full range of his debating talents to attack the Opposition and buoy the spirits of his own supporters. Fraser ignored these flights of oratory and repeated his demand for an early election. Otherwise, the day-to-day administration of government business continued. Like other staffers, on both sides, I came into the office in the mornings and stayed until late at night. Ministers continued to carry out their normal functions. On one occasion during this period I encountered Treasurer Bill Hayden at Canberra airport where he was boarding a plane to Sydney to deliver a speech to a group of businessmen. He was standing beside a huge pile of copies of the speech. I noticed its title: *Business Profits under Labor*. "What's next?" I asked. "Italian war heroes?" Hayden gave me a look of weary contempt that could probably only come from a former Queensland police officer who had seen any number of smart alecks.

During the third week of October the government made a major tactical mistake. It may be that the outcome of the stand-off would have been the same. But it was clear, not only later but at the time, that some members of the Opposition were uneasy about the consequences of blocking the budget bills. There would have been much greater pressure on these individuals if they knew that the money would run out. And the reality was that after the end of November there would not be sufficient funds to pay the salaries of public servants and meet other essential administrative costs. But the government turned this pressure down.

During the second half of October a taskforce from various departments had been trying to work out how the government could carry on financially after the end of November. They devised a scheme under which the government would issue IOUs to public servants for their wages and contractors for their bills and then banks would give loans on the basis of these certificates. Ultimately the government would repay the loans to the banks with interest, either directly or through the customers. Not only would these so-called "alternative arrangements" have required the close co-operation of the banks, who were hardly sympathetic to the government, they reinforced the impression in the community, already created by the Loans Affair, that the government was constantly engaged in activities that were illegal or at least highly unorthodox. It was particularly damaging at a time when the polls indicated that much of the community was sympathetic to the government's position on the budget bills, even though this was not the same as saying that they would vote for the government in an election.

Negotiations with the banks continued during the first week of November. The banks obtained two legal opinions from the Sydney Bar that raised serious legal doubts about the alternate arrangements. The opinions were not available to the government but were forwarded to the Governor-General, Sir John Kerr.

I was more concerned, however, with an earlier legal opinion. In the second week of October a statement had been issued by four of the country's leading professors of constitutional law who argued that the rejection of the budget bills by the Senate "would be likely to do irreparable damage to the parliamentary system as we have known it" and "would be an act which future generations would have cause to regret."[9] This was one of the early shots in the propaganda war but it had received a great deal of publicity. The Shadow Attorney-General, Senator Ivor Greenwood, placed a lengthy question on the Senate notice paper, seeking information from the Attorney-General as to who had prepared the letter and who had paid the costs of sending it around the country to be signed by the various academics. The answer was that I had organised the statement and the relatively minor costs of circulating the document had been met by the government. There was nothing improper in this but I was not looking forward to being in the spotlight when the information was provided and seeing Enderby, who had not been involved, possibly embarrassed. Greenwood's question was never to be answered.

Tuesday 11 November was hot and clear in Canberra's high summer. It was to be a busy day in Parliament House. Both the House of Representatives and the Senate were sitting. The two sides had party meetings in the morning. Cabinet was scheduled to meet in the evening. All this was preceded at 9.00 am by a meeting between Whitlam and Fraser, each supported by two colleagues. Predictably there was no resolution. Fraser repeated his demand for an election for the House of Representatives. Whitlam responded by saying that, unless the budget bills were passed by the Senate later in the day, he would advise the Governor-General to call an election for half the Senate. In one sense this was another tactical mistake, because it forced Kerr to act. Once a half Senate election was called, he would lose any opportunity to dismiss the government and call a general election for both Houses of Parliament. It seems likely, however, that Kerr had already decided to end the stalemate so it probably made no real difference.

I spent most of the morning with one of the Tasmanian Labor Senators, Mervyn Everett, looking at some legal questions arising out of the proposed half Senate election in that State. Enderby was out of the office. He had gone to the Remembrance Day ceremony at the War Memorial and, together with Sir John Kerr, laid a wreath in memory of the fallen. He was due to see Kerr again that evening at a meeting of the Executive Council at Yarralumla. Shortly after

12.30pm John Iremonger and I drove to the ANU staff club to meet Susan Ryan, who had been endorsed as the Labor Senate candidate in the ACT. This would be the first Senate election in the Territory and Susan wanted to discuss her campaign with the two of us. We had a sandwich and a glass of wine, sitting in the sun close to the shores of the lake – as good a place as any for a last supper.

When Iremonger and I walked back into the office, just on 2.00 pm, one of the staff said that she had heard that the Governor-General had taken some action. Iremonger seemed unimpressed and went in and sat down at his desk. I felt vaguely uneasy and decided to walk around to the office of the Foreign Minister, on the Senate side, where the tall and angular Geoff Briot was chief of staff. He always seemed to know what was going on in Parliament House. I opened the door to a scene of confusion. Most of the staff were throwing piles of documents into large cardboard boxes. I knew the answer before I called across the room to Briot: "Is it true?" "Yes. I knew we couldn't trust that bastard." This was not hindsight. Briot had said precisely that when Kerr was appointed. I ran back to Enderby's office.

Whitlam and his ministers had been dismissed shortly after 1.00pm by Kerr. The rest followed quickly. The final formality was the reading of the proclamation dissolving both Houses of Parliament by the Official Secretary to the Governor-General on the front steps of Parliament House. Along with many government staffers, I stood nearby. In front of Parliament House a crowd of about two thousand milled about, some crying, most simply dazed. They were electrified when Whitlam lead the 92 members of the Labor Caucus in single file through King's Hall and down the steps into the crowd.

By this time many of the ministerial offices had been largely packed into boxes and moved to Labor's own building in Canberra. This may seem an over-reaction in retrospect but there were no longer any Labor ministers and it seemed quite possible that their former departments might reclaim all this material and leave nothing for use in the coming campaign. Charlie's Restaurant in the centre of Canberra was the scene of an emotional wake that started early in the evening and went until dawn. My last memory is of a conga line snaking out into one of the main streets, waking up a few hours later and going into Parliament House because there did not seem anything else to do.

Ahead lay the campaign trail – with the election on 13 December. The first problem was that most of the Labor staffers had been swept away with the ministers. There were now just the four leaders – two in the House (Whitlam and Crean) and two in the Senate (Wreidt and Willesee), who were entitled to any significant staff entitlements. Whitlam's office selected a small group from the former ministerial advisers who could be attached to one of these leaders and so travel on the campaign. I finished up on a list of three advisers to Senator Ken Wriedt, Labor's Senate leader. I did not really know Wriedt and I do not think that I ever had a conversation with him in the course of the campaign. There was, however, a sharp reminder of my changed circumstances when I received a telegram later in the week from the Secretary of the Department of the Special Minister of State:

> IN ACCORDANCE WITH THE GOVERNMENTS DECISION YOU ARE REQUIRED TO CEASE DUTY IN MR ENDERBY'S OFFICE WITH EFFECT COB TUESDAY 18 NOVEMBER 1975 AND SUBJECT TO ANY APPROVED LEAVE COMMENCE DUTY IN YOUR DEPARTMENT ON WEDNESDAY 19 NOVEMBER 1975 STOP PLEASE THEREFORE CONTACT YOUR DEPARTMENT WITHOUT DELAY

I did not return to the Attorney-General's Department on the appointed day but organised some leave without pay for the period of the campaign.

It was not only my circumstances that had been changed. On the morning of 12 November I was talking in Whitlam's office with his chief of staff, John Mant. Whitlam came out of his own room to ask Mant what had been arranged for air travel during the campaign. Mant replied that he had tried but so far failed to get an assurance from the new government that the Leader of the Opposition could use one of the RAAF VIP planes for the next month. Whitlam told Mant not to worry – he would use commercial flights. It did not come to that, however, because the new government ultimately approved the use of a VIP aircraft.

During this conversation I looked out of the window to see a striking example of the transfer of power. Walking across the lawns to Parliament House were Clarrie Harders and Pat Brazil. But they were not, as they would have been the day before, walking towards Enderby's office. They were walking towards the office of the new Attorney-General, Ivor Greenwood, and carrying with them a pile of documents for the new minister to sign.

Like many lost causes, there was something exhilarating about the next month. Labor was flooded with volunteers and the crowds at public meetings were large and highly emotional. One day in late November I went to a lunch time meeting in the Domain in Sydney attended by 40,000 people and then an evening meeting at Festival Hall in Melbourne. Although there were only 7,000 at the second meeting, there was not an inch of space to spare and the reception for Whitlam was wilder than any Grand Final crowd.

I assumed that Whitlam was aware that there had been a meeting in his own office of about a dozen staffers and party officials, including myself, where the question of South Australian Premier, Don Dunstan, taking over as Labor leader was discussed. It sounded like a far-fetched idea but there was no precedent for the situation in which Labor found itself. There was a feeling that Dunstan would not be identified with events like the Loans Affair and could claw back some of the losses that the polls were predicting. Martin Nicholls, member for Bonython, one of the safest Labor seats in South Australia in the House of Representatives, had been approached and tentatively agreed to stand aside for Dunstan if he agreed. Not surprisingly Dunstan rejected this deeply poisoned chalice. He could not be blamed for this, after just winning a hard-fought election in South Australia and realising the essential futility of the current campaign. But it was a measure of Labor's desperation that he was asked if he was available.

The low point of the campaign for me was accompanying Enderby to the Mawson Workers' Club – a favourite of builders' labourers – in the Woden Valley of Canberra. After Enderby spoke, I stood on a chair and told the crowd in the bar that the government had been unfairly sacked. They heard me out but they knew that I was not a worker's bootlace!

A few days before the election a candlelight "vigil for democracy" was held outside Parliament House and attended by several thousand people. I was in another part of the country but, by all accounts, it was beautifully stage-managed by John Iremonger, who had a genuine talent for political events. Like the rest of Labor's campaign, however, it did nothing to stem the approaching tidal wave. This hit on the night of 13 December. The swing against Labor in metropolitan seats was 7 to 8 percent. It retained only 36 seats out of 127 in the House of Representatives, with one seat in Queensland, one in Western Australia and none in Tasmania. Six members of the Cabinet had lost their seats, including Enderby. I watched the count in the National Tally Room in an outer suburb of Canberra. It was the first, and only, time I ever went there.

Thirty years later, in 2005, *Illusions of Power* was reissued under the title *The Great Crash: The short life and sudden death of the Whitlam government.*[10] It was launched, or relaunched, by Paul Keating, who had been appointed as a Minister in the Whitlam

Paul Keating launching The Great Crash *in November 2005*
(Sydney Morning Herald)

government a few weeks before 11 November 1975. The changes in the political agenda during those 30 years were highlighted by some of the issues that I saw, in a new conclusion, confronting any Australian government then and in the future:

> Simplification of the tax system, which has become impossibly complicated. One possible but dramatic option is a flat rate of taxation combined with offsetting benefits.
>
> Containing the sharply rising costs of health for an ageing population, although this would probably require reducing the existing role of doctors and pharmacists, both of whom are extremely powerful interest groups.
>
> The right level of immigration for a country that has labour shortages in some sectors but a number of large cities, most particularly Sydney, where even the existing

population has produced acute problems of air pollution, water shortages, traffic congestion and urban crime.

Improved provision of child care for working women, most particularly for children under the age of two where the cost of care has limited its availability.

The adequacy of existing superannuation arrangements for a population that is living longer and retiring earlier. An associated problem is that the legislation governing superannuation requires drastic surgery, given that at last count it numbered almost 28 000 pages.

Whether there ought to be decriminalisation for adult use of some currently illegal drugs that have a widespread use in the community and effectively consume the largest single component of the resources devoted to law enforcement. This is, in some way, an issue for State governments under their criminal laws but the Commonwealth has a major role in this area because of its regulation of imports.

The use of alternative energy sources – but most particularly nuclear power – once it is accepted that the reserves of coal and oil are finite and have significant environmental consequences, especially in the form, of petrol emissions.

Some of these problems were on the horizon in the 1970s but most of them were far from the minds of those watching the world of the Whitlam government vanish before their eyes in the National Tally Room on 13 December 1975.

6

PUBLISH AND BE DAMNED
Re-writing History

I woke up on 14 December 1975 with a good-sized hangover and no job. The second complaint was not strictly true because I was still on the books at the Attorney-General's Department. But the idea of going back to work for the new government was not very appealing. This probably demonstrated a rather unsophisticated view on my part of the political process in Canberra where most public servants saw the bureaucracy as permanent and governments as merely transitory. In any event, with mortgages to pay and careers to make, they could not afford to indulge their personal preferences.

After the time-warp of the campaign, it was almost Christmas. I drove south with Gae towards Melbourne. We left Canberra at dawn and did not stop until we parked outside Jimmy Watson's wine bar in Lygon Street, Carlton. It was early afternoon and I spotted some old faces from law school days. They were highly excited to have two eye-witnesses of the government's fall. The noise was enormous and the wine seemed less potent in the heat of December. It was not, of course, but it acted as some kind of sedative while re-entering the world outside Canberra.

It was good to spend some time with my parents at Christmas. As a result of the years out of Australia and then in Canberra, I had seen little of them in the last four years. They were in their mid-70s but seemed to be in good health. In the case of my father, this did not last much longer. I should have been more conscious of their age but I tended to see them as they had always been and rather foolishly assumed that there was no urgent reason to return to Melbourne.

The truth is that I was not anxious to make any kind of decision about the immediate future. Shortly after I returned to Canberra I wrote a piece for *The Bulletin* which reflected this time of langour:

> It was getting on towards three o'clock but there really didn't seem any reason to move. The sun flickered through the foliage hanging over our table, giving the faces around it a slightly mottled appearance and lending a golden hue to what was a very ordinary white.
>
> A little mesmerised by the intermittent shafts of light I tried to contemplate the future but couldn't see much beyond the shores of Lake Burley Griffin a few hundred yards away. The location was the Staff Club of the Australian National University, a gracious old building set in grounds that run right down to the lake. On summer days, however, only a philistine would take lunch indoors instead of at the tables under the trees. It is a spot beloved of academics and, lately, of some of those who had worked for the Labor government, like the foursome at our table who had all been on the staffs of different ministers.
>
> The campaign and then Christmas had devoured the last weeks of the year. January, however, left time for thought. It also meant rediscovering Canberra – the place in which I had resided but hadn't really lived in for some time. Even when not physically out of town travelling, there was an other-worldly quality to life when it was hard to recall last seeing the house in daylight or going into any room but the bedroom . . .

Meanwhile, back at the Staff Club, people discussed their options. We could always set off for Adelaide, last outpost of socialist civilisation on the continent, ruled by the wise and with-it King Donald. A number of Labor staffers were in fact going, in an expedition that recalled William Lane's attempt to establish the millennium of New Australia in Paraguay after the failure of the great strikes in the early 1890s.

Then, of course, there was the Department . . . A salary to retiring age, regular promotion since no government, whatever its notional philosophies, had ever succeeded in halting the inexorable growth of the bureaucracy for anything but short periods; flexitime, which now allowed an afternoon for golf each week; and generous superannuation from retirement onwards.

No! I just wasn't ready for the Brave New World in 1976. Taking a firm grip on my glass I resolved to leave this bureaucratic Brigadoon into which I had stumbled and return to the real world of Sydney or Melbourne, harsh and frenetic though they were. Self-righteously I rose from the table and marched towards the car, pausing only to suggest same time, same place tomorrow. Well, I really shouldn't make a final decision without seeing if the others had any thought about the subject. The whole question probably should be discussed a bit more. It's just not something to be decided hastily, you understand.[1]

This dream world was, however, abruptly disturbed by the offer of a lectureship in the law school at the University of New South Wales. I decided to take it, thinking I might last one or two years. After the different but striking landscapes of Melbourne University, the University of Virginia and the ANU, UNSW was not a pretty sight. Set on a long but narrow finger of land in Sydney's eastern suburbs, it was a clutter of ill-matched buildings with almost no trees or open spaces. The law school was relatively new. Established in the early 1970s, it was deliberately designed to provide a contrast to the long-established and very conservative law school at the University of Sydney. Instead of lectures for an hour to hundreds of students, classes would be two hours in length and contain a maximum of 35 students, allowing for the kind of question and answer dialogue that was a feature of American law schools.

When I arrived in mid-1976 most of the staff were hardly older than the students and had been recruited from all parts of Australia as well as internationally. Many wanted to make a contribution to public affairs and were engaged in a range of activities outside the university in addition to their teaching and writing commitments. Quite a number of my new colleagues later went on to other careers inside and outside the law, including Ron Sackville and Margaret Stone, as judges of the Federal Court of Australia; John Basten, Terry Buddin and Ian Harrison, as a judges of the NSW Supreme Court; Julian Disney, head of the Australian Council for Social Services; and Susan Armstrong, Deputy Ombudsman of NSW. There was no shortage of debate in the common room at morning tea. Some of these were happy to go into private practice but, for others, Australia lacked the regular interchange between government service and academia that characterised the law in the United States. The English model still prevailed in Australia. This meant that most public offices in the law, including the judiciary, were only attained after many years of single-minded service in practice as a barrister or solicitor.

The chief subjects I taught in the law school in the late-1970s were contract, employment law and constitutional law. In addition to writing articles for academic journals, considered essential for academic advancement, I wrote book reviews and articles on current affairs for *The Bulletin*, the *National Times* and the *Sydney Morning Herald*. In the classes I took during the first few years, I was an enthusiastic practitioner of the question and answer style – the so-called Socratic method – that I had experienced in the United States. While some of the students enjoyed this, others did not, regarding me as an arrogant inquisitor. The majority were indifferent, being chiefly concerned with obtaining a qualification that would enable them to earn a great deal of money in a law firm or at the Bar. I was initially disappointed that many of the students, who came predominantly from affluent households on Sydney's North Shore, had little interest in the policy questions underlying the decisions of courts and especially the broad political questions behind the thin veneer of legal reasoning in constitutional law. But there were enough students, and members of the academic staff, who were happy to argue about these issues, whether in the classroom or in one of the nearby pubs.

The course I most enjoyed teaching was one that had not previously been offered in Australian law schools until I designed it at this time – Foreign Investment Regulation. It looked at the legislative and administrative regime confronting foreign investors in Australia and considered the economic basis for this system of regulation. Partly as a result of my time in Canberra, I had come to see economics as the most important element in the making of public policy. If economics was about allocation of scarce resources, it followed that the aim of government decision-making should be to employ the country's resources rationally and equitably (which does not always mean equally) in fields such as health, education, transport and even the law. This may not sound a very radical political philosophy but it was, and is, bitterly opposed by almost every interest group in society, including industry bodies, professional associations and trade unions, all of whom want special treatment for themselves. This had been shown in the passionate campaigns run against the modest reforms of the Whitlam government by the medical profession, the legal profession and the insurance industry.

The best models for this kind of political program at that time were some of the social democratic parties of Western Europe, particularly in France and Germany. These organisations often had greater resources than the Australian Labor Party but it seemed to me that, at least in law and justice, Labor would benefit from a group of sympathetic lawyers who were not directly affiliated with the party but could supply ideas for existing or future governments. So in late 1976 I approached the NSW Attorney-General, Frank Walker, to suggest setting up the NSW Society of Labor Lawyers. The year before a Victorian body had been formed, comprised initially of lawyers who had signed newspaper advertisements at the end of 1975 protesting against removal of the Whitlam government by Sir John Kerr. Frank Walker, whose cherubic features belied political skills that had made him a Cabinet minister in the Wran government in his early thirties, agreed to convene an inaugural meeting at which a constitution would be adopted and officers elected.

The inaugural meeting was held at Sydney University law school early in 1977. It was clear, not for the first time, that lawyers seldom agree about anything. By the time I arrived, there were more than 100 people present. The first person I saw hissed at me: "Where's the ticket?" In my naivety I had not thought to organise a slate of office-bearers in advance. Those who were ALP members expected to be told how to vote. When the draft constitution was put to the meeting, numerous amendments were moved, some accepted and some rejected. Senator Jim McCelland, who had the status of a former minister in the Whitlam government, was nominated as President. He was rejected, in the event, because he had not come to the meeting. Greg Sullivan QC was elected instead. Most of the other positions were hotly contested. At one stage I looked up to see the Attorney-General counting votes that had been collected in a large plastic rubbish bin, showing that high office had not caused him to forget the mechanics of politics. I became the secretary without having to face an election. The committee was a mixed group that included three future judges and a future minister in a federal Liberal government, Helen Coonan.

Despite relatively small membership in terms of the legal profession as a whole, the new organisation attracted some fierce opposition. Traditionally it was very unusual for lawyers to criticise judges or other senior figures in the profession, not least because of the damage it might do to the careers of the critics. So there was no problem getting publicity for a group of lawyers calling for changes to the legal system and the profession itself. I became something of a regular on the morning radio programs and occasionally on television. One of the society's first press releases attacked sentencing policies in the then NSW Court of Criminal Appeal. The response was swift. Frank Walker was attacked by the Opposition in the NSW parliament for supporting establishment of the society at all. Various lawyers defended the Court of Criminal

Walking out in August 1976 as Sir John Kerr, in the rear, starts his speech, with, from left to right, Susan Armstrong, Julian Disney, Mark Gumbert, Tom Kelly and future federal Minister, Robert Tickner (Daily Mirror)

Appeal in the media, including Malcolm Turnbull, recently returned from Oxford University and a legal columnist with *The Bulletin*. And the committee members responsible for the press statement were summoned by NSW Chief Justice, Sir Laurence Street, to his chambers to provide an explanation – which they did, against my advice, being lawyers as well as reformers and so very conscious of the power of the judiciary.

Six months earlier there had been another confrontation with the legal establishment. The Sydney University Law Graduates' Association had arranged for Sir John Kerr to address their annual luncheon at one of the city's major hotels. There was bound to be a large attendance of judges and other senior members of the profession. Twenty or so young lawyers bought tickets and, as Kerr rose to speak after the main course, we ostentatiously walked out. This was captured in a photo that covered almost the entire front page of one of the evening newspapers. I was in the first rank, buttoning my jacket – a sartorial troublemaker. The *Sydney Morning Herald* editorial next day indicated, however, that some people were very angry indeed:

> The demonstrations against the Governor-General are reaching the point where it may fairly be asked why the community should put up with them. The latest and most childish was the demonstration of bad manners yesterday by a handful of members of the Sydney University Law Graduates' Association who walked out when their invited guest, the Queen's representative in Australia, rose to speak. By so doing they brought discredit on themselves and their profession. They should not be allowed to get away with it. The profession and the association to which they belong should take disciplinary action . . .
>
> The campaign is a sinister one, mounted, co-ordinated and paid for by sinister people for sinister reasons . . .

The purpose of the campaign is to create a climate of violence, intimidation and harassment and to use it to upset the verdict of the electorate last December. The real target is not Sir John Kerr. He is just the convenient cockshy. The real targets are orderly government and the democratic process.[2]

Twenty years later there were still members of the judiciary and other lawyers who held this against me. As president of the NSW Bar Association and then Chief Justice before becoming Governor-General, Kerr had immense stature amongst his contemporaries. They were outraged by this insult to a man they believed had been unfairly pilloried for dismissing what they thought was an appalling government. In one sense, they were right. I still think that Kerr's failure in November 1975 was not to tell Whitlam what he was thinking. And it would seem from Sir Anthony Mason's account of his discussions with Kerr during this period that Kerr had a long time during which he might have raised this question with Whitlam.[3] According to Mason, Kerr first raised with him the possibility of removing the government in August, well nigh three months before 11 November.

Mason's own role in these events was extraordinary. Although a judge of the High Court, he advised Kerr constantly in the weeks prior to 11 November and even drafted a letter on 9 November, which Kerr ultimately did not use, terminating Whitlam's commission for Kerr to hand to Whitlam. On the afternoon of 11 November he was still advising Kerr as to how he should respond to Labor's parliamentary response to the government's removal. This was a clear abuse of Mason's position on the High Court and constituted a complete confusion about judicial functions and responsibility.

In some ways, Kerr was not the right target for protests. The real criticism for the events of November 1975 should have been directed at the then Opposition, Malcolm Fraser and his colleagues, who blocked the Budget in the Senate rather than wait eighteen months until the next election when they would have been swept into office with a landslide. It is also true that Kerr was deeply affected by these kinds of public protests. They were certainly a factor leading him to resign as Governor-General at the end of 1977 and to live abroad.

By the late 1970s there were branches of the Labor Lawyers in every State and Territory. Each year there was a national conference where papers were presented on current legal issues and later discussed over long lunches and dinners. At one of the first of these, in Brisbane, the guest of honour and speaker at the main dinner was John Mortimer QC, creator of *Rumpole of the Bailey*. I looked after Mortimer and his wife on the evening of the dinner. Mortimer, an owlish upper class Englishman with little in the way of small talk, was very much an observer of events around him and this was reflected in the Rumpole stories which were an uncannily accurate portrait of some of the most common types of judges, barristers and solicitors, whether in England or Australia. It was an evening to remember – or perhaps to forget. Several hundred lawyers sat down in one of Brisbane's hotels and started drinking the wine that was available on each table. But after an hour, when no food had arrived, the wine was starting to exact a toll. I went to the kitchen with one of my colleagues to investigate. There was a problem with the ovens. It was impossible to discover whether the ovens were not working or whether they had worked too well and incinerated the meal. But there was no food to be served. I returned to the dining room where the roar from the tables was now enormous. Much later some kind of main course was served and Mortimer rose to speak. He surveyed the scene with understandable apprehension. He told some very old legal jokes, most of which I had heard as a student in law school, and sat down. The roar resumed. So much for my evening with one of Britain's most famous writers of the post-war years.

According to his biographer, however, Mortimer had no complaints about the dinner:

> Busy though Mortimer was, he took Penny off to Australia to promote sales of the Rumpole books. They loved it: the restaurants, the wines, even the people. They swam at Bondi Beach, went sightseeing in a tiny seaplane, revelled in the wildlife of the northern Queensland rainforest, visited the Great Barrier Reef, and John made a speech at a lawyers' dinner in Brisbane where the evening ended in drunken chaos. He said he had not been so happy and carefree for ages.[4]

In mid-1979 the various State organisations formed a national body, the Australian Society of Labor Lawyers, which set up an office in Canberra funded largely by grants from a number of industrial law firms. The meetings between the State representatives to bring this about were often heated, despite the common goal. As one of the NSW participants, it was my first real exposure to Gareth Evans, the convenor of the group and recently elected to the Senate from Victoria. Tall, bearded and fast-moving, Evans was intensely ambitious, enormously energetic and wildly intolerant of anyone who disagreed with him. When, for example, Chris Sumner, the South Australian Attorney-General, mentioned that he had opposed a plan that had turned out unsuccessfully, Evans snarled back from across the table: "You vote no to everything, so I suppose you must be right occasionally!" All this did not prevent Evans from being very good company but there was no doubting the signs of a stormy career ahead.

The Canberra office was to provide the kind of think-tank role that I had originally hoped for in New South Wales and for some years it did. But the funds dried up and, like so many voluntary bodies, the Labor Lawyers, at both the State and national level, retreated to spasmodic publications and largely social events.

All this makes those years seem more earnest than they were. I had bought a small house near the beach in Clovelly, later a very expensive area but then quite unfashionable. Gae often appeared from Canberra at weekends. I restarted my tennis career with the White City Club in the Sydney Badge competition – long afternoons chasing balls that skidded off the closely mown grass courts. And, together with one of my colleagues in the law school, Denis Harley, I acquired a small sail boat. It was easy to be struck by the beauty of the Harbour when the boat sliced through the dark blue water under full spinnaker and the sun dipped below the bridge. But I was still sceptical about many aspects of Sydney. It was not only its subtropical climate in contrast to Melbourne, its beach culture, its choked streets, although these were all part of the city's style. It was also a place where the differences between rich and poor seemed much sharper than in the rest of the country. There was a brashness, or candour, about the desire for money and success that was not as apparent in other parts of Australia. It was probably a more open society but one that was more tolerant of violence and corruption both in public and in private life. Even the faces in Pitt Street looked different from those in Collins Street, as if the harsher climate and more hectic pace of life had aged many of its residents more rapidly.

Academic life provides time to write. Although there had been a number of books published on the Whitlam government soon after its removal, none was based on real access to the government's internal documents. Because so many documents had been moved out of Parliament House in the days following 11 November 1975, there was plenty of such material, including a full set of Cabinet papers stored in the roof of a former minister. The importance of this kind of material in the writing of history is that it provides at least some contemporary record of events. It is true that any document must be composed by someone and that person may have reason to distort the account of their own actions or the conduct of others. But documents have usually proved more reliable in my experience than memory. Oral versions of earlier events by participants in them will often vary wildly and, not often, but sometimes, quite honestly.

The title of the book that I wrote over the next two years struck a melancholy note: *Illusions of Power: The fate of a reform government*. It was published by the English firm of George Allen & Unwin. It owed much to John Iremonger who had recently joined their Australian office and acted as editor, designer and indexer. The book was launched at the National Press Club by Bob Hawke – still ACTU President – in July 1979. Many reviewers had

Bob Hawke, then ACTU President, launching Illusions of Power *at the National Press Club in July 1979 (Canberra Times)*

assumed that it would be a eulogy for the Whitlam government and seemed pleasantly surprised that it was not. Some of those who were part of the government or had worked for it, including Gough Whitlam himself, did not enjoy the scenes of chaos and confusion that were recreated. The reasons for their dismay are reflected in one reviewer's assessment:

> Parts of the story are necessarily tediously familiar, though Sexton is sometimes able to give them new twists, with new information and new perspectives. What is not stale is a move away from the concentration on the single, simple explanation of 'we was robbed' to a sub-theme that the government displayed such a high degree of incompetence, lack of preparation, lack of unity, foolishness, timidity and naivety that it was heading inescapably to total internal disintegration and electoral annihilation and was only saved, in a sense, by the martyrdom of November 1975.[5]

The sharpest critics came not from the conservative side of politics but from the Marxist perspective. Andrew Theophanous, later a Labor member of the House of Representatives from 1984 to 2000, asked what was missing from the book:

> To answer this question, one must introduce the major missing element in Sexton's account: a class analysis of Australian society. It is because these top public servants are committed to the present distribution of power and wealth, that they will act in every way to oppose any re-distribution from the wealthy, usually foreign, owners of Australia's productive and natural resources to the Australian people as a whole . . .
>
> Unfortunately, because Sexton himself does not appreciate the nature and dynamics of this ruling class, his account of the fate of the Labor government often takes on the

character of an *ad hoc* listing of much of the empirical material without showing the underlying forces which were at work.

In my view, this leads Sexton to a major error. He sees the trade unions as one of the major forces which were opposed to change and therefore frustrated the plans of the Whitlam government. There is no justification for the claim – which is based on the failure to distinguish the working class forces from the ruling class ones mentioned above.[6]

Theophanous was quite right. I did not see this kind of Marxist analysis as useful in Australia. If the problem for all governments is how best to distribute limited community resources, including taxes collected, it was especially demanding in Australia where a large arid continent with a few urban clusters on the coast resulted in higher costs but much lower revenue than in most Western nations. There are class differences in Australia but they do not explain, or solve, this central problem.

A number of his former staffers conveyed the message that Whitlam had not enjoyed some parts of *Illusions of Power*. I was not greatly concerned. In 1975 I had not had a great deal to do with Whitlam personally. I was, however, surprised at how deferential most of his own staff seemed to be. There was no denying the fact that he had almost single-handed led Labor into government after 23 years in opposition. But, unlike many others, inside and outside Parliament House, I felt no need for a hero to worship.

So I was quite casual when I next saw Whitlam, in the queue for coffee at a political seminar at which we were both speaking. He had just delivered a furious attack on a range of characters, but especially on Kerr and Barwick. I mentioned the number of targets and added: "There was so many I thought you might get to me". He did not smile but glared back: "Not today. I was only dealing here with the very biggest bastards!" I grabbed my coffee and dashed for safety.

Although *Illusions of Power* was published in England and the United States as well, almost all the copies were naturally sold in Australia. Late in 1979, however, while in London, I visited to the head office of George Allen & Unwin. After being led through a maze of corridors, I was pushed into a room where complete darkness was broken only by a small shaft of light thrown from a desk light. The shadowy figure behind the desk was Rayner Unwin, head of the firm. I was introduced as one of his Australian authors. He rose from his chair, shook hands and said how pleased he was to meet with me. Then he sat down again and resumed work. I retreated through the darkness and never saw him again.

One of my other activities at this time was the NSW Council for Civil Liberties. In the 1960s the CCL had been in the forefront of challenges to laws imposing censorship, restricting freedom of assembly and denying any rights to persons in prison. It might seem hard to believe now but this was a time when Nabokov's *Lolita* was banned from entry into Australia and any demonstration against the Vietnam war – no matter how peaceful – risked being forcibly broken up by the police.

When I joined the committee of the CCL late in the 1970s, this climate was beginning to change. There were still important questions to debate. I spent some time during the next five years preparing submissions to government bodies on, for example, the powers of the Australian Security Intelligence Organisation and the Special Branch of the NSW Police Force. Both these organisations spent much of their time investigating ineffectual groups that would have conventionally been described as on the political left. But the Wran government, which came to power in New South Wales in 1976, introduced legislation, largely through Attorney-General Frank Walker, that picked up many of the CCL's policies. At the same time, some of those who had been active in the CCL in the 1960s and the early 1970s became judges or senior figures in the law. Suddenly the organisation was no longer bohemian but rather respectable.

In many ways, the CCL never adjusted to the fact that much of its agenda had actually been implemented nor to some of the changes that took place in Australian society in the 1980s and the 1990s. Seemingly oblivious to the growth of serious crime and the concerns of members of the community for their families and homes, the CCL began to oppose any proposals for increasing the powers of law enforcement bodies and any measures, such as DNA testing or listening devices, that would improve crime detection. As a result, it became marginalised with very little influence on politicians who were naturally alive to the concerns of the electorate.

At about this time Gae moved from Canberra to Sydney and took up a post in the New South Wales bureaucracy. I was conscious that this was not especially advantageous to her long-term career and that, while my life was enormously brightened, she had made a considerable career sacrifice. She was first and foremost an economist and probably would have been able to put these skills to better effect in the private sector than in what was still at that time a very hidebound State bureaucracy.

Like all universities at the time, the law school had a system of sabbatical leave. This meant that, after three and a half years, I was entitled to spend six months abroad working on writing projects. Given that, even in normal years, the summer vacation runs to nearly three months, academic life provides the blocks of time that books usually need. My next project was a book on Australia's entry into the Vietnam war. Because I wanted access to many of the documents on the American side, Washington DC seemed the ideal location. For several months early in 1980 I took up a post as

Visiting Scholar in the International Law Institute at Georgetown University in the American capital.

Georgetown is one of the oldest and most stylish quarters of Washington but the Institute was located downtown, closer to the hub of law and government. I slipped quickly back into the Washington I had known in the early 1970s, although this time I was living in the Capitol Hill area. John Edwards, Washington correspondent for the *National Times*, had returned to Sydney for several months to be married and I was the house-minder. Some of my American colleagues were alarmed as this had long been a largely black neighbourhood, and so considered unsafe for whites in what was still a sharply-segregated city, but I enjoyed its closeness to the Institute and to the city's markets. During the next decade gentrification turned this area into a very fashionable part of town.

I used some of my time at the Institute to make requests for documents from the Vietnam period to various government agencies under American freedom of information legislation. Some of these documents were produced; some were not; and some were supplied with portions blacked out. I was particularly anxious to read the unpublished manuscript by William Bundy, who had been Assistant Secretary of State for East Asian and Pacific Affairs in the Johnson administration. In this role he had been the link on the American side between Canberra and Washington. When I saw him at the Council on the Foreign Relations in New York, he was reserved but with the assurance that comes from Groton, Yale and the senior levels of the CIA. He offered me the use of the Council's library to read more than a thousand A4 pages and make notes on the way through. He seemed unconcerned when I made it clear that I thought the war was a terrible mistake for the Americans. It was many years later that I realised from Kai Bird's biography of Bundy and his brother McGeorge, National Security Advisor to both Kennedy and Johnson, that Bundy had had his own doubts in the mid-1960s but never spoken publicly of them.[7]

The starting point for my own research had been a large bundle of highly-classified Australian documents given to me a year earlier. Most of the documents came from the last months of 1964 and the first months of 1965. This was the crucial period when the decision was made in Washington to put a substantial ground force in Vietnam; and in Canberra to offer a battalion of Australian troops. The documents included much of the cable traffic between Canberra, Washington and the Australian embassy in Saigon. Almost all were stamped in red with one of Canberra's security classifications, which ran from CONFIDENTIAL and RESTRICTED to SECRET and TOP SECRET. Some also carried the additional stamp of AUSTEO (Australian Eyes Only).

There was then a general rule in Australia that Cabinet papers are made public thirty years after coming into existence. But some defence and foreign affairs documents have always remained classified even after this period. It seemed unlikely, therefore, that the documents in my possession would be publicly available before 1995 and perhaps not even then. This caused two legal problems. One was the probability of the Commonwealth government asking the courts for an injunction to prevent the publication of a book using this material. The second was the possibility of criminal proceedings against the author and the publisher. I knew the relevant provisions of the federal Crimes Act made it an offence for a public servant to leak official information and an offence for anyone to receive it if the recipient has any reason to believe it was not officially authorised. No doubt such leaks happen everyday in Canberra, especially from ministerial offices, but it is never a defence to a criminal prosecution that others have been allowed to get away with the same conduct. I explained all this to Brian Johns, head of Penguin Books, who had been enthusiastic about the project from the start. Later General Manager of SBS and the ABC, Johns had been a journalist, chiefly with the *Sydney Morning Herald*, before working in the Department of the Prime Minister and Cabinet during the Whitlam years. He had the appearance of a large and engaging teddy bear but was quite shrewd and determined underneath. He loved everything about books and intended to see this one published. I told him there was a small risk we would both go to prison. He refused to take this seriously.

The threat of an injunction, however, was very real. In November 1980 the Commonwealth government went to the High Court to stop publication of a book containing documents from various agencies in Canberra, particularly the Departments of Defence and Foreign Affairs, concerning East Timor and American military bases in Australia.[8] Extracts from the book were to be published in the *Sydney Morning Herald* and the Melbourne *Age*. But the day before, a brochure for the book turned up in the federal Parliamentary Library. Instead of ordering the book, the librarian passed the brochure on to the government's legal advisers. Shortly after midnight that same day the High Court ordered the two newspapers not to publish.

When the merits of this temporary injunction were argued before a single judge of the High Court a few days later, I was sitting in the back of the court room to see whether it would still be possible to publish the Vietnam book early in 1981. It had the tentative title of *War for the Asking: Australia's Vietnam Secrets*. The case for the newspapers was argued by two of the country's leading barristers, Tom Hughes QC and Jeff Sher QC. It did not occur to me that a few years later I would be confronting them myself at the bar table in some hard-fought encounters. On this occasion, however, their talents were not enough. Justice Mason found that the government had not shown any likelihood of damage to national security from the proposed publication but that it had copyright in the documents, because they had been prepared by public servants, and the book would be a breach of this copyright.[9] This was a very artificial use by the Commonwealth of a law designed to protect the works of authors and musicians. It was nevertheless sufficient to stop publication.

There was a good argument that *War for the Asking* was in a different category. Instead of being a collection of documents with a small amount of text, it was largely my text with some extracts from Australian documents and other extracts from American material. There would be no breach of copyright if a substantial proportion of the Australian documents had not been reproduced. There is, however, no certainty in litigation. Brian Johns and I agreed that the book should be on the shelves in bookshops before receiving any publicity. We thought that action by the Commonwealth was less likely once the book was in the public domain. But there are many practical problems for a publisher distributing thousands of copies

Working on War for the Asking *on Gae's dining room table in Canberra in 1980*

of a book to book shops and extolling its merits while otherwise trying to keep the whole exercise secret.

Yet all this effort was justified, in our view, by what the documents revealed. They showed that in late 1964 and early 1965 the Johnson administration had debated whether to introduce significant ground forces into Vietnam. It is very likely that the Americans would have made the decision to commit these forces in any event. But the documents showed that, far from weighing up the benefits and risks of this step, senior politicians and bureaucrats in Canberra and Australian diplomats in Washington had urged the American administration to widen the war and made every effort to ensure that Washington asked for Australian troops. Technically the request should have come from the South Vietnamese government but it was treated as a cipher by both Washington and Canberra. Eventually a 'request' from Saigon was obtained, but not until after Sir Robert Menzies had made the announcement on 29 April 1965.

The real point, therefore, of the book was the almost desperate effort by some ministers and public servants to involve Australia in this conflict. Another important aspect of the story was the failure of the policy-makers in Canberra, and in Washington, to foresee the likely outcome of the war they wanted so badly. This was not a judgment made in hindsight. At the time there were officials in both administrations who expressed the view that the Saigon regime could not be propped up indefinitely. One of the obvious sources of useful information was recent history. It was little more than a decade since several hundred thousand French troops had withdrawn from Vietnam in 1954 after suffering a comprehensive defeat at the hands of the North Vietnamese forces. These events underlined the military capacity of the Hanoi regime and the political weakness of the Saigon government.

So there was a failure of judgment in Canberra and Washington. But there was a more sinister strain on the Australian side. Some, at least, of the decision-makers in Canberra did not seem to care whether the war went badly or not. They were not concerned with what happened to South Vietnam or its government. Nor did they care what happened in the long run to the American military campaign, or the lives of Australian troops. The object of the exercise was simply to put the United States in Australia's debt. Although the war continued for the next ten years, the Australian government was never prepared to make any significant military or financial commitment despite its intense anxiety to be involved at the outset. This remained a puzzle to the Americans. But it is explicable if the Australians considered that they had already achieved their aim in April 1965.

Two communications from January 1965 are sufficient to indicate the anxiety in Canberra that the Americans were vacillating over whether to initiate a full-scale war in Vietnam, a war that the key decision-makers in Canberra wanted to go ahead. In the early days of this month, Paul Hasluck, Minister for External Affairs, sent a note to the head of his department:

> Yesterday I received from Waller [Australian ambassador in Washington] personal letter dated December 21 commenting on our telegram about prospects in Vietnam and expressing his own *grave concern both at hesitancy of United States in taking decisions about future operations and at American inability to control political situation in Saigon*... Today this and other recent messages regarding South Vietnam were discussed by Senator Paltridge [Minister for Defence] and myself. We are both gravely concerned at outlook and the necessity of taking whatever steps we can to advance Australia's vital interest in securing success in South Vietnam and not merely hanging on until the eventually steady erosion brings disaster. [emphasis added][10]

Later in the same month, Hasluck sent a cable to the Australian ambassador in Washington:

> Cabinet is gravely concerned about the outlook. At the earliest opportunity you should try to see Rusk [US Secretary of State] with a view both to obtaining as much further information as you can about American thinking and taking advantage of whatever opportunity may arise of *helping to bring certainty to American policy and planning* ... Furthermore the effectiveness of what we say may be increased if it can be presented in a way and at a time that enables it *to reinforce the persuasion of any likeminded elements within the United States Administration.* For these reasons I have refrained from drafting a note from myself to Rusk and am asking you to seek a less formal discussion and to choose the phrases best suited to the occasion. [emphasis added][11]

The initial commitment of Australian troops was 1,000 but by October 1967 this had increased to 8,000. Apart from the United States, whose forces climbed to 525,000 in mid-1967, the only other significant contribution was the South Korean contingent. As it became clear that the war could not be won, American troop withdrawals began in mid-1969. The first Australian withdrawals took place in April 1970 and by the end of 1971 there was no Australian military presence in Vietnam. Almost 500 Australians had died and 2,500 had been wounded in the previous seven years. The Americans lost 55,000 dead and 300,000 wounded. The last American civilian personnel were evacuated from Saigon on 30 April 1975 – the day on which North Vietnamese troops entered the city. More than two million people in what was originally called Indo-China had been killed and twice that number wounded. Twice as many again had been made refugees.

On 6 May 1981 *War for the Asking* was safely in the bookshops and featured on the front page of the *Sydney Morning Herald* and the Melbourne *Age*. The stories were by Paul Kelly and Laurie Oakes, who had been given advance copies and proved capable of keeping a secret. On the same morning I was on the road, shuttling between radio and television stations for interviews. It was a good week for publication in the sense that the Fraser government in Canberra was distracted by a number of internal problems. Obviously, in deciding whether to try to suppress the book, there were no active survivors from the Menzies Cabinet of 1965 to protect but the Department of Foreign Affairs and the Attorney-General's Department both considered whether any action should be taken and prepared answers for questions that their ministers might be asked in Parliament. The Attorney-General's Department did carry out the exercise, which would have taken some days, of comparing the full documents and cables to the extracts in the book to assess the strength of any copyright claim by the Commonwealth.

While waiting for this decision I had taken no chances with the original documents that had been given to me. I did not want these seized by the federal police if any legal proceedings were taken against the publisher and myself. So they were hidden on a rural property outside Canberra. This all seems rather melodramatic in retrospect but it seemed to me better to be safe than sorry.

A number of the reviews of *War for the Asking* were heavily influenced in their approval or disapproval by whether the reviewer saw himself – they were all men – as on the left or the right of the political spectrum. Both groups seemed to be under the misapprehension that the book was anti-American. It is true that it describes the United States involvement in Vietnam as a disastrous error. But, as someone who had studied and worked in America, and almost taken up permanent residence there, I had none of the hostility to America that appeared to be an article of faith amongst many of those who considered themselves on the left, including some sections of the Labor Party. One of the points of the book was to argue that the Australian government had not done the United States any favours by encouraging its intervention in an unwinnable war that caused substantial loss of lives and bitter divisions in American society. Forty years later Vietnam still lingered amongst many Europeans as a cause for suspicion of all American foreign policies.

One of the most interesting reviews of the book was by Graham Freudenberg in the *Sydney Morning Herald*. Freudenberg had been on the staff of Labor leader, Arthur Calwell, when the initial commitment of Australian troops was announced by Sir Robert Menzies on 29 April 1965. Freudenberg wrote the speech that Calwell delivered a few days later in the House of Representatives opposing the decision. The review was pessimistic about the prospect of the book's revelations changing the way in which these decisions were made:

> This book does exactly what it sets out to do. It shows how Australian politicians and diplomats put pressure on the United States Administration to ensure that Australia was invited to a war in which our Vietnamese hosts and possibly even our American sponsors never really wanted us.
>
> Yet I predict this book will fail to achieve its deserved result of changing the processes by which great and fundamental foreign policy decisions are made in Australia.
>
> It will, I fear, become yet another "gallant failure" in our military and diplomatic annals.[12]

Twenty years later, in launching a revised edition of the book, Freudenberg was happy to be able to say that his fears had been unfounded in the sense that any Australian government would now very much want to avoid the allegation that it had acted as the Menzies government acted in 1965.[13]

I had spent some time before *War for the Asking* was published looking at the federal Crimes Act so that I could tell Brian Johns the worst about what might happen to us. In the middle of 1983 I was able to use this knowledge in a case involving Mick Young, Special Minister of State in the Hawke government that took office in March 1983. During these university years I had written a good deal about the law but never really practised it, except for the occasional advice on industrial law prepared for some of the public sector unions. But this was a good cause. Young was one of the most attractive characters in Australian politics in the post-war years. With black curly hair and winning Irish smile, he was generous, gregarious and genuinely funny. But he was also highly capable and, in the lead up to the election of the Whitlam government in 1972, he had been Labor's national secretary and played a large part in its victory.

Suddenly, in July 1983, Young's political career looked to be finished. He had been stood down from the Cabinet for leaking information about national security. The leak occurred in a conversation between Young and his closest friend, Eric Walsh, a Canberra lobbyist, in the car park of the 19th Hole Restaurant in Canberra, not far from Parliament House and a place I knew from several lunches and dinners in 1975. Young had mentioned to Walsh that the government planned to expel a Soviet diplomat, Valeri Ivanov, on the ground that he was a spy and had drawn a number of Australians into his circle. After the expulsion, there was a Royal Commission into Ivanov's activities, among other things, and the car park conversation emerged in the course of evidence before the Commission.[14]

I was asked by Michael Eyers, who was acting as Young's lawyer, to help with submissions that would be made to the Royal Commission. Not only was Young's political future at stake, there was a question as to whether he would be prosecuted under the Crimes Act with the possibility of a gaol sentence. There was no prosecution but the Royal Commissioner said the conversation was "unauthorised and improper." Normally this would have stopped Young returning to the Cabinet but, over Hawke's objections, the Labor caucus insisted on his reinstatement, another example of how likeable and highly regarded Young was. Usually there is not much room for sentiment in politics.

Young was never really the same after this incident. Later, at the Bar, I saw many people broken by court proceedings. It seemed to me, during the Royal Commission and afterwards, that Young had lost some of his spirit, not least because the whole saga had its origins in a conversation with someone who was like a brother to him. It was no surprise to me when, a little more than four years later, still only 51, he resigned as a minister and gave up his parliamentary seat in the wake of allegations, never made out later, about his dealings with campaign donations.

A few months later my mother called from Melbourne to say that my father had died. Until his mid-70s, my father enjoyed a decade of active retirement but then began a long deterioration from Parkinson's Disease. I thought then that it was a terrible thing to see a person's body become almost useless while their mind remained completely unimpaired. Now that the reverse is so common with Alzheimer's Disease, I am not so sure. I had visited Melbourne frequently, but not often enough. Although I was probably more like my mother and, as an only child, very conscious of both my parents, I realised that, for a son, the death of a father marks the end of a generation. It is also a reminder of who will be next.

The funeral service in Melbourne was conducted by Bishop Arthur Fox, one of the Church's strongest supporters of the Santamaria forces in Melbourne. In view of my father's refusal to become involved in that crusade, it did not seem a very good choice but the arrangements had been made before I could intervene. The burial took place in a corner of the Melbourne General Cemetery in Carlton. In a sense, my father had come full circle. It was just a hundred metres from where he had been born and spent much of his early life.

7

MAN AND MACHINE
The World of Politics

When I settled in Sydney in 1976 I transferred from the Canberra branch of the Labor Party to the Clovelly branch. Clovelly is one of the beachside areas to the east of the city that run along the coast from Bondi to Maroubra. With a staff loan from the bank at the University of New South Wales, I had bought a small semi-detached cottage there, the first house that I had owned.

These ocean beaches had a style that was more like Australia of the 1950s than the 1970s. Unlike the newer suburbs, there were old people who had spent their whole lives in this part of the world. There was still a sense of community, built around pubs, clubs and sporting organisations, especially surf lifesaving bodies. The sights and smells of the coast were all around – sun and salt water, fish and chips, schooners of beer, tanning oil and surfboards. Most mornings I threw myself into the waves at Coogee Beach. It was a good way to wake up.

There was nothing fashionable about these areas in the 1970s. Twenty years later Sydney's real estate boom had swept through this coastal region and pushed prices to dizzying levels. My house had cost $38,000. By the end of the 1990s there were few properties in Clovelly under a million dollars.

The Clovelly branch was one of about a dozen Labor Party branches located in the federal seat of Phillip. It was smaller than some of the other branches with only 30 or 40 members on the books. I became president in the late 1970s and chaired the monthly meetings in the local church hall. Phillip had been a marginal seat over the previous decade, held by the Liberals for most of the 1960s; then by Labor at the 1972 and 1974 elections; and then by the Liberals again in 1975, 1977 and 1980.

Despite the result in Phillip in 1980, Bill Hayden had done extremely well in his first election as Labor leader but Bob Hawke had entered the House of Representatives at the same election and Hayden felt, quite rightly, that his leadership was under constant threat from Hawke's supporters. Early in 1982 the former Liberal Prime Minister, William McMahon, resigned from his federal seat of Lowe, causing a by-election. Hayden knew that he would be vulnerable if Labor did not win the by-election and he wanted a star candidate. He called me and asked if I would sound out Mary Gaudron who was the NSW Solicitor-General. I did but she was not interested – hardly surprising when she held a lifetime appointment for a job she relished and had a good chance of being appointed to the High Court when the next Labor government arrived in Canberra. It did not matter, however, on this occasion. The popular Labor member for Drummoyne, the local State seat, Michael Maher, agreed to stand. He won comfortably. Hayden was safe for the time being.

The next federal election was expected towards the end of 1983. In the first half of 1982 there were pre-selections for Labor candidates in federal seats. I decided to nominate in Phillip. Years later, this still seems a puzzling decision, especially since I knew that I could not win the pre-selection, although I had a strong view that it was important for party members to have choices and I suppose I saw it as signalling an interest for the future. It was also true that I thought Labor's candidate in 1980, who was running again, was not a strong contender. There was an element of bloody-mindedness in standing against someone I thought had little to contribute to public life. This was an expensive self-indulgence. I at once exposed myself to enormous hostility from a large section of the Labor Party in New South Wales.

The reason that I could not win was that Labor's branches in Phillip were largely controlled by the so-called Steering Committee. This group had its origins in the 1950s. It saw itself as left wing. It was implacably opposed to the so-called Centre Unity Group, which was commonly described as right wing. These labels had little meaning, as I explained on ABC Radio at about this time:

> I think two general points should be made first. One is that all parties, including the Liberal Party in Australia, have factions, that is groups of people who operate together, and that all State branches of the Labor Party have factions as well. But the situation in New South Wales over recent years has certainly become much more serious and much more debilitating for the Party than in other State branches of Australia. And the reason is that over that period of time the bitterness and the conflict between the two major groups in New South Wales has almost paralysed the New South Wales Party in terms of policy making and debate, and I might say also, in efforts to try and get a national Labor government... The conditions in general are personal and historical factors, I think, rather than ideological ones. The terms 'left' and 'right' don't have a great deal of meaning in this dispute. It's something that has grown up over a period of many decades, and I think it would be difficult for anyone to explain exactly how it has reached the present situation. The fact is, though, that the present situation is extremely damaging to the Party...

In the same way that religion cloaked a tribal conflict in Northern Ireland for many years, differences in ideology played a relatively minor role in this conflict. As Shane Maloney had one of the characters say in his novel, *Something Fishy*:

> The Australian Labor Party is composed of two main factions: Them and Us. Ideologically distinct only at their extremities, their function is the distribution of spoils.

There was no doubting the passion that both sides brought to this long-running feud. Although the Centre Unity Group usually had a two-thirds majority at the State Conference each year, the Steering Committee controlled a number of the major trade unions affiliated to the party and a majority of the branches in many federal and State electorates. As a result, the Steering Committee was able to claim a share of the official positions in the New South Wales Branch and to decide who would be members of parliament, State and federal, from those areas that it controlled. Their candidate in Phillip was Jeanette McHugh, who had run in 1980. A former school teacher, she was married to Michael McHugh QC, then President of the NSW Bar Association and later a judge of the High Court. Although I did not belong to either faction, my decision to stand in the pre-selection in Phillip was seen by all members of the Steering Committee as an attempt to deprive them of one of their hard-won strongholds.

Because I had come recently to this world, I did not really understand the fierce emotions that had been unleashed in this contest for the control of candidates and seats by the rival factions. One of these contests exploded publicly in July 1980 when Peter Baldwin, then a member of the NSW Legislative Council and later a minister in the Hawke government, was savagely bashed at his home. Baldwin was a Steering Committee activist who had signed up many new members for party branches in Sydney's inner west in an effort, largely successful in the long-term, to wrest the local seats from their sitting members. Because I was standing against a member of the Steering Committee I became the enemy of the entire group whose members saw themselves engaged in an heroic struggle against the forces of evil – as, of course, did their opponents on the other side.

I lunched with Graham Richardson, General Secretary of the NSW branch, and Stephen Loosley, the Assistant Secretary, to talk about my campaign. Richardson, still in his early thirties but a legendary fixer and numbers man, was short and squat, with no neck and a sallow complexion that told of a thousand meetings in back rooms. At one level he was smart and funny but, at another, utterly cynical. Richardson and Loosley were the leaders of the Centre Unity Group and veterans of countless political deals. They seemed sympathetic but said they had no influence at all in Phillip. "Good luck, but you're on your own", were their parting words. A couple of days later I read a story in the *Sydney Morning Herald* which said that the real challenge to McHugh would come from another member of the Steering Committee, Stephen Rothman, a union lawyer who later became a judge of the NSW Supreme Court. The story had clearly been written with Richardson's approval. I had no complaint about this. They knew that I could not win and obviously thought it would be easier to live with Rothman than McHugh. But it was a sharp lesson in the factional intrigues of the NSW branch. In any event, the scheme backfired. The Steering Committee did not want to risk a split in its vote in the pre-selection. The next day a letter was sent to the *Herald* signed by McHugh and Rothman in which Rothman said that he had no intention of standing against McHugh. I assumed that Rothman may well have originally wanted to displace McHugh. It was an example of the iron control that both factions exercised over their members.

I lost the pre-selection vote by 184 votes to 74. In the weeks beforehand I had visited most of these branch members and had enjoyed talking with them, even though I knew that nothing I said could deflect them from their factional loyalty. Later, some Steering Committee members told me they had planned to vote for me anyway but, on arriving at the polling station, found that they had to show their vote to another member before it was put in the ballot box. There was no point in complaining about this. It was the way that the factional system operated in the Sicilian world of the NSW Labor Party. In the letter that I sent to all branch members in Phillip I had talked about this system:

> I am not running as part of any organised group either inside or outside Phillip. I have been told by a number of people in the party that it is futile to run for pre-selection without the endorsement of one or other of the two main factions of the party in NSW. I do not believe that any groups in the party should have this kind of power...

These were fine words but the reality was that it was impossible to make any contribution to the party's policies from outside the factions. Membership of all the central policy-making committees was, for example, effectively divided up between the Centre Unity Group and the Steering Committee at State conferences. This situation was not altered by the fact that many of those in both bodies had no interest in policies at all. So which group to join? The Steering Committee seemed out of the question. Apart from the hostility provoked by the Phillip pre-selection, I did not want to be part of a group where it was necessary to maintain – and constantly repeat – propositions which were economic nonsense, especially about taxation, trade and government ownership. Writing in *The Bulletin* in the early 1980s about economic policy, I was guilty of half a dozen heresies in one paragraph:

> The 50s and 60s were the period when the strongly regulated and anti-competitive structure of the Australian

economy was established. Tariff barriers were set in the manufacturing area that produced totally inefficient sectors such as the car industry. The two-airline policy was enshrined in legislation and the importation of aircraft prohibited to ensure that no new service could be established. Banking licences were frozen in the hands of existing holders and the establishment of foreign banks prohibited. Interest rates were tightly regulated and the rates for home loans fixed at an artificially low level. Broadcasting and television licences were issued to existing media outlets and the issue of additional licences or the transference of existing licences closely regulated. A policy of central wage-fixing by the Conciliation and Arbitration Commission was encouraged by the government and adopted as far as possible by the commission . . .[1]

Not that things were much better in the Centre Unity Group. Most of its trade union members would have been likewise horrified by my views. And my opinions on abortion and euthanasia were hardly acceptable to the Irish Catholics who formed a majority of its numbers. But there were some individuals – Paul Keating, Stephen Loosley and Bob Carr, for example – who had a sense of history and a genuine interest in public policy. The last of these, Bob Carr, had been a friend for some years. When he went into the NSW Legislative Assembly in 1983 at a by-election, I was one of a number of friends from outside the area who went door-knocking for him. It was probably the only time I ever door-knocked for anybody. I did not enjoy it. In one of these suburban streets I was doing the houses on one side and Jim Spigelman, later Chief Justice of New South Wales, was doing the other side. Spigelman's manner was brusque. He was little more suited than I was to this exercise. The next street was much better served – it was being done by the vivacious Mary Alexander who, as Mary Easson, was later member for Lowe from 1993 to 1996. It is unlikely I turned any votes but it was a safe seat and Carr was elected anyway. Soon afterwards I joined the Centre Unity Group. There was nothing in writing, only an oral invitation from its power brokers. I thus gave up my unaligned status in the continuing tribal war within the NSW branch.

At about the same time Mark Latham joined the faction, for similar reasons and with a similar lack of enthusiasm. As he later explained:

> My belief in adventurism means that I will always have an uneasy relationship with the NSW Right. Even though I am part of it notionally, its mind-numbing authoritarianism is hard to cop. I joined the Right in the mid-1980s for pragmatic reasons: in a two-faction State you had to join one of them to have any hope of preselection. And the Right seemed to be more realistic on economic issues than the Left.
>
> The faction, however, is based on a culture of anti-intellectualism. Policy is made through a series of deals, rather than the public interest. Power flows from the top down without any debate, goodwill or generosity of spirit.[2]

Latham nevertheless fought his way through the system to win pre-selection for the federal seat of Werriwa and to become, briefly, leader of the party from 2003 to 2005. Like many others, the skills employed in winning these positions proved unsuited to a career in public life.

The 1983 Federal election came early when Malcolm Fraser dashed, unsuccessfully, to Yarralumla on 3 February in an effort to head off Bill Hayden's resignation as Labor leader in favour of Bob Hawke. I had unwittingly made some new enemies amongst Hayden's supporters just before the changeover. The week before I had written a very lengthy piece for *The Bulletin* about Fraser's period as Prime Minister.³ Much of the article was designed to point out, as many of his Liberal colleagues later agreed, that Fraser had not used his twin majorities in the House of Representatives and the Senate to bring about major economic reforms.

At the end of the article, however, I suggested that, even with all these failings, Fraser still had a good prospect of winning the next election scheduled for the end of 1983. This was taken by a number of Hayden's shadow ministers as an attack on his leadership and support for his replacement by Hawke. As it happens I had no idea how close Hayden was to being forced out of the leadership. Because of Gae's time working for Hayden in the Whitlam years, I knew him much better than Hawke and I respected him as one of the few successful ministers in the Whitlam government. Despite Hawke's many talents, he was supported by some of the worst elements of the trade union movement and the business community. I hoped that Hayden would be Prime Minister. It was not to be.

The election was called for 5 March which meant that the campaign would run through the final month of the university vacation. I moved into Labor's national campaign headquarters in downtown Sydney as its resident legal adviser. I was responsible for seeing Labor's advertising survived any legal challenges and monitoring Liberal publications for statements that could be the subject of complaint to the broadcasting authorities or, in the last resort, court action. But, like everybody else in the office, I was pulled into many other jobs for which I was not nominally responsible.

After the disorganised and dispiriting campaigns of 1975 and 1977, the mood in campaign headquarters was relaxed and confident. All the polls indicated a comfortable victory for Labor. Bob McMullan, the party's National Secretary, was in charge. He was good to work with – softly spoken, cool, rational – something of a contrast to the madness that seems to infect many political operators during election campaigns. His deputy, Ken Bennett, Assistant National Secretary, had played in Collingwood's 1958 VFL premiership team as a teenager. He was hard-headed, hard-working and a good organiser.

After the election victory, I returned to the university for what would be my last year in the law school. At the same time, I started to spend some time on Labor's policies at the State and national level. This began with the Legal and Constitutional Committee of the NSW Branch. Together with Ron Dyer, the committee's chairman and a member of the Legislative Council, and Brian Knox from the Bar, I rewrote the party's policies in this area. The existing platform was largely out of date, as it had not been revised since Neville Wran's work on it in the late 1960s.

Being interested in the Senate, this was not entirely altruistic work on my part, but it was a job that I enjoyed anyway. The problem with the Senate was that, at the usual election every three years for half of its members, there were six senators after 1984 to be chosen in each State. Labor and the Coalition could be guaranteed to win at least two each. The remaining two spots were fought out with the Democrats, the Greens and other minor parties. Within the NSW branch, each of the factions took one of the two safe positions on the ballot paper. So the contest for a very limited number of seats was very competitive. Not surprisingly, they had been mostly taken over the years by full-time party officials who had the inside running.

The House of Representatives presented a different challenge. To succeed in this kind of pre-selection in New South Wales usually required years of filling the local branches with supporters and keeping their membership current. There was sometimes a fine line between this exercise and the branch-stacking of the 1990s, where large numbers of persons with no real interest in the party, often from a particular ethnic group, were enrolled so they could vote in a preselection. It was difficult to combine these time-consuming activities with most occupations, which is why it was normally done by people already working full-time in the political world, for ministers, trade unions or the party itself.

The other policy committee on which I worked in New South Wales was Defence and Foreign Affairs, where I took over as the chairman. Although most of the committees were split fairly narrowly between the two factions, the members usually worked quite amicably together during the year. Then at the annual State conference in the Sydney Town Hall they would heap public abuse on each other, only to return a few weeks later to co-operation in the committee room after putting on this show for their factional colleagues. This was particularly true of the Legal and Constitutional Committee, where there was a least the common bond of all being lawyers. It was, however, one of the members of this committee – Greg Woods QC, later a judge of the NSW District Court – who once described my speech to the 800 conference delegates as disgraceful and despicable, shouting at the top of his voice from the stage. In the middle of this tirade, the Conference time keeper, Tony Luchetti, who had been a member of the House of Representatives from 1951 until 1975, collapsed with a heart attack from which he died a few weeks later. Woods could not see what had happened and had to be stopped by others on the stage. None of this affected my relationship with Woods who was normally very agreeable to work with.

The Defence and Foreign Affairs Committee had a number of members at this time who went on to parliamentary careers, although no others like that of a young Steering Committee activist from the Hunter Valley, Milton Orkopoulos, who became a minister in the New South Wales government in 2005 before being charged soon afterwards with a series of sexual assaults on minors for which he was ultimately convicted and sentenced to almost fourteen years' imprisonment.

I sometimes attended the meetings of Labor's national Defence and Foreign Affairs Committee in Canberra. Its membership included a number of the federal parliamentarians, including Bill Hayden, who had become Foreign Minister in the Hawke government. Hayden was highly intelligent, sharp-tongued and sardonic. He was also prickly and suspicious, quite reasonably after the way in which his leadership had been sabotaged by some of his closest colleagues early in the 1980s. He was a very different character from his successor, the wildly extroverted and enormously

With Gae at the foot of the Mont Blanc glacier in 1981

confident Bob Hawke. My first encounter with Hawke was in the late 1970s when Gae and I were having dinner in an Italian restaurant in Kings Cross with an academic economist. Hawke was at another table but came over to talk to Gae, whom he knew from her time in Canberra. The economist obviously wanted to meet the great man and got up to join them. Smiling, he said who he was and put out his hand. "Fuck off", said Hawke savagely, "I'm talking to Gae." And so he did, reeling back to our table.

Hayden was more introspective. He said that one of the things he enjoyed about being Minister for Foreign Affairs was that, no matter what he wrote on their submissions, the diplomats always responded: "Minister, that is the best analysis of the problem we've ever seen." Surely that must be terribly boring, suggested Gae. "Not at all", Hayden smiled mirthlessly. "It's rather pleasant after a while." No doubt a thinly-veiled reference to the readiness of many staff in the Whitlam government to argue fiercely with ministers as they reached their decisions.

I saw more of Hawke and Hayden at Labor's national conference in Hobart in 1986. I was one of the 99 delegates, as a member of the NSW team. After the victory of March 1983, the Labor government had been re-elected in December 1984. The leader of the Centre Unity contingent from New South Wales was federal Treasurer, Paul Keating, although the organisers of the faction at the national level were Graham Richardson, by then in the Senate, and Senator Robert Ray from Victoria. In a piece in *The Australian* shortly before the conference, I had suggested that the government would have been better off to have accepted Keating's proposals for tax reform in 1985:

> The taxation package announced by Treasurer Keating in 1985 was one of the most wide-ranging in political history and featured a number of measures, such as the abolition of negative gearing and the institution of taxes on fringe

benefits, that were never at any time considered during the seven years of the Fraser government.

Mr Keating himself had, of course, proposed an even more radical restructuring of the taxation system by means of the introduction of a consumption tax but was defeated by an alliance that included significant sections of the business sector and union movement and those very groups inside the Labor Party who complained most bitterly that Labor governments never made significant changes.[4]

This was not a popular view in Labor ranks but my point about a consumption tax, or any other indirect tax, was that it could not be easily avoided. Few wealthy individuals pay income tax on a significant scale. They have lawyers and accountants to ensure that this does not happen. The same is true for large corporations,

At Labor's 1986 National Conference in Hobart with Tricia Kavanagh, later a judge of the NSW Industrial Court; Michael Egan, later NSW Treasurer; and Bob Carr, later NSW Premier

particularly those that operate internationally. Indirect taxes are regressive, in the sense that they take a higher proportion of the earnings of a person on a lower income. But it is similarly as regressive to have a system where the bulk of income tax is met by one section of the community, and far from the richest section. Moreover, it is possible to ameliorate this problem to a large extent through the social security system, community service programs and targeted infrastructure expenditure. Keating's proposal of a consumption tax was, ironically, picked up by John Howard who brought in the GST in 2000 without losing office.

The most divisive question at the 1986 conference was not, however, anything to do with economic policy but the matter of a national system of pre-selection. The model proposed would have brought about a change for lower house seats in New South Wales by giving a central panel as much weight as the local branches. This was the system that already existed in Victoria where it had certainly produced a more talented group of parliamentarians overall than in New South Wales. The Steering Committee in New South Wales reacted violently, fearing the loss of control over the pre-selections it controlled. The day of the vote I was sitting with Kim Beazley at breakfast. He was keen for me to go to Canberra and optimistic as usual: "When this goes through, you'll find a seat soon enough."

Later in the day I found myself in the wash room, standing next to John Faulkner, the Steering Committee's dour and flinty leader and one of the two assistant secretaries from New South Wales. "How's it going?" I asked, really only to break the silence. "Much better than yesterday," said Faulkner grimly. "I think we've got the numbers to stop this happening." He was right. The Centre Left group, which held the balance of power at the conference, withdrew its promised support and voted with the Socialist Left group to defeat the proposed change. Not that this was a problem for Faulkner himself who went into the Senate, became a minister in the Keating and Rudd governments and is now portrayed by the media as a severe critic of party factions and the damage they inflict.

In contrast with the stylised, if essentially synthetic, confrontations between the factions at the NSW State conferences, the national meetings were already heavily stage-managed. There were few genuine debates. Usually the factional operators had agreed on a consensus resolution before the issue hit the conference floor. The session on a national system of preselection was, however, very different. In a memorable display of cold rage – shown on national television – Robert Ray accused the Centre Left on going back on their word and selling out to the Socialist Left. It was a rare occasion, and one of the last, when genuine emotion, whatever its merits, spilled over, raw and open.

One of the leaders of the Centre Left was Victorian Senator John Button, Industry Minister in the Hawke government. Button was small, almost elf-like in appearance, but clever and determined. We shared an interest in books and the Geelong Football Club. He had sounded me out on the idea of being one of the founders of a Centre Left group within the NSW Party. I took the view, however, that there was no real prospect of creating a third force between the two warring tribes. What eventually happened was that internal divisions developed within the two factions and sub-factions were effectively created. But there was no formal change to the familiar historical pattern.

On the last night of the conference most of the NSW Centre Unity delegates gathered for a drink in one of the hotel rooms at the Wrest Point Casino, where the meeting sessions were held and most of the delegates stayed. The star of the show was Paul Keating. Even after his many years in public life, Keating was essentially a shy person. But like many shy people, he had a theatrical side. He was warm to his friends but spoke with open contempt about his opponents, most of whom were in the Labor party and many of whom were in his own faction. At one point, I noticed an ABC television unit filming Keating in full flight – and his audience. I took no further notice. This was a mistake. The film was for use in a *Four Corners* program about the conference. It was shown the following week.

The reaction to my cameo appearance – I was standing in a corner of the room but had no speaking part – was almost uniformly hostile. The most common view amongst Phillip Street lawyers was that any formal association with political life was unsavoury. This attitude often cloaked some very strong informal associations.

At home in the dining room in 1986 with son Jack born at the end of 1985

The most dramatic reaction, however, came from those with Labor sympathies. Most of them, including some who were life-long party members, saw Paul Keating as a devil figure who was intent on destroying all the party's traditions. Some of them simply stopped speaking to me. Only a few years later, when he was Prime Minister, the same people adopted Keating as a hero, much preferring him to any other Labor leader of the post-war years, except for Whitlam. I never understood why it was necessary to divide the entire universe into saints and demons.

There were less fireworks at the other two national conferences, 1988 and 1990, that I attended as a delegate. The 1990 conference was specially convened to allow the Hawke government to privatise Australian Airlines and Qantas. This required a change to the existing national platform. The government also wanted support for its proposal to deregulate telecommunications in Australia. These were examples of the kinds of issues I thought could be the subject of useful debate through the Fabian Society. The Fabians had always been close to the Labor Party in Britain and Australia but their role was educational rather than electoral. In the mid-1980s I became chairman of the NSW Branch. Writing about the Society in *The Bulletin* in December 1985, I set out some of its modern goals in response to an attack on its history in a recent edition of the magazine:

> The original Fabian view of legislation as a means of remedying social ills was developed in the latter part of the 19th century and the early part of this century when there was very little regulation of economic and industrial matters. In the 1980s, with an abundance of legislation in these areas, few persons would suggest that more is needed or even that existing legislation should not be stringently reviewed. It is certainly arguable that the Whitlam government over-legislated as a reaction to Labor's enormous period in opposition ...

The notion of Fabianism as embodying a pervasive anti-Americanism is simply a fantasy. Australian Fabians have traditionally identified this country as a member of the Western group of nations ...

The question of sympathy for the Soviet Union entails another ... delusion about the Fabians. There has always been a very heavy emphasis in the Fabian tradition on a parliamentary system of government. This is hardly surprising considering the origins of Fabianism in Britain at the turn of the [19th] century. Nor is it surprising that this emphasis has been heavily criticised by Marxist writers.[5]

The range of ideas canvassed at NSW Fabian functions during this period is indicated by some of the speakers – Donald Horne; Michael Kirby; Peter Hollingworth, then Anglican Archbishop of Brisbane; Barry Jones; and the future Prime Minister of Britain, Gordon Brown. The secretary of the Society for some of this time was Mark Latham, still in his twenties but determined on a life in politics and already with the intensity that marked his future career.

Many of these debates were about the economic policies of the Hawke government. In its early days I had defended it in *The Australian* against the charge that it was not a "real" Labor government:

> To some extent, the criticisms of the Hawke government ... reflect a disenchantment with the whole parliamentary system of government, although this is seldom articulated.
> ... the sentimentalists inside and outside the Labor party ... love rhetoric, they relish sound and fury. They are bored by administration and detail. The problem is that government is all about administration and detail. Most of the time it is not glamorous or exciting but plain hard work.[6]

By the end of the 1980s, however, it was clear that this was not the whole story. Hawke was certainly the most remarkable politician I witnessed at close quarters. He is possibly the most talented person, except perhaps for Menzies, to hold the office of prime minister. He had no intellectual interests but the sharpest of minds and the capacity to dominate almost all those around him. He was usually a flat public speaker but highly persuasive in small groups, including the Cabinet. Neville Wran had the same skills and was additionally a good public speaker but he did not have, nor did anyone else in Australian public life before or since, Hawke's magnetic appeal to most of the community.

Hawke used all his talents in leading a government that introduced some of the most important economic policies since federation – deregulation of financial markets, floating of the dollar, substantial reduction of tariffs and overhaul of government business enterprises. There was, however, a long-term problem. The government in its later period became heavily dependent for its advice on the corporate sector and Canberra bureaucrats who shared the same values (or lack of them). This was reflected at the very top in Hawke's tolerance of many characters from the dark side of business like Sir Peter Abeles, Laurie Connell and Alan Bond. One consequence of its limited range of advisers was that it never confronted the question of "regulatory capture", exemplified, for example, in transport and communications where the industry groups and the government bodies supposedly supervising them combined to maintain the status quo and resist any changes to their existing positions. It should be added that the Howard government did not take on this problem either.

In the middle of these debates on domestic policy I had a sudden opportunity to make use of my interest in foreign affairs. In April 1988 the ALP National Executive decided to send a delegation to Fiji to recommend what Labor's policy should be towards the new regime in that country.

The preceding twelve months in Fiji had been stormy. Between 1970, when it became independent from Britain, and 1987, Fiji was governed by the Alliance Party led by Ratu Sir Kamisese Mara. The Alliance Party was an association of Fijian chiefs, wealthy Indians and the European, largely Australian, business interests. The main opposition party was the National Federation Party. It had its origins in the Indians brought to Fiji in the 19th century to work sugar cane farms but drew its support from the Indian community generally. In April 1987 the National Federation Party and the Labour Party, newly set up in 1985, fought the general election as a coalition and won twenty-eight seats in the lower house of the national parliament to the Alliance Party's twenty-four. Dr Bavadra, an ethnic Fijian, was commissioned by the Governor-General as Prime Minister.

On 14 May 1987, soldiers, led by an army colonel named Rabuka, marched into the parliamentary chamber in Suva in the middle of a debate. They took Coalition members into custody at gunpoint. The following month the Governor-General dissolved the parliament and set up a council of advisors comprised principally of Alliance members. In September 1987 the Coalition and Alliance parties agreed to establishment of a council, with each party having three members and the Governor-General presiding, pending a review of the existing constitution.

Within days Rabuka, now a brigadier, rejected this proposal and seized complete control of the Fijian government. Two months later a so-called interim government was established with Ratu Mara as Prime Minister, Rabuka as Minister for Home Affairs and other portfolios held by members of the Alliance party or prominent supporters.

The other members of the ALP delegation were Don Dunstan, former Premier of South Australia, and Ray Hogan, a trade unionist and President of the Victorian Branch. I looked forward particularly to working with Dunstan. In the 1960s and 1970s he had been that very rare combination of effective leader, thinking reformer and capable administrator. Objective observers considered him the outstanding contributor out of all the federal and State politicians on both sides at the annual Premiers' meetings in Canberra in this period. There was often talk in Labor circles of Dunstan moving into national politics but this would have put a much brighter spotlight on his openly gay lifestyle, a dangerous political gamble at that time, as Dunstan realised better than anybody.

The visit had a lively start when Rabuka put out a press release on the first day saying that any report by the delegation would be "biased and prejudiced".[7] Appointments with a number of ministers had been made by the Australian High Commission but these were cancelled after the Fijian Cabinet made a decision that there should not be any dealings with the delegation. The various heads of departments also, except one, cancelled meetings that had been organised. The Chief Justice and his fellow judges of the Court of Appeal did, however, meet with us. Then we spent a week of discussions with political, religious and community groups in Suva, in the major provincial cities and the rural areas surrounding these towns. Our chief guide in much of these travels was Harrish Sharma, leader of the National Federation Party, who had been Deputy Prime Minister in the deposed government. We were usually followed, at a polite distance, by the local police. They were not hostile and made sure that we did not miss any of our flights. After travelling through sugar cane farms by day, we would stop for dinner at night and listen to Dunstan's memories of law and politics in South Australia, most of them stories that had never reached the press. He had spent part of his childhood growing up in Fiji and was very bitter about the destruction of its parliamentary system of government.

The real problem lay in the fact that the population was almost evenly divided between ethnic Fijians and Indians, with almost no inter-marriage. The Indians were resented because they largely dominated the business world and the professions but in many ways the military takeover represented the great power that a small group of chiefs within the ethnic Fijian community had always exercised over the whole country. Some ethnic Fijians, however, including the former prime minister, Dr Bavadra, were strongly opposed to this group. The takeover had resulted in an exodus of Indian professionals, particularly doctors, lawyers and teachers, often to the benefit of Australia.

Our report recommended a series of political and diplomatic measures to exert pressure on the regime in Suva to move towards a restoration of parliamentary democracy. We realised that even these measures would be opposed by the Department of Foreign Affairs in Canberra. Dunstan was in favour of proposing economic sanctions, given that Australia was the dominant foreign investor in Fiji and also the major supplier of its imports. I convinced him that this would give Foreign Affairs more ammunition to discredit the report and, in any event, the history of economic sanctions was that they had never worked.

These events in Fiji spilt over into my work at the Bar when I acted for the ABC and SBS after they were sued over a television program about the 1987 takeover. The defamation action was brought in the New South Wales Supreme Court by Jeffrey Reid, managing director of the Emperor goldmine in Fiji, and the company that ran the mine.[8] This was one of the country's most important commercial enterprises and the source of considerable export earnings. Reid argued that the program showed him as promoting civil unrest in Fiji in an effort to bring down the Bavadra government because it represented a threat to the activities of the company. The Alliance

Party government had given large subsidies to the company's mining operations. It seemed unlikely that the new government would continue these benefits. Moreover, Bavadra had called for nationalisation of the mine during the election campaign.

This case would have provided a fascinating opportunity to examine some of the events surrounding the overthrow of the Fijian government in the Australian courts. But, like so many defamation actions that are started, it did not come to trial. After preliminary skirmishes and considerable work by the lawyers on both sides, it was settled on terms that, as usual, were not to be disclosed by the parties.

By the late 1990s it seemed that Fiji had returned to a form of parliamentary democracy. But, following an election in 2000 in which the leader of the Labour Party became Prime Minister, sections of the army arrested senior ministers, including the Prime Minister, and deposed the government. Although a subsequent election was conducted, this was followed by a further military coup. The next election took place in 2014 but it remains unclear whether this has settled some of the deep-seated divisions within the Fijian community.

In the early 1990s I started to withdraw from most of these political sidelines. This was partly a result of the demands of my work but also the realisation, however belated, that many of the decision-makers in the Labor Party had little interest in public administration. As Arthur Schlesinger Jnr remarked of the Democratic Party prior to the election of Franklin Roosevelt as president, "politics was its business – a way of life rather than a way to get things done."[9] I always remained puzzled by individuals who wanted to spend their working lives in politics but saw it as no more than a well-paid job with a great deal of travel.

This was underlined in the early 1990s when Graham Richardson resigned from the Senate and was replaced by Belinda Neal, wife of the NSW Branch Secretary, John Della Bosca. I was under no illusions that I was a likely replacement for Richardson. The most obvious candidates were Michael Easson, Secretary of the NSW Labour Council, and Patricia Staunton, head of the nurses' union in New South Wales. It was, however, a sharp vision of the future. As it happens, Belinda Neal had a spectacularly unsuccessful parliamentary career, attracting bad publicity on an extraordinary scale. At about the same time Eddie Obeid was elected to the NSW Legislative Council at the head of the Labor ticket. This appeared a bewildering choice on its face, as Obeid clearly had not the slightest interest in political ideas or public policy. Twenty years later he was to attract an avalanche of bad publicity.

Writing in the *Sydney Morning Herald* in October 1998, Gerard Henderson complained about the quality of some Labor members in safe seats:

> A quick glance at who is in Federal Parliament – and who is not – demonstrates the problems facing the NSW and Victorian ALP.
>
> There are many low-profile disappointing performers holding safe ALP seats . . .
>
> Yet in recent years the NSW ALP has failed to find seats for the lawyer and author Michael Sexton and the former diplomat Michael Costello. Also Mary Easson was not found a relatively safe seat after losing Lowe. All three were capable of high Cabinet office. Men and women of quality have also failed at winning ALP preselection in Victoria.[10]

Henderson may have been right but there are no second prizes in politics. And it was time to recognise that seats in parliament on the Labor side were being largely taken by those who started running while still in high school. As Rodney Cavalier observed in his book on modern Labor:

Inside one generation, the catchment for parliamentary preferment is increasingly restricted to those who work on the staff of a minister, the ALP Office or an affiliated union . . .

The consequence conforms with the laws of nature. The ALP has been narrowing the gene pool from which MPs might emerge. Life's experiences become limited. After graduation from university (or after dropping out), those aspiring to be MPs reckon their best chance is employment in a union or on the staff of a minister. One can scarcely blame the ambitious for adapting their campaigns for preselection to the changing realities of advancement. The result is an adaptation of life's arc to meet rigid factional expectations about mobility, mating, tribal loyalty, ideological carapace and camouflage.[11]

The one political activity that I kept up was to provide some assistance to Bob Carr, who had become Leader of the Opposition in the NSW parliament after the destruction of the Unsworth government at the polls in 1988. He had been forced by the State Labor organisation to take the job because most of the senior ministers in that government had retired or lost their seats. Carr was passionately fond of books, interested in ideas and wickedly funny in private conversation. He was also a highly skilled and sometimes ruthless politician. Although he had always intended to move on to federal politics, he put this ambition aside and worked relentlessly in the barren world of opposition. I sometimes saw him do half a dozen radio interviews from his car while on the way to lunch.

There was one problem of opposition where I could provide some tangible help. Unless their attacks on ministers and officials are made in parliament, which does not sit for much of the year in New South Wales, the Leader of the Opposition and shadow ministers are potentially exposed to defamation actions. I often gave advice as to how far these attacks could go – and then hoped that I had got it right. There was a small group of lawyers, which included John McCarthy QC, Greg James QC and Tim Robertson SC, as well as myself, available for informal advice whenever legal questions arose. This had been organised by Bruce Hawker, himself a lawyer, who was Carr's chief of staff and an excellent political strategist.

There was another small group, chiefly political staffers with some writers, which met regularly with Carr to try to capture the Opposition's assaults, and the government's mistakes, in short, sharp statements that could be used in the media and the parliament. This came to be called the "One-liners group." Looking at my notes for one of these meetings in 1990, there was a discussion as to how the premier, Nick Greiner, could be portrayed as the rich kid from the North Shore squandering the assets of New South Wales. And how his Education Minister could be described as a mad professor experimenting with the State's children! There were also debates about policy questions but these meetings provided a lot more fun than most of the political activities that I took part in over those years.

In the year preceding the 1991 State election Carr came close to losing the leadership. As is frequently the case in opposition, none of his efforts seemed to be reflected in the polls. The life of an Opposition leader in contemporary Australian politics is often nasty, brutish and short. But he survived and did not make the mistake that Hayden did in 1982 of giving his opponents a second chance. He cold-bloodedly, and quite rightly, finished off the political careers of his two chief opponents, Peter Anderson and Deirdre Grusovin. In 1991 Labor won back almost all of the seats that it had lost in 1988. The election was essentially a tie with a handful of independents exercising the balance of power in the lower house and deciding to support a Greiner government.

Less then a year later, Greiner himself was gone. He resigned after criticisms of his conduct by the Independent Commission Against Corruption. He had proposed the appointment of one of the independent members of parliament, a former minister in his government, to a senior public service position. This would have caused a by-election and the government expected to recover the seat. There was something of an irony here. Many of Labor's power brokers had opposed the establishment of the Commission in 1988, fearing that it would rake over the Wran and Unsworth years. They pressured Carr to take this stand in the parliament. He refused and made some enemies on his own side. I had seen this confrontation in Hobart at Labor's National Conference. As Marilyn Dodkin recorded in her biography of Carr:

> Carr was summoned to . . . a meeting in the room of NSW general secretary Stephen Loosley. Press secretary Malcolm McGregor went with Carr to the meeting. In the room Loosley, Senator Graham Richardson and barristers John McCarthy and Michael Sexton talked to Carr about Greiner's proposed ICAC legislation. When he returned to Sydney Carr recorded in his diary, on 16 June, that Loosley, Richardson and McCarthy had quietly tried to persuade him against supporting ICAC legislation, which they said was "outrageous and should be blocked or thoroughly amended". Loosley and Richardson were concerned about the ICAC being used as a witchhunt against the Labor Party, while McCarthy, a friend of Carr's, reiterated the Bar Association argument that elements in the Bill would result in the legal and medical professions being forced to breach client confidentiality. Despite those fears, Michael Sexton had advised Carr that "the legislation had to be supported from the point of view of Carr's credibility as a new leader, whatever the consequences for any individuals from past administrations".[12]

Even Greiner's departure provided some work for Carr's legal team. Lawyers acting for the former premier demanded that Carr withdraw the press release he had issued on the ICAC's findings and apologise to Greiner. Some of Carr's staff were nervous at this threat of litigation but he was reluctant to back down. I took the view that Greiner would not sue and gave this advice. Greiner did not, so the gamble paid off.

Labor won the 1995 election by a narrow margin. On the Monday following the election, with the result still in some doubt, Carr had lunch with his old friend, the journalist Paddy McGuinness, and myself. "Perhaps we won't get the seats", he said, "and I'll be able to retire to Paris." "Not a chance," we said cheerfully. "You're going to have to be Premier of New South Wales, like it or not." Carr already knew that.

In moving out of the organisational side of politics, I did not plan to keep my ideas and opinions to myself. I intended to speak and write about public issues whenever I had the opportunity. This was discouraged by much of the Bench and Bar, not least because it indicated some strong interests outside the law. I saw the law as closely associated with government and politics. Perhaps I should never have tried to combine these activities. Bismarck once said: "Politics is no science, it is an art, and anyone without the knack for it should leave it alone".[13] Was all that time in committee meetings and at conferences wasted? Yes and no. I think that I had always wanted to see political life at close quarters, whatever the outcome. I had done that and it was time to move on.

8
MEET THE MYSTIQUE
Taking on the Bar

I tilted my book to avoid the sharp glare as the sun glanced off the waters of the lake. A few metres below the courtyard a small swell splashed against the walls of the hotel. The place was Limone on the western shore of Lake Garda. It was the middle of 1983 and I had used some of my time out of Australia to think about the future. With some doubts, I thought it was now or never if I was to leave the university and start practising as a barrister.

The last few months in France and Italy were a reminder that this would mean big changes. Academic life provided time for writing and visits overseas. Gae and I were travelling with her younger sister, Jill, and our old colleague from Parliament House in Canberra, Geoff Briot. Although we had covered a lot of countryside, we were happy to stop in two places apart from Paris. One was a small village, Romanèche-Thorins, a little south of Macon in the Beaujolais region. Here the Hôtel de Commerce, the French equivalent of the Commercial Hotel found in many Australian country towns, was run by a sulky but skilful cook. Set in the surrounding countryside – at intervals of three or four kilometres – were another half a dozen villages, each with a church spire to advertise its location amongst the surrounding slopes.

Almost every piece of ground in between had been methodically planted with the vines that produce the light reds and whites of the district. The locals were good company. On one occasion when we had walked some kilometres out of Romanèche to a restaurant for dinner, the proprietor closed up early to drive us back in a rainstorm, even though he knew we were staying in the village with his hated rival.

The other stopping point was Lake Garda. It was a very different landscape. With both sides of the lake rising sharply into the mountains, it was more like a Norwegian fiord, but under a hotter southern sun. We had become students of the countryside in France and Italy by searching out picnic spots. Lunch most days was bread, cheese and wine beside a river or on the edge of a forest. But we awarded the prize location to Lake Ledro, a much smaller body of water that lay deep in the mountains above Garda. A meadow of flowers ran down to the shores of the lake, which was itself surrounded by still more mountainous country. The idyllic quality of this meal was disrupted only by my failure to pack the wine glasses. So we drank Chianti in turn from the bottle.

All this was something of a last supper before the reality of Phillip Street. This was where most barristers in Sydney had their chambers, called offices by everyone else. One of the steepest barriers to entry at the Sydney Bar at that time was the cost of chambers. This was not always a problem. I knew that many barristers had independent means, sources of income apart from their legal practice, and that a surprising number came from established legal families. One of the reasons for this was the high cost of setting up at the Bar. It was possible to rent chambers but to buy into one of the more fashionable floors cost as much as a substantial house. During the early years of practice work might be sparse and payments slow. Not all newcomers to the Bar face these problems but I had no guarantees of work. I knew a number of lawyers in Sydney but the really useful contacts for a barrister are solicitors who conduct a high volume of litigation in the courts.

In addition, I was very old, by the standards of the time, to be going to the Bar. This was normally done ten years earlier by people in their mid to late twenties. I would be starting at the bottom at a time when most of my contemporaries were well settled in their careers. I had taken some advice from several lawyers I knew. Most were encouraging but cautious. Mary Gaudron QC, then Solicitor-General of NSW, was typically hard-headed. "Good luck", she said "but be careful. You wouldn't want to make a fool of yourself."

There was a final problem. The last book that I had written while at the law school, together with Laurence Maher, by then practising as a solicitor in Melbourne, was *The Legal Mystique*. The book examined the various functions that lawyers, including judges, carried out around the country. But, as the title suggests, it rejected the notion that value judgments were not involved in many judicial decisions:

> To a large extent the law is seen as a set of immutable principles that have always and will always exist, and lawyers as the priests who reveal these principles to laymen, always with a remoteness and neutrality, especially in the case of judges, that transcend any question of personal values or interests.
>
> Even if the law were made up of immutable principles, it will be obvious . . . that judges have often been entrusted with social and economic questions that affect the distribution of power and resources in Australian society. But does the law really exist in another world where there are no choices between competing and conflicting values? The most cursory glance at the Australian legal system demonstrates that this idea of the law is a myth . . .
>
> This is not a novel point about the law and judges. It was put forward as a serious explanation of judicial decisions

in the early 1920s by a group of American law teachers at Yale and Columbia universities. Because they insisted on looking for the real reasons for court decisions they were dubbed the "realists". Their point was that, even if a judge gave the impression that he had simply discovered and applied a legal principle already in existence, it could be demonstrated by looking closely at his judgment that his choice of legal principle was often determined by his own broad social and political values. Similarly, the realists demonstrated that in most cases it was possible for another judge to choose a different starting principle and then, with what seemed impeccable legal reasoning, arrive at precisely the opposite conclusion. This is what sometimes explains the three-to-two and four-to-three decisions of the High Court and of other Australian courts. Four judges can start from one basic assumption, three from another.[1]

This was not really a criticism of judges but just a statement of the obvious. These kinds of thoughts were not, however, calculated to win friends in Phillip Street. But worse was to come. We had looked at the members of the Victorian and New South Wales Supreme Courts and arrived at a judicial profile. Not surprisingly, at this time, all the judges of both courts were male; former barristers, usually specialising in commercial and corporate work; generally educated at private schools; often members of socially exclusive all-male clubs; and predominantly resident in a handful of affluent suburbs. This profile has changed during the last thirty years, particularly with the appointment of many women to the bench, although it still fits many judges. Our survey concluded with a piece of economic analysis:

> One of the most interesting of these figures is the twenty-five years that elapsed, almost exactly in many cases, before these barristers were appointed to the Supreme Court bench, usually at the age of about fifty, therefore. It

is reasonably clear that this is an economic judgment. At a certain age a successful barrister will have maximised his income at the Bar and still have enough working years to maximise his superannuation entitlements under the judges' pension fund arrangements. So the bench is in many ways the bar's superannuation plan and, as such, even more valued as its exclusive preserve.[2]

I suppose that I must have realised that the description of judicial office as a superannuation plan would be taken as an insult by many judges. But I was not quite prepared for the hostility that followed publication in June 1982. It did not help that the book received a lot of publicity after it was launched by Justice Lionel Murphy of the High Court, himself a controversial figure in legal circles. Nor did it help that the *Australian Financial Review* carried a front page story about the book under the headline "Why judges are biased". The story started off:

> Australian judges are usually old, rich, male, educated in non-catholic private schools and have limited social experience. They have friends and social contacts who are almost exclusively other lawyers, and they come from a very small proportion of the legal profession. What's more, being a judge is almost a matter of heredity.[3]

One judge was prepared to respond. Justice Frank Hutley of the NSW Court of Appeal launched a 5,000 word attack in *Quadrant* magazine. He commenced:

> The law and lawyers have been the victims of an inordinate amount of denunciation and preaching lately, almost all ill-informed; *The Legal Mystique* is no exception. The only fact which makes it worthy of attention is that it has been advertised by the ABC and commended in the press . . .[4]

When Justice Hutley said that the book had been "advertised by the ABC" he did not mean that the national broadcaster had been paid to publicise it but that the ABC had covered the launch in one of its television current affairs programs. At least he was prepared to put his views on the record. Most of those who shared his opinions were not interested in the notion of public debate.

There were, however, a small number of reviewers who thought the book was not nearly radical enough. Humphrey McQueen, a Marxist historian, conceded that "no criticism can take away from the usefulness of what Sexton and Maher have done." But he went on to say:

> It takes a hefty wrench for any Australian to make a radical analysis of the state and of its dominant class. Sexton and Maher have not done so, nor did they intend to. Their assumptions are liberal, progressive, reformist; their analysis of the legal system is further curbed in order to retain an audience of lawyers unaccustomed even to such mild criticism.[5]

Kevin Bell, later a QC at the Melbourne Bar and judge of the Victorian Supreme Court, had a similar complaint:

> The book will leave readers better informed about the issues raised ... But many readers will find it unsatisfactory because it goes only so far in analysing the issues, and does not attempt to provide answers to the criticisms it raises. Readers who have thought about the twin problems of inequality and poverty in Australian society, will be frustrated with the liberal democratic philosophy, albeit unstated, that permeates the book.[6]

We thought it was obvious that we had a liberal democratic philosophy. Professor Robin Sharwood of Melbourne law school certainly made this assumption[7]. He thought the book "to be without doubt the best short account and critique of the legal profession in this country which has yet appeared," but added shrewdly that "the authors take a somewhat radical stance, but my emphasis would be on the word 'somewhat' ".

In many ways the book's criticisms of some, but by no means all, lawyers was summed up in one of its quotes from Justice Harlan Stone of the US Supreme Court. He had worked as a corporate lawyer on Wall Street but said in 1934:

> Steadily the best skill and capacity of the profession has been drawn into the exacting and highly specialised service of business and finance. At its best the changed system has brought to the command of the business world loyalty and a superb proficiency and technical skill. At its worst it has made the learned profession of an earlier day the obsequious servant of business, and tainted it with the morals and manners of the market place in its most anti-social manifestations.[8]

Again, this was not likely to win many friends in Phillip Street, or in the large law firms from which I would now be looking for work.

There were two things that I had to do before I could start practising as a barrister. One was to find some chambers and the other was to find someone to read with. This second requirement meant, theoretically, at least, being supervised during the first year by a barrister who had been in practice for at least seven years. For some new barristers, particularly those with a guaranteed stream of work, this could be an essentially formal arrangement, but, in many cases, master and reader spend a considerable amount of time together and sometimes form a strong bond. I asked Terry Tobin if he would take me on as a reader. I was looking for someone who practised especially in media law – defamation, contempt, breach of confidence – and this was a large part of Tobin's practice. His biggest client was the ABC. Like an incident from Anthony Powell's *A Dance to the Music of Time*, we had a past association but had never met. Tobin had started at Melbourne University some years before me but studying English Literature. He had come later to the law school and seldom attended any classes. My room mate in final year, Joe Edmonds, had been in the same year at high school as Tobin and asked me if he could give Tobin some of my own lecture notes. I said yes but thought no more about it.

It was not as if Tobin could not have mastered the courses himself. He is small, with finely-chiselled features and one of the sharpest minds in or out of the law. In court he spoke softly and persuasively to judges and juries but there was an element of quiet menace in his cross-examination of an obstructive witness. He had a complete grasp of legal principles with a sure sense of the strategy and tactics that best suited a particular piece of litigation. He was a formidable advocate.

Initially, however, this looked like an odd match. Tobin had worked in Canberra in the early 1970s on the staff of Jack Kane, deputy leader of the Democratic Labor Party. I had written harsh things about the DLP and its supporters. Some of my friends had advised me to read with another barrister who had a more conventional background in the law. And Tobin may have had his own reservations about me. But it was a tradition of the Bar that requests to read were agreed to unless someone else had got in first.

At the Melbourne Bar readers spent this first year in the master's room (the term "master" was changed sometime in the 1990s to "tutor" on the basis that this was less sexist and less reminiscent of the 18th century). The custom was different in Sydney, so I still faced the problem of chambers. This grand title really meant a room on a floor of barristers and, in my situation, probably a shared room.

I was taken in as a tenant by Serge Galitsky, who combined being a barrister with teaching law in the Business School at Macquarie University. He had a room in University Chambers – so-called because they were next door to Sydney University Law School in Phillip Street. They were not fashionable chambers but there were some good lawyers and some good company on the floor. One of the best lawyers was Galitsky himself. A white Russian, born in Shanghai after his parents had fled the Soviet Union, Galitsky had come to Australia as a child in the 1950s. Behind his almost theatrical old world manner there was a very clear mind that could quickly go to the heart of almost any legal problem. He was a source of much useful advice but perhaps the best was: "You'll see all the issues in a case. Then you will worry about how to deal with them. It's often better at the Bar not to see too much. But it can't be helped. You won't feel so bad after a while."

My real problem was that while I knew, or thought I knew, a good deal about the law, I knew next to nothing about the procedures in court. Appearing in court is like being in a play where everyone has their stage directions. But I was not at all familiar with the script. I did not enjoy the daily prospect of looking foolish, especially when I was older than most of the other new barristers. Some judges took a particular pleasure in humiliating beginners, although many were surprisingly helpful.

One of my earliest cases took me straight into the rough and tumble world of criminal law. The case went for the best part of a week in the Magistrates' Court at Campsie in Sydney's western suburbs. My client was a security officer, less formally, a bouncer, at the Canterbury-Bankstown Leagues Club. He was charged with assaulting a young man one Saturday night on the floor of the Club's disco. There was no dispute that the young man was being removed for noisy behaviour and that he had hit the floor. But, after that, there were several witnesses on both sides with radically different accounts. There was no permanent damage suffered but a complaint was made to the police and they had brought the criminal charges. I prepared for my cross-examination by wandering through the deserted disco by day to look at the location of tables and measure out distances. This was slightly obsessive but a good lesson. It is always an advantage in court to have actually seen the place where the events occurred. I always tried later to do this if the location was in any way important to the legal issues.

The bouncer was big, although, like many big people, quietly spoken. The victim, by contrast, was a small but aggressive young man. He looked to me like someone who could easily provoke a punch in the nose. But I did not have to be concerned with the merits of the case. That was the magistrate's problem. After several days of conflicting accounts by the eye witnesses, he dismissed the charges with a rather bad grace, making it obvious he felt that many of the witnesses were lying. No doubt some were, although it would not have been easy to be dogmatic about events that occurred in a few seconds on the floor of a half-lit and crowded nightclub. At any rate, it was a win. More importantly, I had spent almost a week on my feet questioning witnesses and sparring with the police prosecutor.

Another early case taught me a very valuable lesson, namely, having some confidence in my own judgment. The brief came from a former student at the law school. His client produced a range of red and blue elastic body protectors under the name "Thermoskin" and was being sued by a Swedish company that marketed a similar product in Australia. The allegation was that the Thermoskin products were designed and packaged to confuse customers into thinking they were buying the Swedish model. I thought this claim of deceptive conduct, under the federal Trade Practices Act, had no merit.

The Swedish company was represented by very experienced solicitors and barristers and had obtained an interim injunction against the Australian company. The proceedings in the Federal Court would be expensive and might wipe my client out if it lost and had a costs order made against it. My chief problem was that I could not understand why the other side was going ahead with the case. My concern was no doubt obvious on our side. Just before the case was due to start, my solicitors brought in a silk from the Melbourne Bar as a leader. I was not offended. I was very new at the Bar. The clients were paying the bills and the stakes, for them, were high. The case was heard by the Chief Judge of the Federal Court, Justice Nigel Bowen. After several days of evidence, he found that there was no deceptive conduct at all on the part of the Australian company. I was relieved that I had not missed something blindingly obvious, which was what I had feared. Even so, I never lost the habit of spelling out the risks of litigation to clients in very clear terms. This is done automatically by most lawyers, but not, unfortunately, by all.

At about this time, Tobin involved me in some of the cases he was doing for the ABC. This marked the start of a long association that continued to the end of my time at the Bar. The links became stronger in the late 1980s when Bruce Donald took over as the head of the ABC Legal Department in Sydney. After our time together as associates at the High Court in the early 1970s, Donald had become a partner in one of Sydney's largest law firms but he had abandoned this during the early 1980s to take up a position as legal adviser to the Central Land Council in the Northern Territory. He was a highly talented lawyer with considerable political and bureaucratic skills. In addition to defending the ABC in court, I found there was plenty of work in advising on programs before they were put to air. This was constructive work, like preventive medicine. With any luck, those parts of a program that gave rise to a problem of defamation or contempt could be rewritten to minimise the risk of litigation. It was seldom possible to eliminate the risk completely, at least without taking all the punch out of the story, but the prospects of being sued could certainly be diminished. Most ABC programs had few such problems. Others, such as *Four Corners*, *The Investigators* and the *7.30 Report*, had them all the time.

No program had more legal problems than *The Moonlight State*. It went to air in May 1987. Some weeks before it was scheduled to be telecast, Bruce Donald called to warn me that *Four Corners* was working on a program that contained some explosive allegations: "We will be spending quite a bit of the next few weeks out at the studio." There was one piece of goods news: the reporter was Chris Masters. Masters was part journalist and part detective, with genuine investigative skills and enormous attention to detail. Otherwise the news was bad for the lawyers. The script made allegations of corruption against a number of highly-ranked Queensland police officers, including the Commissioner, Sir Terence Lewis. It also raised questions about what senior ministers, including the premier, Sir Joh Bjelke-Petersen, knew about the links between organised crime and the police force in Queensland.

At one point Masters and I went to Cairns to take a statement from a potential witness. This journey broke down some barriers between Masters and myself, as he recorded in his book *Inside Story*:

> When a report is defamatory, the publisher will frequently seek independent analysis of the risks involved. So the inquisition was not to be conducted by Bruce [Donald] alone. He brought in one of Sydney's sharpest defamation lawyers, Michael Sexton.
>
> Michael is tall, slim and neat in both appearance and vocabulary. The torture was resumed with my new interrogator slipping easily into the role of devil's advocate. Every sentence of the script was subject to scrupulous

punishment and as usual I became petulant and over-defensive.

There is an important lesson here too, which as usual was learnt the hard way. Michael and I travelled back up to Queensland to re-interview a key witness. He wanted to secure a signed statement. The statement would not be needed for the broadcast but was of value if we were later challenged in court.

On the plane I discovered there was more to my companion beyond the talent for ruthless cross-examination I had witnessed so far. My steely-eyed interrogator was gentle and amusing, a human being as well as a lawyer. I came to realise while sitting beside him that the sharp questioning was not personal. He was attacking the proposition and not the person. This is something every witness should know and every lawyer should make as clear as Michael managed to do.[9]

This was flattering but the real point was why the program needed so much legal work. The range and seriousness of its charges were indicated by its consequences. A Royal Commission was set up to investigate the allegations. It became known as the Fitzgerald Commission after Tony Fitzgerald QC who conducted the inquiry. In its aftermath, Sir Terence Lewis was sentenced to 14 years in prison for taking bribes. Some of his most senior colleagues in the Queensland police force only escaped prison by giving evidence against him and others. Four ministers in the Queensland government also went to jail. Sir Joh Bjelke-Petersen was charged with perjury on account of his evidence before the Fitzgerald Commission but survived because the jury could not agree and the prosecution decided against a re-trial.

Out of all this there was only one person who sued in defamation. But it was a very expensive action for the ABC and took a different kind of toll on Chris Masters. The case was brought by in Queensland by Vincenzo Bellino. He complained he had been accused of drug trafficking and corruption of police in the program. I could not do the case because at that time practitioners from other States could not be admitted to practise in Queensland. It became a legal saga that continued for almost a decade, with two trials and several appellate hearings in the Queensland Court of Appeal and the High Court.[10] The ABC won in the end. It had cost a great deal of money. And it left Masters very disillusioned with the legal system.

All the work for the ABC was essentially defensive. In some ways, it was much more fun being on the other side and acting for the plaintiff – lighting the litigation fuse and watching the other side react. This is illustrated by another case from 1987 which had its origins in one of Britain's most sensational post-war scandals.

In 1963 John Profumo was Secretary of State for War in the Conservative government led by Harold Macmillan. Profumo was introduced by a London osteopath, Stephen Ward, to a young woman named Christine Keeler and started a brief affair with her. The meeting had taken place at the country home of Lord Astor. Ward sometimes lived rent-free in a cottage on the property and brought girls down from London for Astor's parties. One of Keeler's other sexual partners was Eugene Ivanov, a KGB officer at the Soviet Embassy in London.

This obviously had the makings of a good story. It was first reported in March 1963 in *Paris-Match* and the following month in the Italian *Il Tempo*. In an amazing act of bravado, Profumo brought libel actions in the French courts against *Paris-Match* and in the English courts against the distributors of *Il Tempo*. He obtained a retraction in the French action and was awarded costs and nominal damages in the English proceedings. Profumo denied any involvement with Keeler to the Prime Minister and then to the

House of Commons. By early June, however, he realised that the game was up. Keeler had sold her story to the *News of the World* and Ward was arrested on a charge of living on the earnings of prostitutes. While waiting for the jury to return with its verdict at his criminal trial, he killed himself with an overdose of drugs.

This was the start of a long chain that led to proceedings, brought in the New South Wales Supreme Court twenty-four years later, by John Burrows against *The Australian* newspaper and Phillip Knightley, an Australian writer and journalist who had lived in England for many years. Tobin, now a QC, and myself took the case for Burrows. He had been a detective sergeant in the London Metropolitan Police and one of the team who conducted the investigation of Stephen Ward prior to charges being brought against him. He later migrated to Australia and served in the South Australian police force and then the Australian Federal Police before retiring to the south coast of New South Wales.

The action arose out of a book written by Phillip Knightley and Caroline Kennedy and published in May 1987 under the title, *An Affair of State: The Profumo Case and the Framing of Stephen Ward*.[11] The book was published in Britain, the United States and Australia. At the same time it was serialised over four weeks in Britain in the *Sunday Times* and in this country in *The Australian*. Burrows' complaint was that the book, and the articles, alleged that the police officers investigating Stephen Ward intimidated some witnesses and persuaded others to give false evidence in order to have Ward convicted on charges that they knew were bogus. This was a grave allegation, especially as Ward killed himself as a result of the charges being brought.

There was really only one defence that could be mounted to Burrows' claim and that was truth. In other words, it would be necessary for the author and the newspaper to demonstrate that Burrows had taken part in some kind of conspiracy with the other police officers to bring charges against Ward and that they knew these charges to be without any basis at all. This would have been a difficult exercise in any case after almost twenty-five years, but it seemed to us particularly far-fetched here. It is not always easy to make a judgment about clients but, if anyone looked and sounded as straight as a die, it was John Burrows. And he denied absolutely that the police officers had done anything but collect the available evidence and present it to the Director of Public Prosecutions. Again, it is always difficult to know how any person will stand up to fierce cross-examination in court, but Burrows gave every appearance of being an ideal witness. In addition, he had displayed great bravery in his time with the Australian Federal Police by rescuing a young girl being held hostage at Sydney airport by a man armed with a knife, an event which had received considerable publicity in all the Australian media.

For the next year British and Australian lawyers for the defendants spent considerable time in London trying to dig up material that would assist their case. All this was no doubt very expensive. We would have liked to be in London as well but our client did not have the same resources as book publishers and newspapers, so we waited to see if anything turned up. It did not and there was a substantial settlement. Knightley described the process in his book, *A Hack's Progress*:

> In Australia our lawyers started to defend the case. Our main problem was that we had taken a risk over the fourth detective and this had not paid off. The fault was ours and there was a very real prospect we would lose. We had not spoken to him, we had not tried hard enough to find him, and I felt he was right to complain. There was also another problem, a commercial one. If we went to court it would be a virtual rehearing of the Old Bailey trial of Stephen Ward. We would have to round up all the usual witnesses

and bring them all to Sydney. "Sydney!" I said when they told me this. "You saw the trouble we had getting them to Gray's Inn." The hearing would probably last three weeks to a month. A conservative estimate of the cost would be one to two million dollars. As might be expected, our insurance company was shouting, "No. Settle, settle." So our Australian lawyers played legal poker with the other side's lawyers – a game that went on almost to the steps of the [Supreme] Court – and then our lawyer went along the corridor to the other side's lawyer and made him an offer his client could not refuse. He accepted and it was all over.[12]

From a purely professional point of view, Tobin and I were disappointed. The trial would have been sensational. Better still, we thought we could not lose. But no litigation is free of risk and this was a retired police officer taking on the global empire of News Limited. Our client made the right decision and we told him we agreed with it.

By this time I had moved from University Chambers to the Fourth Floor of Selborne Chambers on the other side of Phillip Street. *The Legal Mystique* continued to cast a long shadow. Another floor that I had applied to join at about the same time rejected the application after one of its barristers circulated photocopies of selected pages from the book to its colleagues. I did not know which pages but I knew the result.

My new room was small and expensive but I needed some space of my own. My next door neighbour was Nick Cowdery, later Director of Public Prosecutions in New South Wales. I tried to keep up some writing outside the law. I continued to review books for the *Sydney Morning Herald* and most of these articles were uncontroversial. One exception was a review of a biography of Queen Mary, wife to George V, and mother of Edward VIII and

George VI.¹³ After starting with the proposition that "there is no longer running soap opera than the House of Windsor", the review gathered speed:

> It is remarkable that, right down to the present day, the House of Windsor has produced so many persons of below-average physical and mental qualities. One reason for this is undoubtedly the extensive in-breeding that has taken place over the past two centuries in European royalty in general and the House of Windsor in particular. The present Queen Elizabeth II and Prince Philip are cousins, as were Queen Mary and George V.

Then came a brief but colourful guide to the Windsors in the first half of the 20th century:

> The palace bureaucracy had been quite happy to see Mary wed to Prince Eddy despite his retarded condition. When he died they were equally happy to see her passed on to his younger brother, George . . . Her father-in-law became King Edward VII in 1901 at the age of 59. His chief amusements were stuffing the pockets of his guests' dinner jackets with sticky sweets and squirting them with bicycle pumps filled with water.
>
> Her husband, who became king George V in 1910, relaxed by shooting 4,000 pheasants in a day on his estates at Sandringham after they had been flushed out by 100 beaters. George V's eldest son was Edward VIII, who succeeded to the throne in 1936 and abdicated the same year to marry Mrs Simpson. He was succeeded by George VI, his stuttering and dipsomaniac brother.

The conclusion was a mixture of political science and straightforward invective:

> The classic objection to monarchy as an element of government is its inconsistency with democratic political

theory. This objection is, of course, impossible to overcome. What this book demonstrates, however – no doubt much against the author's wishes – is that even apart from political theory, it is insulting to have such a talentless and unattractive family as the constitutional rulers of Australia.

The literary pages are part of Saturday's *Sydney Morning Herald*. When the phone rang at about 7 am on Saturday morning I picked it up. The voice was female and upper class: "Are you the person who has written about Queen Mary in this morning's *Herald*?" "Yes," I answered automatically, even though I had not yet seen the newspaper. "I want to say that it is one of the most disgusting things I've ever seen in a respectable journal." And so on. I let her finish and then hung up. The phone rang again at once. I left it off the hook. After the weekend there was a storm of letters to the editor in the same vein. The literary editor, Margaret Jones, was philosophical: "I thought this might cause some excitement. But it will blow over by the end of the week." I had quite enjoyed the debate although I realised that this would not improve my reputation with some sections of the Bench and Bar any more than *The Legal Mystique*.

In March 1985, about a year after I had started at the Bar, my mother called from Melbourne to say that she was going into hospital for a couple of days to have a lung biopsy. She was now 82 but still living by herself and still walking to the local shops and the church. Whenever I visited Melbourne, she still preferred dinner at a restaurant to eating at home. I called her doctor. He said that she had been complaining of about being short of breath but that he did not expect to find anything. I decided to travel to Melbourne anyway. As soon as I walked into my mother's room at the hospital, I knew that she was dying. The change since I had seen her a few months earlier was striking, at least to me. At this stage there was no result from the biopsy but the next day the doctor confirmed that, to his surprise, it indicated a malignant lung tumour. He said it would be necessary to find a hospice for the remaining months. I doubted this estimate when I left my mother late that afternoon. The doctor called shortly after midnight to say that she had died. I was glad that I had not yet told her the truth.

Early that morning I drove across town to the home of my mother's sister – Aunt Molly as I had always known her. For some reason, I wanted to tell her in person. We spent the morning making arrangements for the funeral. I have almost no recollection of the next few days, even at the church and the cemetery. By the time I returned to Sydney, my mother had joined my father in his shaded corner of the Melbourne General Cemetery. It was a peaceful place that I had often walked past in my university days. Just a few weeks later Gae discovered that she was pregnant. Our son, John, was born at the end of the year. Even though she had not lived to see him, my mother would have very much approved.

One of the important strands of my practice, as time went on, was prosecution of complaints against doctors in the Medical Tribunal. This work started with a case brought by the health authorities late in 1985 against Dr Geoffrey Edelsten. Edelsten was a flamboyant public character, best known as pioneer of twenty-four hour medical centres and owner at one time of the Sydney Swans AFL team and the Cronulla Rugby League Club. The case continued in various tribunals and courts, including the High Court, for almost ten years. It was a brief well worth having. As so often in the early years of the Bar, there was a large element of luck. Tobin had been briefed by the health authorities with a junior barrister. Suddenly the junior barrister took silk and had to drop out. Tobin pounced and I was in the case.

Only one of the complaints against Edelsten concerned treatment of patients. This resulted from removal of tattoos in a number of his medical centres where some of the patients made allegations of infections and serious scarring. Then there were the other complaints: that he had induced doctors in the medical centres to over-service patients by paying the doctors a commission if they referred patients to specialists or pathology companies associated with Edelsten himself; that he had engaged in a fraud on the federal Health Insurance Commission by inflating claims for ultrasound tests; and that he had tried to obtain the assistance of a notorious criminal to intimidate one of his former patients. This last complaint was the most sensational aspect of what was already a high profile hearing.

The notorious criminal was Christopher Dale Flannery. Flannery had a reputation in Sydney as a contract killer. He disappeared early in the 1980s, doubtless murdered, but no body was ever found. There was an enormous amount of argument in the Medical Tribunal and in the courts about whether a tape of one of Edelsten's telephone calls should be admitted into evidence. In the telephone call, intercepted and recorded by a private investigator, Edelsten spoke with his wife about the possibility of setting Flannery on to the former patient who was in a dispute with Edelsten about his medical treatment. After years of argument, the tape was finally played in the Tribunal:

> Edelsten: Did I what?
> Wife: Talk to that bloke.
> Edelsten: Yeah I did. And he was the one that said that he thought that he was very dangerous and odd and I ought to get someone to bash his brains out.
> Wife: Head beaten around, broken nose and broken arm and broken leg.
> Edelsten: Mm Mm.
> Wife: So that he's out of action for a little while.
> Edelsten: Um.
> Wife: So that he'd think twice about it.

Edelsten: Mm.
Wife: Will he do it?
Edelsten: Pardon?
Wife: This bloke.
Edelsten: Oh this bloke will do it for ten grand.
Wife: Maybe he's charging you ten grand.
Edelsten: Pardon?
Wife: Maybe he's just charging you ten grand.
Wife: Maybe if I asked him he wouldn't charge you ten grand.
Edelsten: Oh I think he would.
Wife: You think?
Edelsten: Yeah I helped him and he just said he doesn't drop his price for anybody and that's it. He said "I'm a professional – it's my livelihood."
Wife: Beats people up?
Edelsten: Mm.
Wife: Is that all he does?
Edelsten: He kills people.
Wife: Does he?
Edelsten: Yeah, nice young fella . . .
Wife: Has he got a nice house?
Edelsten: Pardon?
Wife: Has he got a nice house?
Edelsten: I don't know. I've never been to his house. He's just a patient and the police introduced me to him . . .
Wife: Who did he kill?
Edelsten: Um a standover man, someone who was standing over a restaurant owner trying to extort money from him and ah –

Wife: He killed him.

Edelsten: He was hired to come from Melbourne and kill him.

In April 1988 the Medical Tribunal found the financial complaints and the Flannery complaint to be made out and ordered that Edelsten be struck off the roll of medical practitioners. There were numerous legal challenges in the courts to this order over the next five years but all failed.[14] In the meantime, Edelsten faced criminal charges. In addition to the charge that he asked Flannery to assault the former patient, there was a further allegation that he had perverted the course of justice by giving Flannery a false medical certificate so that he could delay the hearing of a trial where he was accused of murder. Edelsten was convicted on both counts and sentenced to a year in prison.[15]

Sometimes our legal team functioned as much as detectives as lawyers. Much time was spent on financial complaints, mulling over bank statements and balance sheets to work out the money trails. We tracked down former staff from the medical practices who had moved to other parts of the country. We held up documents to the light and found figures had been altered. There is a danger in all this. I had seen other prosecutors and investigators become intoxicated with the thrill of the chase and obsessed with their pursuit of the quarry. I like to think that we kept a balance in the Edelsten case but, the longer this kind of proceeding continues, the harder it is to be detached about the outcome.

9

THE HUMAN FACTOR
Victims of Law and Medicine

It is not easy in any barrister's career to single out one case as the most dramatic. If forced to choose, I would nominate the so called "Mr Bubbles" case. It sparked a media frenzy for much of the 1990s, particularly in Sydney but also in the rest of the country.

The source of this controversy was a series of sensational allegations about sexual abuse of kindergarten children. In the last two decades there has been a sharp rise in the number of these allegations. The legal system has struggled to deal with them. This derives from two conflicting values. Everyone knows that some children are sexually abused and these cases must be prosecuted. But an allegation, once made, will almost certainly destroy the career and reputation of the person against whom it is levelled, whether it be true or false and whether or not criminal charges are ever made out. And, as in the case of many allegations of sexual assault on adults, there are usually no witnesses and often no useful forensic evidence. It has become quite common for allegations to be made about incidents 20 or 30 years in the past where any external evidence that did exist would have long since been lost or destroyed.

The "Mr Bubbles" story began just after 6 am on the morning of Sunday 6 November 1988. Tony Deren opened the front door of his home on Sydney's northern beaches. He saw half a dozen burly men. One of them said: "We are the police. We have a warrant to search these premises." He went back to the bedroom to get his wife, Dawn.

Dawn Deren had set up the Seabeach Kindergarten not far from her home. What she did not know was that ten days before the police raid, one of the children who attended the kindergarten, aged almost four, had told her mother in the local pizza parlour that she and two other children had been taken from the kindergarten to see "Mr Bubbles" and had been asked to take their clothes off. One of the other children was asked the next day whether Mr Bubbles took pictures of the children with their clothes off. The answer was "yes", he did. Another child was also questioned and described parties where baths and showers took place and photographs were taken. Five children were given a medical examination which revealed nothing in the case of four of them and, in the case of the fifth, a condition that might or might not have resulted from sexual interference.

The Derens were taken to the local police station. They remained until close to midnight. The kindergarten was searched. Various books, records and photographs were seized, together with a small gold-painted wand from the end–of–year production of Cinderella. At the police station Tony Deren took part in a form of line-up where, according to the police, he was identified by one of the children, although she had earlier described Mr Bubbles as a robot with yellow curly hair and a red stripe on his neck. The Derens were then fingerprinted, photographed and stood in a dock to be formally charged with five counts of sexual assault.

Next day, one of the city's two afternoon newspapers carried the front page headline: "PRE-SCHOOL SEX PARTIES" and underneath this article:

A North Shore pre-school principal and her husband have been arrested over 'sex parties' with children less than five years old.

Police said today the couple indecently assaulted six youngsters after giving them sweets and toys to create a party atmosphere.

The children, aged between three and five, were probably hypnotised before the assaults and on one occasion were enticed into a bubble-bath with the man, police said. They said the sex parties were photographed or videotaped by the 45-year-old teacher and her husband, 47.

Examinations have shown the children were sexually interfered with – and two toddlers have displayed psychological disturbances.[1]

The following day Dawn Deren's licence to conduct the kindergarten was withdrawn by the NSW Department of Family and Community Services. It never operated again. The story was now running in all newspapers, radio and television. One newspaper report quoted a member of the police media unit who said that photographs or videos of the assaults would be presented in court as evidence.

Although the Derens were not named in most of these reports, it was now well known that Seabeach was the kindergarten under investigation. It had also been named on Sydney's highest-rating morning radio program.

The Derens were charged with the sexual assault of another twelve children after a series of police interviews with former pupils at the kindergarten. The NSW Police Royal Commission later gave a scathing account of these interviews:

> The probationary constable at times interviewed the children alone. As she found it difficult to record the conversations, much was lost, and the detail noted could

not be relied upon as accurate. There were other times when she carried out interviews in the presence of other children. This created an unacceptable risk of contamination. The statements that were ultimately produced were inaccurate and, in many respects, bore little resemblance to the notes she had made either contemporaneously or immediately after the interviews.

She also had difficulty dealing with the parents, who were understandably very anxious. She was concerned whether the children were repeating things that they had heard from them or from other children. She found that while the parents had been asked not to talk to their children about the case, they continued to pass on information to them. She soon found herself out of her depth.[2]

Two weeks after the police raid, the Derens appeared in person at Manly Local Court with hundreds of people outside screaming insults and holding abusive placards. These scenes were shown on the television evening news and reported in next day's newspapers. Shortly afterwards two other women teachers at the kindergarten were charged with the sexual assault of a number of children.

Seven months later the Derens faced committal proceedings in the local court to determine whether they would go to trial before a judge and jury in the District Court. After a five week hearing the magistrate dismissed the charges against the Derens and the two teachers, at the same time ordering the police to pay $225,000 towards the Derens' legal costs. This verdict did not, however, satisfy those who thought the Derens guilty. The problem was that the magistrate had ruled out evidence by any of the children. He did this for two reasons – first, that they were too young to understand the notion of telling the truth; and, secondly, that their evidence had been contaminated by suggestions put to them by parents and police officers.

During the next twelve months there was a highly-organised campaign to have the charges against the Derens reinstated. Six months after the charges had been dismissed, *New Idea* magazine carried a story on the Seabeach kindergarten that began on the front cover:

> EXCLUSIVE – Live animals were ripped up in front of our children. Sexual abuse . . . torture . . . satanic rituals . . . the horror of Sydney's kindergarten outrage – at last the desperate parents speak out.[3]

There was much more detail on the inside pages:

> But more chillingly, in a confidential medical summary obtained by *New Idea*, some of the children also describe how they were allegedly forced to take part in horrific daytime rituals in private houses. They say these satanic-style rituals included witnessing animals being dismembered alive and then having the blood of the 'sacrifices' smeared over them. The children allege more than eight adults were involved in these depraved acts.

The editor of *New Idea* wrote in her column of "depraved, vicious mongrels, passing themselves off as normal human beings, while they prey on the innocent and helpless children".

At about the same time the case was raised in the NSW Parliament. The Deputy Leader of the Labor Opposition in the Legislative Council, Deirdre Grusovin MLC, called for the Derens to be sent to trial by the Attorney-General:

> I have moved to adjourn the House to seek justice – justice for all those little children who have been physically and emotionally abused and scarred for life, justice for the parents whose lives have been shattered by the events, and justice for the people of New South Wales who can no longer have any trust that the criminal justice system in

this State can protect their children against sexual abuse. The Mr Bubbles case has tremendous ramifications for the whole justice system in Australia.[4]

In the following months Grusovin and her colleague, Franca Arena MLC, read into the parliamentary record many of the interviews conducted by police with children from the kindergarten.

Then, in mid-1990, the Nine Network's *60 Minutes* broadcast a program on the Mr Bubbles case. This included interviews with parents of four of the children from the kindergarten. Disguised with wigs and false beards, they insisted that sexual assaults had taken place. It was said that one child had been threatened with death if she told her parents. There were also re-enactments of police interviews with some of the children and an interview with a doctor who had examined a number of children and expressed the view that five of them had been sexually abused.

In the middle of all this, the Derens came to see me in my chambers, together with the young solicitor, Stephen Hahn, who had represented them at the committal proceedings. Dawn Deren was in her late 40s, friendly but, I thought, very determined. Tony Deren seemed about the same age, dark and sallow, more wary of a stranger. They wanted advice about what legal action they could take against the police. After listening to them for several hours and hearing their vehement denials of all the charges, I knew that there were only two possibilities – either they were monsters who had committed appalling crimes or they were the victims of a terrible injustice. I did say, however, that the truth would almost certainly come out in any civil proceedings that they brought against the police. They said they wanted to proceed. I suggested an action in defamation against the police on the basis that various police officers had told the media of the existence of video tapes and photographs of the assaults and also referred to hard medical evidence. None of this was true. But it had to suggest to any reasonable reader who recognised the kindergarten as Seabeach that the Derens were guilty as charged. The newspapers could have been sued as well but the Derens' real complaint was against the police and we needed the help of the various journalists to explain how they had obtained the information contained in the articles. So there was only one defendant – the State of New South Wales as the employer of the police officers.

It was, however, almost eight years before the trial began in February 1998. There had been some lengthy disputes about preliminary legal questions and then several years were lost waiting for the report of the NSW Police Royal Commission which looked at the Seabeach investigation. When the report came out in mid-1997, it was highly critical of the conduct of the police investigation but it did not consider the question of what, if anything, had actually happened at the kindergarten.

The trial was conducted in the Supreme Court before Justice Alan Abadee and a jury of four women. I appeared with Kylie Nomchong, who had just come to the Bar and been reading with me, supported by Stephen Hahn. We were opposed by Bruce McClintock SC and Lucy McCallum. I gave an opening address and then called our first witness, Dawn Deren, to explain to the jury the normal routine at the kindergarten. One puzzle was what the tactics of the other side would be. Two months before the start of the trial they had said that they would not be calling any of the children as witnesses and would not be suggesting that sexual assaults had taken place. This was hardly surprising in view of an internal police report into the Seabeach affair. The officer who wrote the report concluded:

> I do not believe a Royal Commission will resolve this matter, nor do I accept the fact that all the alleged victims

were sexually abused by the same person, if they were sexually abused at all . . . The Magistrate heard evidence from a number of experts about the manner in which the alleged victims had made their disclosures and in my opinion the statements had been tainted by leading questions and a lot of fantasy by the children clearly indicating that they were too young to be called to the stand.

One of the crucial tasks in litigation is bringing the witnesses to court. When one of the journalists we wanted to call could not be found, Stephen Hahn showed his skills. He tracked the witness down and got him back to Sydney. Then, because the journalist had no clothes fit for court, he sent him into the witness box wearing a pair of his own trousers. This is what wins close cases.

After the journalists had given evidence that they obtained the information in their reports from the police, we closed our case. Then it was the turn of the defence. One of their witnesses was the officer from the police media unit who had referred to videos and photographs at a press conference, even though shortly afterwards he learnt that there were no photographs and no one had yet watched the videos that had been seized from the Derens' home. I cross-examined him on this:

> Q. Would you agree with me, Sergeant, that the reference to videos and photographs at the morning media conference would suggest to anyone who was attending the conference that there were some videos and photographs in existence in relation to the Seabeach matter?
>
> A. Yes . . .
>
> Q. And in those circumstances what I was suggesting to you, and tell me if you agree or not, that it was unreasonable to release that information at that time to the media?
>
> A. Well, taking into account what I found out later; one would have to agree, yes.

Q. And you didn't know at the time you released that information what was in any photographs or on any videos.

A. No.

There was, of course, nothing incriminating in any of the photos or videos.

The real point of the defence case, however, was an attack on Tony Deren for conduct far removed from the Seabeach kindergarten and 26 years earlier. When the Derens had lived in Port Moresby, Tony Deren had touched some teenage girls on the outside of their swimming costumes at the local pool. When he was approached by the police, he admitted this and was fined in subsequent court proceedings. He admitted it again to the jury in this case when he gave his evidence. But there was a much more damaging allegation in the *60 Minutes* program which contained an interview with a young woman who said that at about the same time in Port Moresby, when she was five or six years old, she had been the subject of a serious sexual assault by Tony Deren. The judge ruled, however, that she could not give evidence of this allegation because it was not relevant to what had happened at the Seabeach kindergarten many years later.

Both sides made closing addresses to the jury. I tried to leave them with some sense of what was at stake for the Derens:

> Finally, can I say this to you, that you might think, looking back on this case over the last two weeks and what you now know, that in November 1988 Mr and Mrs Deren were two persons whose life revolved around their work and family and whose life was shattered in November 1988. Sometimes it is possible for all of us to put ourselves in the position of a person who is bringing an action. You might think, however, it is difficult for any of us to put ourselves in the position of the Derens, given what has happened to

them over the decade. Perhaps the most remarkable thing is that they have come to the legal system, they have come to you, the jury, for justice in view of those events. What you do, of course, will determine how they face the world, really for the rest of their lives. We can all walk away from the case – probably after Monday – but not the Derens, of course, because they have to bear this result for the rest of their lives.

The judge summed up to the jury for almost two days and then sent them out to consider their verdict. After they had been out for about five hours, the judge's associate telephoned to say that the jury were ready to give their decision. I had often looked at the four women on the jury over the last few weeks. The jury box was only a couple of metres from my end of the Bar table. They had all followed the trial very closely, in some cases taking notes, but they had been careful not to give any indication of their thinking. There was dead silence in the court room as they approached the jury box. They had been given a long series of questions to answer but the answer to the first question would tell the story. The judge's associate read out the first question. When the jury's spokesperson answered in our favour, I felt a flood of relief. The final verdict came to just over $530,000 for Dawn Deren and almost $415,000 for Tony Deren. But the important thing for the Derens was that everyone in that court room, including the jury, knew that no children had been sexually abused at the Seabeach kindergarten.

The State of New South Wales appealed against the verdict and this was argued for three days before three judges in the Court of Appeal. The award of damages to Dawn Deren stood but the Court of Appeal ordered a re-trial in the case of Tony Deren on the basis that the defence should have been allowed to call the evidence of the woman who was interviewed on *60 Minutes*[5]. I still think the Court of Appeal were wrong on this point and the trial judge right, but the Derens could hardly be expected to go through the same exercise again, so there never was another trial. The two teachers from Seabeach, who had also sued, did not have to face a trial because the cases were settled, on the basis of substantial payments of damages to them by the State. The reality was, however, that all four individuals had had their lives radically changed, if not destroyed, by these events which had their origin in a child's conversation in a local pizza parlour. There have been similar cases in other countries.

All allegations of child sexual abuse should be thoroughly investigated. This case was simply an example, all too common in recent history, of innocent people caught up in and ground to pieces by the great machine of the law.

Many of the cases that I was involved in during these years received considerable publicity, not least because they were cases where I was acting for media organisations. But, after the Mr Bubbles litigation, the most sensational matter in which I took part was the Chelmsford Royal Commission and its aftermath in the courts.

Chelmsford was a small private hospital on Sydney's Upper North Shore. Between 1963 and 1979 it was used by one of Sydney's leading psychiatrists, Dr Harry Bailey, to administer Deep Sleep Therapy (DST) to approximately 1200 patients. Twenty-four of these had died; nine had committed suicide shortly after the treatment; and hundreds later brought claims of permanent, physical and mental injury.

I was introduced to this legal saga late in 1988 when the NSW government set up a Royal Commission to inquire into DST at Chelmsford. One case from the many hospital records that I saw gives a graphic picture of the treatment itself. The patient was a young woman of 26, a child of Italian immigrants, who was admitted to the hospital in mid-1977, seemingly with a diagnosis of depression. Given a cocktail of barbiturates that induced a coma, she remained in this condition for almost two weeks, receiving some liquid nourishment by means of a tube that ran through the nose and down the back of the throat into the stomach. Most days she was given shock treatment through electrodes attached to her head. At the end of this period she died, probably from an infection leading to pneumonia, or possibly from some respiratory complication. Because Dr Bailey falsified the death certificate, the cause of death could never be authoritatively established. Her parents took the body to Italy for burial and never returned to Australia. The Royal Commission tried to make contact but could not find them.

Bailey himself emerged from the evidence at the Royal Commission as a person of enormous energy and self-confidence who exercised a high degree of control over patients and almost anyone else who met him. But these were second-hand impressions because Bailey had killed himself in 1985, seemingly as a reaction to the increasing range of civil and criminal litigation he was facing in the coming years.

In addition to depression, other conditions that were common in DST patients were drug dependency, alcoholism and anorexia. Some patients had severe psychiatric disorders and were in a desperate condition even before DST. Some, however, were hardly ill at all and should never have been in any kind of hospital.

The Royal Commission was conducted by a retired judge, Jack Slattery of the NSW Supreme Court, and continued for almost two years. I appeared with Terry Tobin for the NSW Department of Health. We knew we had a tough job because it would be said that the department had not tried to stop DST being administered. This was true, although the department had no real power over private hospitals and many members of the medical profession in NSW had been aware of Bailey's activities but had said nothing about them.

The most moving part of the Commission's hearings was evidence given by a large number of former patients. In addition to their own stories, their evidence underlines the problem of mental illness in modern society. In many cases their families had been unable to cope with conduct resulting from severe personality disorders and had willingly accepted Bailey's assurances that he could improve these conditions. The problem is even more acute where a patient is dangerous to family members and to strangers. Some of these conditions can be treated, but not cured, by sedating drugs. This is only a solution so long as the drugs continue to be taken.

The Commission's final report was damning about the various doctors who had administered DST at Chelmsford. Tobin and I were then given the job of having the doctors, except for Bailey, struck off the medical register. The doctors challenged these proceedings on the ground that there had been a failed attempt to strike them off early in the 1980s and this ruled out a second effort – a principle known in the criminal law as double jeopardy. We said these were different charges but we lost this argument in the NSW Court of Appeal, by two judges to one, and in the High Court by three judges to two.[6] These results illustrated how different judges can take different views of the same question but the result was final.

The doctors were enmeshed in other webs of litigation. One was a series of civil actions for damages by 130 former Chelmsford patients. I was brought into this litigation because the department was sued, in addition to the doctors, on the basis that it had provided the licence for the hospital and conducted sanitary inspections of its premises. The real grounds for joining the department as a defendant was that it obviously had the resources, like the doctors who carried indemnity insurance, to pay any verdict against it. The basis for the department's liability seemed thin but one practical problem for the defendants was that these cases would take years of court time and legal costs. As a result, almost all of these cases were ultimately settled prior to being heard, although even this process took until the end of 1998.

In all these cases I was arguing about the law with other lawyers. In many ways it is a more difficult task to demystify the law for non-lawyers because it requires much clearer and simpler language. Once a week, for several years in the mid-1990s, I tried to do this as the legal commentator on ABC Radio National's morning program. This was presented by Peter Thompson, tall, lean, with a sharp mind, a clear radio voice and the ability to ask an awkward question. Our subject every week was the most topical legal issue of the time, whether this was how to prosecute war crimes in Bosnia or what should be the rules governing IVF pregnancies. I would prepare a series of questions and answers in advance but Thompson was able to expand the discussion in ways that few of his colleagues in radio and television were able to do.

Although I had done quite a number of television interviews over the years, I much preferred radio. There never seemed to be enough time in current affairs television to discuss any issue for more than a few minutes. And there could be no sudden movements that might distract the viewers from what was being said. In a radio studio, by contrast, it was possible to stretch out behind the microphone with a cup of coffee and explore matters in some detail. It is true that there might sometimes be a million people listening but it was still a conversation with one person on the other side of the desk.

My radio appearances sparked hostility in some sections of the Bench and the Bar. It was impossible sometimes not to criticise the decisions of courts or the conduct of lawyers. Feedback from listeners, however, about the legal spot was very positive. The program's producers seemed pleasantly surprised by this but I had always felt many people in the general community had a keen interest in how the law worked, even if it was hard to find legal issues discussed in plain English. I doubted, however, that this was the view of some members of the profession.

During this period I made a number of applications to take silk. Originally King's or Queen's Counsel were appointed in England to appear for the Crown and were entitled to wear a silk gown. In Australia they were appointed by the Attorney-General, although largely on the recommendation of the president of the Bar in some States, including New South Wales, or on the recommendation of the Chief Justice in others. Early in the 1990s, however, the system was changed in New South Wales so that appointments were made by a Bar committee – headed by the president – and the new silks were called Senior Counsel. One way in which the system had not changed, however, in New South Wales or elsewhere, was that one person, or sometimes a very small group of persons, had a great deal of power over the future careers and earning capacity

Taking silk in October 1998

of those who had applied for silk. There might be 100 applications and a dozen appointments so there was a lot of room for personal opinion. It was true that most of the other applicants had been at the Bar longer than I had but only a few had done as many big cases by themselves. When two of my applications were rejected, I had my suspicions about the real reasons. The selection committee was required to consult with various members of the Bench and some of these had never enjoyed works like *The Legal Mystique*. Others, however, were very supportive. Justice Michael Kirby, by then on the High Court, wrote to me:

> Dear Michael,
>
> David [Kirby's brother and a judge of the NSW Supreme Court] told me last night of the list of silks. He and my brother Donald were both outraged that you were left off.
>
> I just want to offer a note of encouragement and an assurance of the very high opinion I have of your skills as a lawyer and an advocate. Don't let this little reverse discourage you too much. Just go on being yourself.
>
> With encouragement,
>
> Michael

Good advice, although being myself was no doubt part of the problem. Next year, however, I received a letter to say that I had been appointed Senior Counsel. I still did not much like the system but at least I had managed to slip through the net.

Chelmsford had been my first real exposure to the world of psychiatry but I soon discovered at the Bar that it was a very common feature of litigation. In criminal cases a psychiatrist is often called by the defence to say that the accused is not fully responsible for his or her actions. In civil claims for damages there is likely to be psychiatric evidence that the plaintiff has not only suffered physical injuries but severe mental distress as well.

One problem about this kind of evidence is that psychiatrists, more so than any other doctors, are heavily dependent on what they are told by their patients because there is often little physical evidence of the illness. The other problem, largely confined to criminal cases, is that many psychiatrists seem to start from the proposition that no one is ever really responsible for anything they do. Everyone accepts that persons with a severe mental illness should not be convicted of a criminal offence (although it may be that they cannot be released into the community). But in any criminal justice system the scope for avoiding the consequences of an individual's actions needs to be limited, if only because the effects of those actions are the same for victims and their families whatever the mental state of the accused.

I found a graphic example of this problem when I provided the legal advice for Phil Cleary's autobiography in the late 1990s.[7] Cleary was a well-known Australian Rules footballer in Melbourne and had been elected to the House of Representatives as an independent when Bob Hawke's retirement in 1992 caused a by-election. Cleary played the role of working class hero and it paid off because there was much truth in it. The biggest legal problem in the book came from the killing of his sister in 1987. Vicki Cleary was a kindergarten teacher. She had been stabbed to death outside the pre-school where she worked by her former boyfriend. He had a criminal record stretching back to childhood that included violent assaults and abduction and sexual assault of a small child. Not a great choice for a boyfriend but she was the victim of a shocking crime. At the trial the accused put forward a defence of provocation, designed to reduce the charge from murder to manslaughter, on the basis that the victim had verbally abused him when he confronted her with a carving knife – a normal reaction, it might be thought, by almost anyone. The defence argued that he suffered from alcohol-induced depression and so lost control more easily than a normal person. Two psychiatrists gave evidence that he was depressed. This evidence was one of the factors that influenced the judge to allow the defence of provocation to go to the jury. The jury brought in a verdict of manslaughter and the killer finished up serving three and a half years in prison.

Cleary blamed the trial judge for this result and his vitriolic comments about him raised the question of the little-used but still-existing form of contempt known as "scandalising the court". Whatever the judge's role, however, it looked like a case where the jury had abandoned their common sense. However it happened, the outcome of the whole exercise, including the psychiatric evidence, was simply bizarre. It is only necessary to look at the result to know that something had gone wrong. It could only undermine the faith of the general community in the criminal justice system.

By this time there had been some changes on the home front. In 1992 a house that I had always wanted to buy came onto the market. It was in Petersham, on the edge of Sydney's old Italian quarter in Leichhardt. I knew the house because we had some friends in the same street and I often drove past. The area was bohemian by standards of most lawyers, who lived on the North Shore or on the peninsular east of the city. There had always been a number of cafes and restaurants in Leichhardt but this had now expanded into the kind of area more commonly found in some parts of Europe than in Australia. Home life was also improved by Gae's retirement from full-time work in the NSW bureaucracy and a move onto the boards of a number of statutory bodies, including Taronga Park Zoo and the NSW government's property developer, Landcom, in a good use of her skills as an economist.

Towards the end of 1995 I received a telephone call from the Minister for Transport in the NSW government, Brian Langton.

I had met Langton on occasions and thought that he might want some legal advice. Without any preliminaries he asked me to take the job as chairman of the board of the State Rail Authority (SRA). He said it was a part-time position but obviously time-consuming. After overcoming my initial surprise, I agreed and, during the next three years, periodically moved into a completely new world.

The SRA's rail network stretches 470km from north to south and 160km inland from Sydney to the west. It carries almost one million passengers per day and in 1995 cost more than $1.6 billion a year to operate. This is a very large commuter rail system by world standards. Those cities whose systems carry more passengers, like New York and Chicago, do so because they have a subway system as well. I had been appointed, like the last emperor, to preside over partial dissolution of this empire. Most of it remained with the SRA as the body running city and country trains. There were, however, two new organisations – one which owned the tracks and one responsible for maintenance. This never seemed to me to make much sense but it was the brain child of some economic theorists in the Cabinet Office. The theory never worked in practice. In 2004, all these functions were put back into the one organisation. There was also, for a short time, a separate entity that operated the freight rail business before that was sold to the private sector. This split took place six months after I arrived and each of the three new organisations then had its own board.

I also became a member of the Public Transport Authority, a collection of the heads of the various transport services, trains, buses, ferries and roads, that looked at transport policy across the board. Sydney's problems of traffic congestion and air pollution were, and are, very severe by the standard of Western cities. The PTA's forecast showed that these problems would increase sharply in the next 20 years as the city's population continued to grow and its boundaries were pushed further in every direction except where they were blocked by the sea.

It has become obvious that the size and spread of population in the Sydney basin has long passed its optimal level. The New South Wales government cannot, however, control this growth because the federal government sets the immigration intake to Australia and the majority of those migrants arrive in Sydney and stay there. The supply of government services, including transport, to this area will become increasingly expensive. It would be possible essentially to ignore public transport and concentrate funding on freeways in the way that Los Angeles has done. Few people would consider this a desirable model, although it is a much simpler solution for governments. Even then, however, it would be impossible to match the road system of Los Angeles because of the difference between the financial capacities of governments in the United States and Australia.

One reason that public transport is a difficult option for governments is that it almost always has to be run at a loss. This is only a loss by accounting standards. From the point of view of an economist, it brings other benefits to the community including, in Sydney, by preventing traffic flows coming to a halt altogether. There have been attempts in recent years, chiefly in Victoria, to privatise trains, trams and buses. But, as the Victorians have found, privatisation only works when the purchasers of the government business can run services at a profit and this is seldom so in the case of public transport. Government transport systems should be run efficiently so that public subsidies can be kept as low as possible, but it is unrealistic to expect that these services can be provided without some government contribution.

These are difficult long-term political problems because they can only be solved, if at all, by substantial government expenditures. On a day-to-day basis, however, there was intense political pressure on the SRA. If the trains ran on time, nothing was ever heard about it. If they did not, it was front page news and the government felt it was under threat from voters. This political insecurity led to storms at the SRA. The other six members of the board were also new appointments because all the former directors had been suddenly removed by the government. Chief executives were sacked on a regular basis. The one who was there when I started lasted another year before the axe fell. I was called at home by the Premier, Bob Carr, who told me what was going to happen. I said that anyone else would have the same problems and it might be too early to act. He said that he was not asking for advice but letting me know what was happening. I prepared to work with a new person. This turned out to be David Hill, the former head of the SRA and the ABC, a man of great energy and charm but with a ruthless streak and often a brutal style. We had a good working relationship. But, as at the ABC, Hill had either loyal supporters or fierce enemies amongst SRA management.

Most of the men and woman at the SRA had spent their working lives there. I came to realise that the rail industry was in many ways a world of its own. This is true not only in Australia but for the rail operators I met from other countries. In contrast to the legal world, they could see the results of their work every day as passengers and goods were moved across the landscape. They usually had an infectious enthusiasm for what they did that made them good company.

Like all forms of transport in Australia, rail had the problem of vast distances outside the major cities but a small pool of passengers by international standards. During my time in the SRA there was yet another proposal for a high speed train between Sydney and Canberra. I had always taken the view that this project could never deliver a return to investors unless it was heavily subsidised by the governments in Canberra or Sydney. There may be a good argument why taxpayers should contribute these funds but this was never the basis on which the proposal was put forward by its promoters. In any event, the push made in the late 1990s came to nothing and the economic arguments were put away for next time. There was, however, always a next time. During the next decade consultants were engaged, with taxpayer funds, to do further studies on the feasibility of high-speed rail between Sydney, Brisbane and Melbourne. Confronted by the usual financial problems of the project, governments simply put these reports on the shelf.

In addition to the financial battles with the Treasury and the political problem of on-time running, there was a constant concern at the SRA with the question of safety. It was always on my mind that I could wake up any morning to find that there had been a rail crash with serious loss of life. This did not happen during my term but it certainly happened not long before and not long afterwards. There are so many train movements in the course of a day on the Sydney network that, as in the airline industry, it only takes one serious mechanical failure or human error for a disaster to occur. It did not help that many of the work practices had not changed for decades and that the rail unions resisted the slightest attempts at modernisation.

The relationship between the minister, the chairman and the chief executive is crucial to whether a statutory body operates effectively. To a large extent their roles are not legally defined and have to be worked out by the individuals who occupy these posts. There is plenty of scope for conflict here but I was fortunate with the two ministers and three chief executives with whom I worked. The biggest dispute took place inside the board over the appointment of one of these chief executives. When David Hill's temporary return ran out in late 1997, the job of chief executive was advertised inside and outside Australia. When it came to a choice, the board was split between two candidates. Three of us were in favour of Simon Lane, a relatively young but thoughtful Englishman with a big reputation internationally in the rail industry. He had been running the train system in Melbourne. The other was a senior executive in the transport industry within Australia. Four board members wanted the other candidate. One of those four was John Menadue who had been head of the Department of the Prime Minister and Cabinet under the Whitlam and Fraser governments and then Australian ambassador to Japan. Even on a board that contained a number of strong personalities, Menadue was a very formidable character. He was used to being in charge and did not shrink from confrontations. When one of his supporters changed sides, on the ground that I would be spending a lot of time with the chief executive and should have the person I thought I could work with, he sent me a formal letter complaining about "unfairness" and "unprofessionalism." These are strong terms to put on paper in a boardroom debate.

After the board had made its recommendation to the minister, a fierce battle broke out inside the government over the two candidates, with politicians and bureaucrats taking sides. In a meeting with Brian Langton I said that there did not seem to be enough time to organise the paperwork so that he could put Simon Lane's name before the next Cabinet meeting. Langton replied sharply: "It has to be the next meeting. I couldn't get it through in another week's time. There is too much pressure." I knew that I was lucky to have Langton's support and his political judgment. The paperwork was done in time and it did go through.

I never regretted the turmoil surrounding Lane's appointment. I thought that he was one of the best rail operators on the international level. Naturally, some years later, after I had left the SRA, he was also forced out, like all his predecessors, largely as a result of hostility from the rail unions who opposed some of the changes that he wanted to introduce. This was, indeed, the history of the SRA. I had to give up the post of chairman when I became Solicitor-

General of NSW at the end of 1998, but, despite all the political and financial dramas, I was very satisfied by having been part of an organisation that delivered a major community service on a daily basis – something that very few lawyers ever get to do.

10
FREE SPEECH
Theory and Practice

In the late 1980s and the 1990s about half of my practice at the Bar was in media law – defamation, contempt, suppression orders, breach of confidence and copyright. These legal issues could arise out of television and radio programs, newspapers and magazines, books, movies and even musical recordings.

The ideal situation was to get the material well in advance of publication and then try to minimise the risk of litigation. This is particularly important in the case of books and films, which are much more vulnerable to a court's restraining order than a daily newspaper or a one-off television program, although these have also been stopped from publishing on occasions. I say minimise the risk of litigation. The worst lawyer can take all the risk – and all the interest – out of a good story. The real skill is in avoiding the greatest dangers while keeping the story essentially intact.

Using this standard, the work on the ABC's *Moonlight State* was almost perfect. Given the number of targets and the gravity of the allegations, it was remarkable that only one person sued in defamation and, as so often happened in my experience, it was not one of the major characters. But that litigation went for the best part of a decade and, although the plaintiff ultimately lost, it cost the ABC a great deal of time and money.

The ABC was a very attractive client for any media lawyer. It had a number of radio and television programs on the cutting edge of investigative journalism, with the highest profile being *Four Corners* and the *7:30 Report*. Some weeks I spent almost as much time at the ABC television studios at Gore Hill on Sydney's North Shore as I did in my chambers in Phillip Street. The in-house legal department of a dozen lawyers, headed by Bruce Donald, with Judith Walker as his deputy, was more than a match for any of the big firms. They were on a tighter budget than their rivals in the private sector but this was very much to my advantage. Instead of briefing a silk to lead me when cases did come to court, they were happy for me to appear by myself. This meant that I was able to run cases against many of the leaders of the Sydney and Melbourne Bars. Initially this was nerve-racking but I was at a stage where I wanted to run cases by myself.

Most practitioners in the field of defamation work on both sides of the street. This is a contrast to other fields of the law, including crime, personal injury and industrial relations, where lawyers tend to be identified with one side or the other. As a result, I appeared almost as often for plaintiffs as defendants and frequently found myself taking cases against large media organisations, as in the Burrows case – but not against the ABC, which put me on a retainer so that I could not take cases against them. This interchange of roles is reflected in the underlying concept of defamation law. It is designed to strike a delicate balance between protection of individual reputation and freedom of speech. Media organisations have always complained that the balance is tilted too heavily against freedom of speech. Of course, they would say that. But what is the reality?

The first question that has to be answered in any defamation case is what the publication means. This is often the subject of a hot dispute. The plaintiff will not get to first base unless he or she establishes that the publication contains one or more defamatory allegations, that is, allegations that would lower the reputation of the individual in question in the eyes of ordinary reasonable members of the community. If these kinds of charges are set out in a media publication, it always seemed to me that in most cases there are only two defences that could stop the plaintiff getting an award of damages. One is the defence of truth. The other is the defence of fair comment.

In Australia the defence of truth requires proof – on the balance of probabilities – that the allegation is "true in substance and in fact." This leaves the big problem for a defendant of producing the evidence that will meet the high standard of proof that the courts employ.

The defence of fair comment also requires proof of some facts. The defendant claims that the defamatory allegation is an expression of opinion on facts that are set out in the publication or are so well known to readers that they do not need to be set out. It might be reported, for example, that a company manager had employed a whole series of relatives and so was not fit to be in charge of the organisation. What has to be shown is that the relatives were employed and then the question of fitness can be a fair – which is not the same as reasonable – comment on those facts. Most comment defences fail because at least some of the facts in the publication are wrong.

In 1997 the High Court considered whether an additional defence should be available to the media for publications about politicians and political issues. The case had been brought against the ABC by David Lange, who was Prime Minister of New Zealand from 1984 until 1989. In April 1990 *Four Corners* broadcast a program made and already put to air by Television New Zealand. This meant that there was no scope for legal changes to be made to the program by the ABC, as there would have been with one of its own productions. The main argument of the program was that the New Zealand Labour government of the 1980s had raised substantial campaign funds from the business community and tailored some of its policies to benefit business in general and some individuals in particular. I acted for the ABC in the action brought by Lange and several other New Zealand politicians and public figures. If the makers of the program were looking for a reaction, they certainly got it. The New Zealand Prime Minister, Geoffrey Palmer, described it as "the most dishonest, distorted, deceitful and disgraceful program that I have seen". Most of those involved in the production at Television New Zealand were forced out of their jobs and several came to work in Australian television. For some reason Palmer sued Television New Zealand but not the ABC. If he had, I would not have taken the case as I still counted him as a friend after the time we spent together in the US.

David Lange may well have thought that it had been a mistake to take this case to the High Court on a legal question that was never central to his claim. He did not need to make some new law which was bound to be an expensive and time-consuming exercise. The case was finally settled on terms not be disclosed, although Lange said that he was prepared to settle for little or nothing except an apology and his legal costs because he just wanted the saga finished.

This was not the only problem about the hearing in Canberra. The High Court itself was deeply divided about what kind of extra defence, if any, should be available for publications about political questions. All seven judges ultimately put their names to a joint judgment but this compromise meant that some of the legal issues were never fully explained and this has caused difficulties in trying to interpret the decision ever since.

At any rate, the High Court said that there was a new defence available for publications about political subjects, based on an implied freedom of political communication in the Constitution.[1] This was an extension of the old defence of qualified privilege at common law. Traditionally this doctrine had always protected very limited publications, such as a reference by an employer or a parent's letter to a school principal complaining about a teacher. But the defence had only been available to media publications in very unusual circumstances. This was changed by the High Court for discussions of political questions but there was a large qualification – the publication had to be reasonable. Normally this would require the publisher to have some basis for believing that the defamatory charge was true; to take proper steps to verify the accuracy of its information; and to seek a response from the person against whom the charge was made and to publish that response at the same time. This kind of test, at least in the way it has been interpreted by judges, has always been too high for journalists to meet. It is relatively easy for a cross-examiner to undermine the credibility of a journalist in the witness box when the whole point of the case – in the absence of a defence of truth – is that the journalist got some things wrong in the story. If everything in the story was accurate, the case would never have started. I often cross-examined journalists in this way when appearing for plaintiffs. When I was on the other side, however, I was very wary about calling the writer of the story as a witness and hardly ever did.

The standard of care for publishers is the real issue in any debate about striking the balance between protection of reputation and freedom of speech. What kind of evidence should be necessary before, for example, an allegation of taking bribes is made against a politician – or against anyone? The American solution to this problem has been to say that publications about "public figures", which includes not only politicians but movie stars, television personalities and sporting heroes, will only give rise to a successful defamation action if there was malice on the part of the publisher.[2]

This usually means knowledge that the charges were false or there was reckless indifference as to whether they were true or not.[3] Although these decisions of the United States courts have tilted the balance in favour of publishers in comparison with Britain and Australia, it is still open to a plaintiff to ask the court to look at the journalist's research and sources. And, if these are simply inadequate, there may well be a finding that the journalist did not care whether the story was correct and so was acting with malice.

To take this approach in Australia, however, would be too big a step for the courts. It would require legislation by the various States and Territories. When I had a chance later to propose some changes to legislation in New South Wales, I suggested adopting the American approach, at least in part, but I found it hard to find support for this idea. In 2001, as Solicitor-General for NSW, I persuaded the Attorney-General to set up a four-person task force

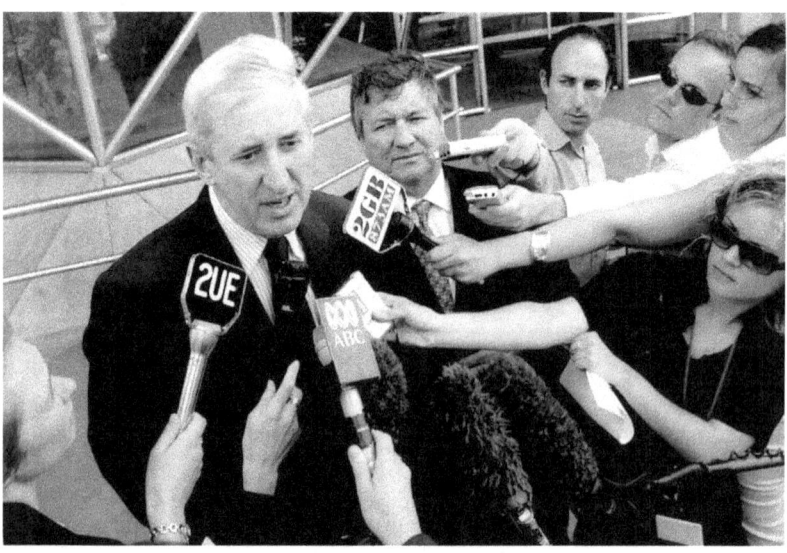

With NSW Minister for Industrial Relations, John Della Bosca, at a joint press conference in December 2005 outside the courts in Sydney to announce a challenge to the Howard government's workplace laws (Australian Financial Review)

to look at existing NSW legislation on defamation. The task force recommended a number of changes, including the removal in most cases of a corporation's right to sue for libel and a less stringent test for what is reasonable conduct by journalists. These changes were made to the NSW legislation and included in the uniform legislation, based largely on the NSW model, adopted by all the States, the Australian Capital Territory and the Northern Territory early in 2006.[4] There was quite a lot of criticism by some lawyers of the removal of most corporations' right to sue in defamation but I had always taken the view that the reputation of companies did not need protecting in the same way as that of individuals and, in any event, large corporations had a bevy of public relations staff who could respond to any unfavourable media publicity.

I was not able to get enough support on the task force for the American approach to public figures which made it harder for them to sue successfully in libel. Because public figures can easily put their side of a story in the media, it did not seem to me that they needed the same level of protection as private individuals, although, even in the United States, they will still succeed in the courts if there is simply no factual basis for what has been published. This is because the absence of any factual basis would normally lead to a finding of malice – that the publisher knew the allegations were false or did not care whether they were true or false. But even if this change to the law had been recommended by the task force, there was no chance it would be accepted by the NSW Cabinet, all of whom were politicians and so public figures themselves.

During the late 1980s I had been writing a text on defamation law in Australia, with Terry Tobin. This did not consider policy questions of what the law ought to be, but what it was. There were two English texts that most Australian lawyers in the field used regularly but nothing from this country. We had piles of cases sitting in our rooms and decided to draw this material together.

It was published as *Australian Defamation Law and Practice* by LexisNexis in 1991. Tobin had wanted to have a handsome leather bound volume. I also would have liked this but it would have been out of date within six months so the text emerged as a loose-leaf publication that we had to update three times a year. It is still going and has become a web-based service as well.

A practice in media law inevitably meant looking at, not always with their approval, the affairs of some of the country's best-known characters. During these years I did the legal work on biographies of Kim Beazley by Peter FitzSimons, Graham Richardson by Marian Wilkinson, Kerry Packer and Alan Bond, both by Paul Barry, as well as the autobiography of Bill Hayden. These two strains of business and politics came together in John Elliott who sparked one of the longest-running and most expensive sagas in Australian legal history. In the late 1980s Elliott was often put forward as the next Liberal prime minister. Bluff, straight-talking, hard-drinking and chain-smoking, he was chief executive of the conglomerate, Elders IXL; federal president of the Liberal Party; and president of a Melbourne institution, the Carlton Football Club. Then, in February 1990, the ABC's *7.30pm Report* reported, just four days after the calling of a federal election, that the National Crime Authority (NCA) was investigating a corporate takeover in which Elliott was involved. There was a volcanic legal reaction. Elliott immediately sued the ABC in the Supreme Court of Victoria, not only on the basis that the *7.30pm Report* was defamatory but also that the ABC was responsible for every television, radio and newspaper follow-up story in every State and Territory. I had not advised on the program before it went to air but came into the case for the ABC as soon as Elliott started his action.

When I first looked at the legal issues with Bruce Donald, we realised that there was an intriguing, if somewhat alarming, conundrum at the heart of the case. How could the ABC prove in court that the NCA was conducting this investigation? It would not be possible to call as witnesses anyone from the NCA because under federal legislation its inquiries were secret. Even if we found some other way of proving the existence of the investigation, we suspected that Elliott's lawyers would argue that this evidence should not be allowed because the whole point of an NCA investigation was that it did not become public unless and until criminal proceedings were instituted.

We were right. In the first skirmish between the parties in the Supreme Court of Victoria Elliott's legal team was headed by Jeff Sher QC. Then in his fifties but still slim and dark, Sher was a formidable opponent, a skilled technical lawyer, a powerful jury advocate, tenacious, ferocious and cunning. Sher said that what the ABC had done was illegal because it was contrary to federal law. I disagreed and invited Elliott's lawyers to walk several blocks to Melbourne Police Headquarters and try to have some charges laid: "Don't think we haven't already tried that!", snarled Sher from the other end of the Bar table.

While waiting for this case to come to a hearing, the ABC became embroiled in more litigation with Elliott. The NCA brought criminal charges against Elliott and a number of other Elders directors. These charges did not relate to the company takeover referred to by the *7.30 Report* but concerned an allegation of fraud by means of sham foreign exchange transactions involving $66 million. Elliott had asked the Federal Court to stop the charges being laid but this was refused. At the same time Elliott issued a claim for damages in the Federal Court against the NCA and various other parties including the ABC. This action was based on an alleged conspiracy between several ministers in the Hawke government, including Hawke himself, and a range of other people to injure Elliott's reputation and his business career. As part of the conspiracy, it was said that the Minister for Police in the Victorian Labor government, Steven

Crabb, had given the information about the NCA investigation to the *7.30 Report*.[5] Sher argued that the ABC broadcast had changed the course of the federal election campaign. I responded that it was a fantasy to suggest that the ABC was involved in a conspiracy to damage Elliott.

I thought from the start that this action had no legal basis and could never succeed. Together with the other defendants, I argued this point over a week in the Federal Court in April 1994. Although the action was not struck out, the Court agreed that it could not succeed in its present form. Elliott's lawyers were ordered to reformulate it. Early in 1996 Elliott's trial on the fraud charge was due to start in the Supreme Court of Victoria. Instead, however, of a jury being sworn in and the prosecution giving an opening address, the normal opening of a criminal trial, several months of legal argument took place about what evidence the prosecution could call. In the end no jury was ever sworn in because Justice Frank Vincent ruled that much of the prosecution evidence was inadmissible because the NCA had exceeded its statutory powers in conducting the investigation into the foreign exchange transactions. Elliott and the other directors were acquitted by order of the judge, except, in a bizarre twist, for one who had already pleaded guilty.

Although it was an academic exercise, because Elliott and the other directors could not be tried again, the prosecution challenged Vincent's decision in the Court of Appeal. The Court of Appeal said that Vincent had been wrong and added that the history of the case suggested that "criminal proceedings in this State are in some respects out of control". The Court of Appeal thought it extraordinary that after four years of protracted legal proceedings, the charges had never gotten before a jury.[6]

This was not, however, the end of the legal saga. In 1998 the battle over the conspiracy action resumed in the Federal Court when the NCA again attempted to have it thrown out. I did not have to appear for the ABC because earlier that year Elliott agreed to halt both the defamation action and the conspiracy case against the ABC, although not against the NCA and some of the other defendants. But it was not until the end of 2001, after several more years of argument, that the remainder of the conspiracy action, except for the case against Crabb, was struck out by the Federal Court.[7]

None of this showed the legal system at its best. This decade of litigation had provided many lawyers, including myself, with considerable work. But the criminal proceedings were a fiasco and the civil claims an enormous waste of court time. In later years Elliott's own career continued to spiral downwards. No government would consider appointing him to any public position. The Australian Securities and Investment Commission successfully went to court to have him disqualified from being a company director. And he was even forced out of the presidency of the Carlton Football Club.

Despite all the time I had spent on Elliott's affairs, I had never actually met him, although he had been present in court at some of the hearings. It was about the same time that I gave legal advice on Paul Barry's biographies of Alan Bond and Kerry Packer. Again, there was something strange about knowing so much about a person's life without having any actual contact with them. It is presumably something like the kind of relationship that biographers have with their subject when writing about a person who is long dead, or still alive but unwilling to cooperate with the author.

Cases on constitutional law are usually few and far between at the Bar but I had kept up my interest in this area from teaching days and used it to take part in the debate that started in the early 1990s as to when and how Australia might become a republic. In 1967 I had been one of the foundation members of the Melbourne University Republican Club. We had an inaugural meeting but never met again. There did not seem anything useful to do at that stage. These sentiments did not, at least on my part, reflect any hostility to England or its legacy of law, literature and parliamentary democracy – quite the contrary – but I had always found the idea of an hereditary monarchy offensive, the more so when it was embodied in the tasteless and talentless group that comprised the House of Windsor.

Initially I argued in various publications that the change to a republic could take place without the necessity for a president as head of state. The Prime Minister would be head of state and head of government in the same way that both offices are filled by the President of the United States. This would have required some changes to the existing parliamentary system, including preferably the introduction of fixed-term parliaments, so that no one would have the powers that the Governor-General exercised in 1975. It soon became clear, however, that most republicans were desperate to have a president as head of state. As Brian Toohey wrote in the *Australian Financial Review* in November 1995:

> The unprecedented entry into the Australian political debate in recent weeks by the Governor-General, Bill Hayden, has highlighted a little noticed issue for republican supporters: if they don't want a governor-general, why do they want someone in a similar role called a president?
>
> With the exception of a few lonely voices such as that of the Sydney lawyer Michael Sexton, most republicans have taken it for granted that the Governor-General should be replaced by a president.
>
> But even prominent supporters of this position . . . acknowledge it is possible to have a republic without a president.[8]

I did not mind being a lonely voice but I was also happy to join in the general push for a republic, even it was not exactly the model I favoured. So for several years in the 1990s I was a member of the national committee of the Australian Republican Movement. This body had its origins in Malcolm Turnbull's energy and money. Turnbull was a genuinely mercurial figure. Intelligent, articulate, and often charming, he was also brash, ruthless and capable of explosive outbursts of anger. He had the absolute assurance of someone who is rich enough to be able to do almost anything. I found him good to work with but he excited hostility as well as affection on both sides of politics. Turnbull chaired the national committee of the ARM but there was no shortage of other healthy egos when it sat down to meet. Amongst the other members were the authors Tom Keneally and Donald Horne; former head of the ABC, David Hill; former NSW Premier, Neville Wran; and broadcaster, Geraldine Doogue.

The focus on the presidency, however, ultimately became the central weakness of the republican campaign. This led to division among republicans. The ARM supported the proposition of a president elected by a two-thirds majority of the federal parliament. When this proposal went to a referendum on 6 November 1999, other republican groups argued that it should be rejected because it did not provide for a president elected by all voters. The referendum was lost in all States (although the vote in Victoria was almost a tie). It is true that the Prime Minister, John Howard, opposed the proposal but I doubted that this was the real problem. Writing later about the result, it seemed to me to be an opportunity lost:

> The reality is that the referendum at the end of 1999 was lost not because most of the electorate did not want Australia to become a republic but because there were differing views as to how any president should be chosen. As soon as different methods of appointing – or electing – the head of state are canvassed, there is a serious risk of repeating the failure of 1999.
>
> If the office of head of state – with a governor-general or president – is essentially a ceremonial one, why has so

much time and energy been expended by republicans on trying to devise a new method of appointment or election for a position that is expressly designed to be powerless? Of course, if the position were designed to establish a high-profile political rival to the prime minister, that would be a different matter. But presumably no one wants this result, as it would only undermine the existing system of government where the prime minister, as the leader of the party winning the majority of votes, is the head of the country's administration. So what is the intrinsic significance of how the position is filled or vacated?[9]

This was basically an argument for moving to a republic but keeping the Governor-General – perhaps with a name change to president, as a head of state. It would be useful at that time to spell out the powers of the head of state and to keep them as confined as possible. There is obviously a large gap between the present theory, where the Governor-General calls elections and commissions governments, and the political reality of where these decisions are all made on the advice of the government of the day. This is an argument, however, where I seem to be on the losing side. It looks as if any change to a republic will include a president elected in a nationwide poll. This might seem attractive but I suspect there will be problems in the long term between prime ministers and presidents if they have to compete for the same votes. And will the candidates for the presidency typically be television presenters or movie stars on the basis that they are the best-known individuals in the country?

Many republicans in 1999 wanted much bigger changes to the Australian Constitution. There are plenty of improvements that could be made to the Constitution but, if those debates are mixed with the threshold question of whether to change to a republic at all, I doubt that a republic will ever be approved by referendum. One of the most contentious suggestions raised in the debates during the

1990s was for insertion in the Constitution of a bill of rights. Apart from the problem of entangling other changes to the Constitution with the proposal for a republic, my own view was that a bill or charter of rights was, and is, fundamentally anti-democratic at a conceptual level and essentially impractical in its operation. I raised these objections again in 2009 when the Rudd government set up a committee to examine the issue, pointing to what I saw as the consequences of a bill or charter:

> It is no accident that almost all the proponents of a bill or a charter of rights are lawyers. This is not because it would be a financial windfall for some lawyers – although it would – but because they very much want lawyers, especially judges, to have a larger role in dealing with the problems of modern society. This is a key point of difference between the two sides in the debate. Of course, the courts sometimes deal with social and political questions now. Under a bill or charter of rights, however, they would do so in a much more direct way . . .
>
> But one of the real problems about this discussion is what is meant by "rights". Let's assume that there should be a "right" to a fair trial, to freedom of assembly, to freedom of movement, to freedom of political association. It is hard to see how anyone could say that these do not already exist in Australia or are not well protected.
>
> But what about a "right" to decent housing, a good education, a reasonable standard of living? It is difficult to see how these can ever be legally enforced. They are individual aspirations that have always been met with varying degrees of equality in this country and with government support for those particularly disadvantaged. Giving these social and economic questions to a judge to decide does not change them into legal issues – they are still social and economic questions. That is why they are quite unsuitable for litigation in the courts.[10]

The problems of handing over political issues to judges was spelt out by Jonathan Sumption, now a judge of the Supreme Court of the United Kingdom – in 2011.[11] Sumption noted that judicial decisions are preferred by many activists:

> ... because they appear to introduce a higher morality into public decision-making, untrammelled by the impurities of the political process. The attraction of judicial decision-making is that it is animated by a combination of abstract reasoning and moral value-judgment, and the decision imposed by the judiciary's plenitude of power to declare and

With NSW Director of Public Prosecutions, Lloyd Babb SC, in December 2010 in one of the barrister's rooms in the High Court in Canberra

enforce law. To some, this will seem more straightforward than the messy compromises required to build a political consensus. However, for those who are concerned with the proper functioning of our democratic institutions, the judicial resolution of inherently political issues is difficult to defend. It has no legitimate basis in public consent, because judges are quite rightly not accountable to the public for their decisions.

None of this means that governments cannot or should not use laws to attack specific social problems in some areas. An example is the anti-discrimination legislation that exists in all States at the federal level and bans discrimination on such grounds as sex, race and religion. But general notions of rights and responsibilities in a society can only be the result of a consensus in that community. They cannot be imposed by legislation. As the American jurist, Learned Hand, pointed out more than half a century ago:

> Liberty lies in the hearts of men and women; when it dies there, no constitution, no law, no court can save it; no constitution, no law, no court can even do much to help.[12]

This was another case, however, where my view seemed to be running against the tide. The campaign for a bill of rights at both the State and federal level has been conducted for some years by active and well-resourced groups in the legal profession and in law schools. There is no organised body to present the case against a bill of rights. The governments of the ACT and Victoria have succumbed to these pressures. It looked as if some other States would do the same but this has not happened. And the Rudd government decided in 2010 against the bill of rights at the federal level, despite the recommendation that this should happen by the committee that it had established to consider this issue. It can be assumed, however, that those groups that support the proposal have not given up and will continue to exert pressure on future governments.

One of the issues in the bill of rights debate, freedom of speech, was the subject of a piece that I wrote for the *Sydney Morning Herald* at about this time.[13] It was provoked by the *Victorian Racial and Religious Tolerance Act* which seemed to me to be a complete denial of such freedom:

> This legislation makes it unlawful for someone, on the ground of the religious belief or activity of another person or class of persons, to engage in conduct that "incites hatred against, serious contempt for, or revulsion or serious ridicule". There is a similar provision about racial vilification. However, there is a defence of conduct that was engaged in "reasonably and in good faith" in the performance of an artistic work or in the course of a discussion or debate for any genuine academic, artistic, religious or scientific purpose.
>
> ... there is a bigger problem at the heart of the legislation. It is an unnecessary attack on free speech. Free speech has never, of course, been an absolute value. It has always been subject to significant limitations, including the law of defamation and contempt and questions of national security. But the law in this case makes it illegal to incite "severe ridicule" of another person or group. No one enjoys being ridiculed, but why should such publications be unlawful?
>
> It is true that the legislation also deals with the incitement of hatred, and speech of that kind is normally to be deplored. But it does not follow that something that may be immoral should therefore be illegal ...
>
> It is obvious that legislation of this type is a lawyers' picnic but its real vice is that it can be used by all kinds of groups to suppress ideas they don't like. It can just as easily be used by oppressive majorities. Defences of reasonability and good faith are no real protection because a judge's

decision on these questions is just as arbitrary as anyone else's.

I was still arguing this point in *The Australian* in 2012:

> The very point about expressions of opinion that are offensive to some or even most members of the community is that they should be allowed despite their offensiveness. As the American jurist, Oliver Wendell Holmes said a century ago: "We should be eternally vigilant against attempts to check the expression of opinions that we loathe".
>
> It is not the case, as Holmes went on to claim, that the truth will necessarily triumph in the "market" of ideas. But to live with the expressions of others that are untrue or unjust, or just silly, or that *we think* are untrue or unjust or silly, is one of the burdens of a democratic society, as well as of the human condition.
>
> The right response to speech that one finds offensive is one's own speech, not suppression.[14]

In the same piece I attacked the 2012 report by retired Federal Judge Court, Ray Finkelstein, which recommended a new statutory body to regulate the media in Australia:

> Putting aside its almost unreadable style, the Finkelstein report started from the proposition that most members of the community are just not clever enough to make their own judgments about material published in the media without some guidance. The report said that, to engage in public debate, citizens must have the "relevant critical and speaking skills", but that there is "real doubt as to whether these capacities are present for all, or even most, citizens".
>
> This argument that most people are stupid is, of course, the argument of every anti-democrat in history, but the authors of the report, who obviously have no doubt that they

possess the relevant "capacities", argue that regulation of speech is needed to protect democracy.[15]

Not surprisingly, perhaps, this piece was the subject of an effusive editorial in *The Australian* the following day under the heading: "Free speech opens minds":

> In our pages yesterday, the NSW Solicitor-General, Michael Sexton SC, issued an eloquent defence of free speech and sounded a warning about a creeping illiberal attitude to public discourse in Australia ... Mr Sexton's conclusion could not have been more valid or succinct: "The right response to speech that one finds offensive is one's own speech, not suppression."

The question of freedom of speech was at the heart of many of the cases that I had at the Bar. The law of defamation, as already suggested, is an attempt to strike a balance between freedom of speech and protection of an individual's reputation. In the case of the law of contempt, the two competing interests are freedom of speech, again, and the administration of justice in the courts. In the criminal area, this means that it is dangerous for the media to publish prejudicial information about the accused if that information will not be available to the jury, for example, the accused's previous convictions or allegations of similar criminal conduct to the current charges. Lawyers acting for media organisations, as I did for the ABC for many years, are always conscious of the fact that a charge of contempt is itself a criminal prosecution, usually brought by the Attorney-General, and that journalists have on occasion been sent to prison. Although a gaol sentence was an unlikely result, it was common for the courts to impose very heavy fines on media organisations. In 1994 I appeared for the prosecution when *Who Weekly* magazine published a cover photograph of Ivan Milat while he was awaiting trial for the murder of seven backpackers in a forest south of Sydney. It was the prosecution case that publication of the photograph might affect the evidence of any witnesses who could be called to identify Milat as being in the vicinity of the forest. *Who Weekly* was fined $100,000 and its editor $10,000.[16]

There is a real question whether the law of contempt, which has hardly altered in its basic concepts since the 19th century, can continue to apply without change to criminal trials in an age when a juror can find on the Internet everything that has ever been published about an accused's past criminal conduct. In addition, it seems obvious that very little of the vast volume of information that is showered on most members of the community on a daily basis is remembered for any length of time. A number of American studies suggest that juries in fact focus on the evidence presented at the trial rather than anything they might have heard about the accused before they were sworn as jurors. In the United States the test for a contempt prosecution is much higher. There must be a "clear and present danger" to the administration of justice. The result is media coverage before trials that can be very hostile to the accused or, sometimes, to the prosecution.

Outside the criminal law, the problem of prejudicing a jury is now largely academic because few civil cases are still heard with a jury. It has always been assumed, maybe optimistically, that no judge would ever be affected by something published in the media. Another basis for contempt, however, in civil litigation has been any publication designed to force one of the parties to give up their case rather than withstand more bad publicity. This was the case successfully brought by the Attorney-General against *The Times* newspaper in Britain in 1974 when it published a series of articles about actions brought by the parents of children with serious birth defects against the manufacturers of the drug Thalidomide.[17] The articles argued passionately that the manufacturers were responsible for the birth defects and should pay compensation rather than fight the claims. The other basis for the case against *The Times* was prejudgment or "trial by media". It was said by the Attorney-General that the issues in a case before the courts should not be publicly discussed in a way that suggests that one party is entitled to succeed rather than the other.

Writing in 1994, I had criticised these grounds of contempt because of their chilling effect not only on accounts of current cases but also on the history of events well in the past:

> All of these grounds represent a major threat to the ability of writers and journalists to deal with questions that are of significant contemporary or historical public interest. There are still, for example, cases before the court arising out of the sinking by HMAS *Melbourne* of HMAS *Voyager* in 1964. Does this mean that it is not possible to write a book or an article about that naval disaster without running foul of the law of contempt? If the events being discussed in the book about the Christian Brothers orphanages took place in the 1930s and 1940s, how can it be satisfactory that these issues should not be publicly discussed in 1994?[18]

The reference to a book about orphanages run by the Christian Brothers was *When Innocence Trembles* by Kate Davies.[19] It had been published in 1994 but was removed from bookshops when the lawyers acting for the Christian Brothers threatened the publishers with contempt proceedings. More than 200 former inmates of these institutions, in desolate parts of Western Australia with the Celtic titles of Bindoon, Clontarf and Castledare, had sued the Christian Brothers in the Supreme Court of NSW, seeking compensation for physical and sexual abuse.

I was not looking for work when I wrote this article but the publishers of the book saw it and thought they would get a second opinion from me. They had been advised by their law firm to remove the book from sale. When I read the book, I found it a harrowing account of the brutal life of children who had been put in these places. The defendants' lawyers were quite right to think that it would affect anyone's view of their clients. But that did not seem to me to be a reason to ban its publication. I thought that the notion of "trial by media" had never been accepted as part of Australian law and I advised that the book should be put back on sale. It was but I did not win any friends at the publishers' law firm and I assumed that I would not be getting any work from that group in the future.

There was, however, no happy ending for the plaintiffs in the litigation who had spent time as children in these orphanages. Because the events had happened decades earlier, they were out of time for bringing the actions and had to accept a settlement where no substantial damages were paid but a trust fund established to be used for psychological assistance to the victims. It was a hollow victory, although it is hard to see how any damages could have compensated for their lost childhood.

I could not help wondering what my father would have thought of this case. He always seemed to think that he had received a pretty good education from the Christian Brothers. But these orphanages were in remote locations and there were no outsiders to whom the children could complain. Many of the children were not in fact orphans but had been handed over by their family, often a single mother, and in some cases been shipped out from Britain. History indicates that once children are taken from their families and placed in institutions, even including expensive boarding schools, there is a serious risk of abuse from staff or other inmates, although seldom on a scale described by those who went through the gates of Bindoon, Clontarf and Castledare.

Like defamation and contempt, the question of national security also requires the balancing of competing interests in the law. On one side is the ability of organisations like ASIO to work effectively against terrorists and hostile foreign governments. On the other side is the community's right to enough information about these bodies to be able to make some judgment as to their effectiveness and efficiency. In defamation cases I often appeared for the plaintiff and in contempt cases I sometimes appeared for the prosecution. In national security I was always acting for the media and so trying to ensure the publication of information that the security services wanted to keep secret. Often the problem for the publisher was the same as it had been in 1981 with my book on Vietnam – how to get the secret material published before the government found out what was happening and went to court to get an injunction. This was the situation in 1994 when the *Four Corners* team was putting together a program based on interviews with two agents of the Australian Secret Intelligence Service (ASIS) who had operated as spies from Australian embassies in the Middle East, India and Asia. I was taken to a private television studio on Sydney's North Shore to watch the interviews and provide legal advice. The program-makers thought that there was a real risk of the story leaking if the ABC's own studios were used. There was no doubt that the agents worked in a world where mistakes could be lethal. They told how locals in some countries, recruited by MI6 or the CIA, had been killed and how defectors could meet the same fate.

On the night that the program was due to go to air at 8.30pm, I watched the ABC news an hour earlier. Until then *Four Corners* had been advertised as a look at the Russian political scene. At the end of the news, however, the real subject was announced. It was too late for the government to get to the courts. The Foreign Minister, Gareth Evans, complained angrily about the conduct of the ABC but its managing director, David Hill, was an equally forceful personality and defended the deception. Like *The Moonlight State*, however, this program had some long-term consequences. Two days after the telecast the federal government set up an inquiry into ASIS which recommended that the organisation have a statutory charter and that there be some scrutiny of its activities by the Inspector-General of Intelligence and Security and also by a parliamentary committee.[20] And in 2001 these recommendations were largely adopted in federal legislation.[21]

The role of ASIS illustrates the difficult questions that can sometimes confront media organisations or book publishers in deciding whether to reveal classified material. If someone's life is going to be endangered, that is a much better reason not to publish than fear of an injunction. But very often the supposedly top secret information disclosed is simply embarrassing to one of the organisations in the defence and security area. In 1961 the *New York Times* knew about the plans of the Kennedy administration to sponsor an invasion of Cuba by exiles from Castro's rule. Under pressure from Washington, the story was not published. If it had been, it might have aborted the invasion and saved the United States government the humiliation of the Bay of Pigs fiasco.

The various legal cases recounted in this book and the political events witnessed or written about – sometimes both – represent some small pieces of history during the post-war years in modern Australia. It is true that those who have corresponded with that period like myself by being born in the late 1940s and the 1950s – the so-called baby boomers – have largely had good lives in comparison to most of their forbears. Until that time life in this country, if not nasty, brutish and short, was relatively harsh for all but a small section of the community. Inevitably prosperity has brought its own, different problems and it is clear that affluence does not necessarily equate with individual well-being.

The link between the two chief subjects of this book, history and law, is that they both proceed on the basis of limited materials. In the case of the book on the Whitlam government, for example, I was personally present at some of the events described but others who were also there at the same events had different recollections.

Contemporaneous documentary records were often more reliable than individual memory but even they depended to some extent on the view of the author as to what was important and what was not. It became clear to me in writing history that the information selected for inclusion involved considerable choice on the part of the recorder.

In somewhat similar fashion the adversarial process of litigation used in this country for both civil and criminal cases largely depends for its outcome on how the lawyers on each side identify the questions to be decided and select the material that they will rely on to support their client's position. It is obvious that in this exercise accident or human error can result in some evidence being omitted that might have caused the case to be decided differently. There is an appeal process to deal with judicial errors but not to make up for deficiencies in the way the case was presented by one side or the other. There has to be finality in litigation, however, so that a party normally only gets one chance to make out their case.

To this extent, the ideals of historical truth and justice under the law often fall short of perfection. That is not to say that they should not be zealously pursued but only that practitioners of history and law, and their students and clients, need to be aware of the chimera that lies at the heart of both professions.

ENDNOTES

1. Solicitor-General: Centre Stage in the Law

[1] *State of New South Wales v Lepore* (2003) 212 CLR 511; *State of New South Wales v Godfrey* (2004) Aust Torts Reports 81-741

[2] *RPS v The Queen* (2000) 199 CLR 620; *Keir v The Queen* (2002) 127 A Crim R 198

[3] *New South Wales v Commonwealth* (2006) (2) 229 CLR 1

[4] "Bashir sought advice on sacking government", *Sydney Morning Herald*, 11 June 2010

[5] See *Solicitor-General Act* 1969 (NSW) s 3

[6] *Uncertain Justice: Inside Australia's Legal System* (New Holland, 2000, Sydney)

[7] *Uncertain Justice* at 69

[8] *Sydney Morning Herald*, 17 October 2000

[9] *Sydney Morning Herald*, 20 October 2000

[10] See *Crimes (Sentencing Procedure) Amendment (Standard Minimum Sentencing) Act* 2002 (NSW)

[11] *Surveillance Devices Act* 2007 (NSW) s 19 (the previous legislation was the *Listening Devices Act* 1984 (NSW))

[12] *Surveillance Devices Act* 2007 (NSW) s 51

[13] *Surveillance Devices Act* 2007 (NSW) s 20

[14] *Independent* (UK), 7 March 2002

[15] *DPP (Vic) v Scott* (2003) 141 A Crim R 497 at 498-499

[16] *Children (Criminal Proceedings) Act* 1987 (NSW) s 13

[17] *The Queen v T* (2001) 122 A Crim R 206

[18] *The Queen v T* [2003] NSWCCA 357

[19] *Smith v The Queen* (2001) 206 CLR 650

[20] *The Queen v Keir* (2002) 127 A Crim R 198

[21] *The Queen v K* (2003) 144 A Crim R 468

[22] *Jury Act 1977* (NSW) s 68C

[23] See *Attorney-General (NSW) v John Fairfax & Sons Ltd* (1985) 6 NSWLR 695 at 711-712

[24] See *Sheppard v Maxwell, Warden* (1966) 384 US 333

[25] *Keir v The Queen* [2007] NSWCCA 149

[26] *Skaf v The Queen* (2004) 60 NSWLR 86

[27] *Criminal Justice Act* 2003 (UK) Part 11, Chapter 1

[28] *Crimes (Criminal Organisations Control) Act* 2009 (NSW)

[29] *Serious and Organised Crime (Control) Act* 2008 (SA)

[30] *State of South Australia v Totani* (2010) 242 CLR 1

[31] *Wainohu v New South Wales* (2011) 243 CLR 181

[32] *Assistant Commissioner Condon v Pompano Pty Ltd* (2013) 295 ALR 638.

2. The Way We Lived Then: A Child of the 1950s

[1] Launceston *Examiner*, 19 April 1893

[2] *Daily Telegraph*, 10 April 1893

[3] *Daily Telegraph*, 17 April 1893

[4] *The Advocate*, April 1930

[5] Maryanne Confoy, *Morris West: Literary Maverick* (Wiley, 2005, Milton) at 62-63

[6] *The Australian*, 14-15 April 2007

[7] Quoted in Gerard Henderson, *Mr Santamaria and the Bishops* (Studies in the Christian Movement, 1982, Sydney) at 172

[8] Patrick Morgan (Ed), *BA Santamaria: Running the Show: Selected Documents: 1939-1996* (The Miegunyah Press, 2008, Melbourne) at 113

[9] *Catholic Worker*, (No 472) July 1976. See also Bruce Duncan, *Crusade or Conspiracy?: Catholics and the Anti-Communist Struggle in Australia* (UNSW Press, 2001, Sydney) at 252

[10] James McClelland, *Stirring the Possum: A Political Autobiography* (Viking, 1988, Melbourne) at 7-8

[11] *The Advocate*, 15 December 1966

[12] *The Advocate*, 22 December 1966

[13] *The Advocate*, 12 January 1967

[14] *The Advocate*, 2 February 1967

3 Crime and Punishment: Counsel for the Prosecution

1. *Sentencing Act* 1989 (NSW)
2. *Sentencing Act* 1989 (NSW) s 13A; see also *Crimes (Life Sentences) Amendment Act* 1989 (NSW); *Prisons (Serious Offenders Review Board) Amendment Act* 1989 (NSW); *Sentencing (Life Sentences) Amendment Act* 1989 (NSW)
3. *Crimes Legislation Amendment (Existing Life Sentences) Act* 2001 (NSW)
4. *Sentencing Legislation Further Amendment Act* 1997 (NSW)
5. *Baker v The Queen* (2002) 130 A Crim R 417
6. *Baker v The Queen* (2004) 223 CLR 513
7. *Elliott v The Queen* (2007) 234 CLR 38
8. *Crump v New South Wales* (2012) 286 ALR 658
9. *Folbigg v The Queen*
10. *Folbigg v The Queen* (2005) 152 A Crim R 35
11. *Folbigg v The Queen* [2005] HCA Trans 657
12. *Folbigg v The Queen* [2007] NSWCA 371
13. *Thomas v Mowbray* (2007) 237 ALR 194
14. "Violent role models make peace unlikely", *The Australian*, 20 January 2004
15. "Remembering paradise: forever lost in the flames", *Sydney Morning Herald*, 12-13 July 2008
16. "No job veto for judges, Kirby", *The Australian*, 8 June 1999
17. *Burrell v The Queen* (NSW Supreme Court, 19 December 2003)
18. *Burrell v The Queen* [2004] NSWCCA 185
19. *Burrell v The Queen* [2005] HCA Trans 103 (4 March 2005)
20. *Burrell v The Queen* [2007] NSWCCA 65
21. *Burrell v The Queen* [2007] NSWCCA 79
22. *Burrell v The Queen* (2008) 248 ALR 428
23. *Burrell v The Queen* [2009] NSWCCA 163

4 Outward Bound: Melbourne to Washington

1. "The ALP: Is the Party over?", *The Summons* (1967)
2. "A Victorian Era", *The Summons* (1968)
3. Michael Kirby, *Sir Edward McTiernan: A Centenary Reflection* (NSW St Thomas More Society, 1991)
4. Michael Sexton and Lawrence W Maher, *The Legal Mystique: The role of lawyers in Australian society* (Angus & Robertson, Sydney, 1982) at 54
5. John Douglas Pringle, *Australian Accent* (Chatto & Windus, London, 1958) at 199
6. See e.g., *Edwards v The Queen* [1975] AC 648

5 The Great Crash: Inside the Whitlam Government

1. Neil Brown, *On the other hand ... Sketches and Reflections from Political Life* (Poplar Press Canberra, 1993) at 168
2. George Allen & Unwin Sydney, 1979
3. *Illusions of Power* at 138
4. *Illusions of Power* at 148
5. *Illusions of Power* at 135
6. *Illusions of Power* at 151
7. *Illusions of Power* at 166-167
8. *Catholic Weekly*, 18 September 1975
9. *Illusions of Power* at 209-210
10. Scribe, Melbourne, 2005

6 Publish and be Damned: Re-writing History

1. *The Bulletin*, 21 February 1976
2. "Sir John is not the real target", *Sydney Morning Herald*, 5 August 1976
3. See the article by Sir Anthony Mason in *Sydney Morning Herald* and *Age* of 27 August 2012.
4. Graham Lord, *John Mortimer: The Devil's Advocate* (Orion, 2005, London) at 216
5. (1982) 42 *Labour History* 137-139
6. Department of History and Politics, Melbourne State College

[7] Kai Bird, *The Color of Truth: McGeorge and William Bundy: Brothers in Arms* (Touchstone, 1998, New York) especially at 291-295

[8] Richard Walsh and George Munster, *Documents on Australian Defence and Foreign Policy 1968-1975* (Angus & Robertson, 1980, Sydney)

[9] *Commonwealth of Australia v John Fairfax & Sons Limited* (1980) 147 CLR 39

[10] *War for the Asking: Australia's Vietnam Secrets* (Penguin, 1981, Melbourne) at 90-91

[11] *War for the Asking* at 96

[12] *Sydney Morning Herald*, 23 May 1981

[13] *War for the Asking: How Australia invited itself to Vietnam* (New Holland, 2002, Sydney)

[14] See *Royal Commission on Australia's Security and Intelligence Agencies, Report on Term (c)* (December, 1983); David Marr, *The Ivanov Trail* (Nelson, 1984, Melbourne)

7 Man and Machine: The World of Politics

[1] *The Bulletin*, 23 October 1984

[2] Mark Latham, *The Latham Diaries* (Melbourne University Press, 2005, Melbourne) at 39

[3] *The Bulletin*, 8 February 1983

[4] *The Australian*, 29 May 1986

[5] *The Bulletin*, 24 December 1985

[6] *The Australian*, 29 May 1986

[7] *Fiji Times*, 18 May 1988

[8] *Reid v Special Broadcasting Service* [1989] A DEF R 40, 301; see also *Kelly v Special Broadcasting Service* [1990] VR 69

[9] Arthur Schlesinger Jr, *The Age of Roosevelt: Volume III: The Politics of Upheaval* (Heinemann, 1961, London) at 409

[10] *Sydney Morning Herald*, 6 October 1998

[11] Rodney Cavalier, *Power Crisis: The self-destruction of a state Labor Party* (Cambridge University Press, 2010, Sydney) at 51

[12] Marilyn Dodkin, *Bob Carr: The Reluctant Leader* (University of NSW Press, 2003, Sydney) at 13

[13] Christopher Clark, *Iron Kingdom: The Rise and Downfall of Prussia 1600-1947* (Penguin Books, 2007, London) at 521

8 Meet the Mystique: Taking on the Bar

1. *The Legal Mystique: The role of lawyers in Australian society* (Angus & Robertson, 1982, Sydney) at 2-4
2. *The Legal Mystique* at 5
3. *Australian Financial Review*, 25 June 1982
4. F.C. Hutley, "The Role of Lawyers in Australian Society", *Quadrant*, November 1982 at 32
5. Humphrey McQueen, "The Legal Mystique: A Review", (1982) *Legal Service Bulletin* 159
6. Kevin Bell, "Not all the legal masks come off ..." *Australian Society*, 17 December 1982 at 29
7. R.L. Sharwood,, Book Review (1982) *Law Institute Journal* 826
8. H. Stone, "The Public Influence of the Bar" (1934) 48 *Harvard Law Review* 1 at 7
9. Chris Masters, *Inside Story* (Angus & Robertson, 1992, Sydney) at 71-72
10. *Bellino v ABC* (1996) 185 CLR 183
11. Phillip Knightley and Caroline Kennedy, *An Affair of State: The Profumo Case and the Framing of Stephen Ward* (Jonathan Cape, London, 1987)
12. Phillip Knightley, *A Hack's Progress* (Vintage, London, 1998) at 185
13. *Sydney Morning Herald*, 2 March 1985
14. See e.g., *Edelsten v Richmond* (NSW Court of Appeal, 11 November 1988, unreported); *Edelsten v Ward [No. 1]* 1989 63 ALJR 345; *Edelsten v Ward [No. 2]* 1989 63 ALJR 346
15. See *R v Edelsten* (1989) 18 NSWLR 213; (1990) 21 NSWLR 542

9 The Human Factor: Victims of Law and Medicine

1. *Daily Mirror*, 7 November 1988
2. Royal Commission into NSW Police Service (1997) Vol 4 at 7.153-7.155
3. *New Idea*, 20 January 1990
4. NSW Parliamentary Debates (Legislative Council) Vol 213 at 309
5. *State of New South Wales v Deren*, Court of Appeal (NSW) 25 February 1999, unreported
6. *Gill v Walton* (1991) 25 NSWLR 190; *Walton v Gill* (1993) 177 CLR 378
7. Phil Cleary, *Cleary Independent* (Harper Collins, 1998, Sydney)

10 Free Speech: Theory and Practice

[1] *Lange v Australian Broadcasting Corporation* (1997) 189 CLR 520
[2] *New York Times v Sullivan* (1964) 376 US 254. See also *Curtis Publishing v Butts* (1967) 388 US 130; *Greenbelt Cooperative Publishing Association Inc v Bresler* (1971) 398 US 6; *Gertz v Robert Welch Inc* (1974) 418 US 323
[3] *Garrison v Louisiana* (1974) 379 US 64; *St Armant v Thompson* (1968) 390 US 727; *Times Inc v Pape* (1971) 401 US 279
[4] See *Defamation Amendment Act* (NSW) 2002; *Defamation Act* (NSW) 2005
[5] *Elliott v Seymour & Ors* (1995) 119 ALR 10; see also *Elliott v Seymour & Ors* (1993) 119 ALR 1
[6] *DPP (Vic) Reference No. 2 of 1996* (1997) 1996 A Crim R 519 at 523-524
[7] *Elliott v Seymour & Ors* (2001) 116 FCR 100
[8] Brian Toohey, "The Case for a President-less Republic", *Australian Financial Review*, 3 November, 1995
[9] "Think before you rock the boat", *The Australian,* 28 May, 2003
[10] "Why Australia needs its own statute of liberty", *Sydney Morning Herald*,7-8 March 2009
[11] Jonathan Sumption QC, "Judicial and Political Decision-making: The Uncertain Boundary" – FA Mann Lecture 2011.
[12] Gerald Gunther, *Learned Hand: The Man and the Judge* (Knopf, New York, 1994) at 548
[13] "Case for the persecution" *Sydney Morning Herald*, 11-12 October 2008
[14] "From sport to the media, we must be free to offend", *Australian*, 12 July, 2012
[15] The Hon R Finkelstein QC, Report of the independent inquiry into the media and media regulation (Commonwealth of Australia, Canberra, 2012)
[16] *Attorney General for New South Wales v Time Inc Magazine Co Pty Limited (No. 2)* (NSW Court of Appeal, 21 October 1994, unreported)
[17] *Attorney General v Times Newspapers Ltd* [1974] AC 273
[18] *Sydney Morning Herald*, 21 July 1994
[19] Kate Davies, *When Innocence Trembles* (Harper Collins, Sydney, 1994)
[20] Commission of Inquiry into the Australian Secret Intelligence Service, Report on the Australian Secret Intelligence Service (1995)
[21] See *Intelligence Services Act* 2001 (Cth)

ACKNOWLEDGEMENTS

The manuscript of this book was carefully read by my wife, Gae, and my old friend and sometime co-author, Laurence Maher, both of whom made many helpful suggestions. The text was very skilfully edited by John Nethercote who also made numerous constructive comments about questions of substance and style.

The book represents a thin slice of Australian history over the post-war years but most of the persons mentioned in its pages have made their own contribution to the ideas and events of those times.

INDEX

Abadee, Justice Alan 207
Abbott, Mitchell 87
Abeles, Sir Peter 168
ABC Legal Department 188
ACTU 132
Advocate (*The*) 32, 50-1, 53
Agnew, Spiro 87-8
Alexander, Mary 155
Al-Qaeda 61
Anderson, Peter 175
Arena, Franca, MLC 206
Armstrong, Susan 123, 126
Astor, Lord 191
Attorney-General (Cth) 1-2, 5, 33, 48, 65-6, 95-100, 107, 110, 112-3, 115-6, 120, 144, 215
Attorney-General (NSW) 6, 12, 63, 77, 125, 135, 205, 230, 244-6
Attorney-General's Department (Cth) 96, 121, 144
Australian (*The*) 39, 61, 83, 105, 161, 167, 192, 243
Australian Airlines 166
Australian Broadcasting Corporation (ABC) 151, 188-9, 191, 214, 225-8, 232-5, 237, 248
Australian Constitution 3, 109, 238-9
Australian Defamation Law and Practice 232
Australian Financial Review 182, 236

Australian Journalists' Association 99
Australian Labor Party (ALP) 28, 42, 125, 152, 168-9, 173-4
Australian Legal Aid Office 102
Australian National University 97, 103, 121
Australian Republican Movement (ARM) 236-7
Australian Secret Intelligence Service (ASIS) 248-9
Australian Securities and Investment Commission 235
Australian Security Intelligence Organisation (ASIO) 110, 135, 247
Australian Workers' Union 27

Babb, Lloyd, SC 240
Bailey, Dr Harry 211-3
Balding, Janine 58
Baldwin, Peter 152
Baker, Allan 55-8
Bar Association (NSW) 10, 65, 128, 152, 176
Barbour, Peter 110
Barker, Ian, QC 68-9
Barry, Paul 232, 235
Barwick, Sir Garfield 3, 5, 135
Bashir, Professor Marie 5
Basten, Justice John 123

Bavadra, Dr 169, 171-2
Bay of Pigs 249
Beattie, Peter 61
Beazley, Kim 163, 232
Behm, Allan 38
Bell, Justice Kevin 183
Bellace, Janice 89
Bellino, Vincenzo 191
Bennett, Ken 158
bill of rights 239, 241-2
Bindoon 246
Bird, Kai 137
Bjelke-Petersen, Sir Joh 189-90
Blair, Tony 62
Blazey, Peter 106
Bolte, Sir Henry 74
Bond, Alan 168, 232, 235
Bosphorus 82
Bowen, Chief Judge Nigel 188
Brazil, Patrick 95, 116
Briot, Geoff 114, 178
Brown, Gordon 167
Brown, Neil, QC 96-7, 107
Buddin, Terry 123
Bulletin (The) 64, 121, 123, 127, 154, 156, 166
Bundy, McGeorge 137
Bundy, William 137-8
Bureau of Crime Statistics (NSW) 8-9
Burns, John 82
Burrell, Bruce 67-9
Burrows, John 192-3, 226

Business School (Macquarie University) 186
Button, Senator John 99, 164

Cahill, Ron 71
Cahill, Archbishop Thomas 108
Cairns, Jim 104-6, 189
Cairns, Phillip 105
Calwell, Arthur 42, 145
Campbell, Ian 82
Carlton Football Club 232, 235
Carr, Bob 5, 8, 155, 162, 174-7
Castledare 246
Catholic Social Studies Movement 38
Catholic Weekly 107
Catholic Worker 42
Catholic Young Men's Society 32
Cavalier, Rodney 173
Central Land Council (NT) 188
Centre Unity Group 151-6
Chelmsford Royal Commission 211, 213, 216
Christian Brothers 32, 37, 46, 246-7
Cleary, Phil 217-8
Cleary, Vicki 217
Clontarf 246
Commissioner of Police (NSW) 23
Confoy, Maryanne 37
Connell, Laurie 168
Connor, Rex 104-6
conscription 70-1

Constitutional Convention (1973) 109
Coonan, Helen 126
Costello, Michael 173
Costigan, Michael 51
Council for Civil Liberties (CCL) 11, 135-6
Court of Criminal Appeal (NSW) 3, 14-22, 56-7, 59-60, 67-8, 126, 182, 210-11
Cowdery, Nick 194
Cowls, Eric Farnborough Sear 105-6
Crabb, Steven 234-5
Crean, Frank 115
Crimes Act 10, 138, 146
Crimmins, Peter 50
Cronkite, Walter 88
Crump, Kevin 55-6, 58

Dachau 83, 85
D'Arcy, Archbishop Eric 51-3
Dalton, David, SC 68
Davies, Kate 246
Dean, John 88-9
Deep Sleep Therapy 211
defamation law 189, 226, 231-2
Defence Department 38
de Jersey, Chief Justice Paul 22
Della Bosca, John 173, 230
Democratic Labor Party 39, 185
Department of Family and Community Services (NSW) 203

Department of Foreign Affairs 144, 171
Depression (Great) 33, 44
Deren, Dawn 202ff
Deren, Tony 201ff
Director of Public Prosecutions 2, 10, 15-16, 67, 193-4 (NSW)
Diem, Ngo Dinh 39
Disney, Julian 123, 126
DNA evidence 3, 12, 18, 136
Dodkin, Marilyn 176
Donald, Bruce 122, 188-9, 226, 232
Doogue, Geraldine 237
Dunstan, Don 116-7, 169-71
Durack, Senator Peter 96
Durrell, Lawrence 92
Dyer, Ron 158
Dynan, Billy 31, 34
Dynan, Eileen 26, 31
Dynan, Jack 38
Dynan, Michael 31
Dynan, Molly 34, 36-7, 197
Dynan, Rita 34-6

Egan, Michael 162
Easson, Mary 155, 173
Easson, Michael 173
Edelsten, Dr Geoffrey 197-200
Edmonds, Joe 185
Edwards, John 137
Elders IXL 232-3
Elliott, John 232-5
Elliott, Victoria 233-5

Enderby, Kep 98-100, 106-8, 110, 113-7
Essendon Football Club 44-5
Evans, Senator Gareth 130, 248
Everett, Senator Mervyn 113
Eyers, Michael 146

Fabianism 167
Fabian Society 166
Faulkner, John 163-4
Federal Court of Australia 3, 123, 188, 233-5
Fiji 168-72
Finkelstein, Justice Ray 243
Finks Motorcycle Club 23-4
Finnane, Judge Michael 49
Fitzgerald Commission 190
Fitzgerald, Tony, QC 190
FitzSimons, Peter 232
Flannery, Christopher Dale 198, 200
Folbigg, Kathleen 59-60
Foreign Affairs Department 144
Four Corners 165, 189, 226-7, 248
Fox, Bishop Arthur 42, 51-3, 147
Fraser, Malcolm 96, 103, 106, 109-11, 113, 128, 144, 156-7, 162, 223
Freeman, Cardinal James 107
Freudenberg, Graham 145

Galitsky, Serge 186
Gallipoli 32
Gaudron, Justice Mary 1, 150, 180

Geelong Football Club 44-5, 76, 164
Georgetown University 90, 137
Gilham, "Uncle Harry" 105
Gilmore, Mary (Cameron) 30
Governors (State) 5
Governor-General 104, 112-4, 127-9, 169, 236-8
Green, Marshal 97
"Green mango murder" 14
Greenwood, Senator Ivor 112-3, 116
Greiner, Nick 55, 175-7
Griffin, Walter Burley 75
Grusovin, Deirdre 175, 205-6
GST 163
Gumbert, Mark 126

(A) Hack's Progress 193
Hahn, Stephen 206-8
Hand, Justice Learned 241
Harders, Clarrie 100, 116
Harley, Denis 131
Harrison, Ian 123
Hasluck, Sir Paul 142-3
Hawke, Bob 132, 146-7, 150, 152, 156-7, 160-1, 164, 166-8, 175, 217, 233
Hawker, Bruce 175
Hayden, Bill 106, 111, 150, 156-7, 160-1, 175, 232, 236
Hayne, Justice Ken 76
Health Insurance Commission 198
Heffey, Jacinta 71

Hells Angels Motorcycle Club 23
Henderson, Gerard 173
High Court 1, 3-4, 16-17, 23-4, 55, 57-9, 61, 65, 67-9, 76, 78, 80, 98, 128, 139, 150, 152, 181-2, 188, 191, 197, 213, 216, 227-9
Hill, David 221-2, 237, 248
HMAS *Voyager* 246
Hogan, Ray 169
Hollingworth, Archbishop Peter 167
Holman, William 30
Holmes, Justice Oliver Wendell 243
Holt, Harold 71
Horne, Donald 167, 237
Howard, John 61, 163, 167, 237
Howard government 3-4, 168
Hughes, Tom, QC 139
Hussein, Saddam 92
Hutley, Justice Frank 182-3

ICAC 176-7
Iemma, Morris 5
Igoumenitsa 82
Illusions of Power 100, 102-3, 192, 117, 132, 134-5
Independent Commission Against Corruption 176
industrial law 130, 146
Inside Story 189
International Labour Organisation 89
International Law Institute (Georgetown University) 137

(*The*) *Investigators* 189
IRA 62
Iremonger, John 98-9, 108, 114, 117, 132
Ivanov, Eugene 191
Ivanov, Valeri 146

Jaegerstaetter, Franz 50-1
James, Greg, QC 175
Jefferson, Thomas 86
Jesuits 46
Johns, Brian 139-40, 146
Johnson, Lyndon 87, 137-8, 141
Jones, Barry 167
Jones, Margaret 196
Joyce, James 49

Kane, Senator Jack 185
Kavanagh, Justice Tricia 162
Keating, Paul 117-8, 155, 161-6
Keeler, Christine 191-2
Keir, Thomas 17-19
Kelly, Bishop John 48
Kelly, Paul 144
Kelly, Tom 126
Keneally, Tom 237
Kennedy, Caroline 192
Kennedy, John F. 88, 138, 249
Kennedy, Robert 87
Kennedy, Ted 87
Kerr, Sir John 104, 112-3, 125-7
Khemlani, Tirath 104-5

Kirby, Justice Michael 57-8, 66, 77, 167, 216
Knightley, Phillip 192-3
Knights of the Southern Cross 42
Knox, Brian 158

Labourers' International Union 88
Lake Garda 178-9
Lake Ledro 179
Landcom 218
Lane, Simon 222-3
Lane, William 27-8, 30, 122
Lange, David 87, 227-8
Langton, Brian 218-9, 223
La Scala 83
Latham, Mark 156, 167
Laxdale, David 14-16
Law Society (NSW) 10, 65
Legal Aid Commission (NSW) 10
Legislative Assembly (NSW) 5, 155
Lewis, Sir Terence 189-90
Limone 178
Loans Affair 104, 106, 112
Lolita 135
Loosley, Stephen 153, 155, 176
Luchetti, Tony 159

Macmillan, Harold 191
McArdle, John, QC 82
McCallum, Lucy 207
McCarthy, John, QC 175-6
McCarthy, Mary 75

McClelland, Senator Jim 43, 107, 125
McClintock, Bruce, SC 207
McCormack (Dynan), Hannah 31, 34
McGregor, Malcolm 176
McGuinness, Paddy 177
McHugh, Jeannette 152
McHugh, Justice Michael 57, 152-3
McMahon, William 150
McMullan, Bob 157
McMullin, Ross 65
McQueen, Humphrey 183
McTiernan, Sir Edward 76-7, 79-81
Maher, Laurence 24, 78, 97, 180, 183
Maher, Michael 150
Maloney, Shane 152
Mannix, Archbishop Daniel 32, 39-40, 42
Mant, John 116
Mara, Ratu Sir Kamisese 169
Marist Brothers 46
Mason, Sir Anthony 128, 139
Masters, Chris 139, 189-91
MCG 45
Medibank 101
Medical Tribunal 197-8, 200
Melbourne Cricket Club 72
Melbourne University 33, 52, 70-1, 83, 91, 122, 185
Melbourne University Republican Club 235
Mellyn, John 86-7
Menadue, John 223

Menzies, Sir Robert 70-1, 141, 144-5, 168
Milat, Ivan 244-5
Mooney, Ellen 27
Mooney, James 27-30
(*The*) *Moonlight State* 189, 225
Morgan, Patrick 40
Morosi, Juni 104
Morse, Virginia 55-6
Mortimer, John, QC 129-30
"Mr Bubbles" 201-2, 206, 211
Murphy, Justice Lionel 97-8, 110, 182

National Crime Authority (NCA) 232-5
National Times 64, 123, 137
Neal, Belinda 172-3
Neave, Airey 62
New Australia (Paraguay) 27-9, 122
New Idea 205
New York Times 249
Newman College 52, 75
Newport, Barry QC 15
Nicholls, Martin 117
Nixon, Richard 88-9
Nomchong, Kylie 207

Oakes, Laurie 99, 144
Obeid, Eddie 173
O'Connor, Ellen 27
O'Connor, Kevin 76
Olympic Games, Munich (1972) 83
Orkopoulos, Milton 159

Packer, Kerry 232, 235
Palmer, Geoffrey 86-7, 228
Paltridge, Senator Shane 142
Parole Board (NSW) 56
Phillip electorate 150-4
Phillips, Chief Justice John 13
Police Integrity Commission (NSW) 2
Police Royal Commission (NSW) 203, 207
Powell, Anthony 185
Premier's literary awards (NSW) 65
Prime Minister's literary awards 65
Pringle, John Douglas 79
Privy Council 79-80
Profumo, John 191-2
Public Transport Authority (NSW) 219-220

Qantas 166
Quadrant 182

Rabuka, Colonel Sitiveni 169
Raby, Gae 106, 136, 160, 178, 197, 218
Raby, Jill 178
Racial and Religious Tolerance Act (Victoria) 242
Rae, Senator Peter 102
Ray, Senator Robert 161, 164
Rees, Nathan 5
Reid, Jeffrey 171

Richardson, Graham 153, 161, 172-3, 176, 232
Robb, Charles 87
Robertson, Tim, SC 175
Rockefeller, Nelson 88
Romanèche-Thorins 178
Roosevelt, President Franklin D 172
Rothman, Justice Stephen 153
Royal Society of General Practitioners 101
Ruckelshaus, William 97
Rudd government 164, 239, 241
Rumpole of the Bailey 129-30
Rusk, Dean 143
Ryan, Susan 114

Sackville, Justice Ron 123
Santamaria, B.A. 39-40, 42, 51-3, 147
Schlesinger, Arthur, Jnr 172
Seabeach Kindergarten 202-3, 205, 207-11
Selborne Chambers 194
Sellar, Jeff 76, 90
Serong, Michael 82
Serong, Ted 82
7.30 Report 189, 226, 232-4
Sexton, Cyril Francis 26, 32
Sexton, Gerald 27, 45
Sexton, John O'Connor 27
Sexton, Michael 8, 63, 133-4, 173,176, 183, 189, 236, 244
Sexton, Patrick 27

sexual abuse 47, 201, 205-6, 211, 246
Sharma, Harrish 170
Sharwood, Professor Robin 183
shearers' strike 28
Shaw, Jeff, QC 2-3
Sher, Jeff, QC 139, 233-4
60 Minutes 206, 209-10
Slattery, Justice Jack 212
Society of Labor Lawyers (NSW) 125
Sofronoff, Walter, QC 60
Solicitor-General (NSW) 1ff, 54, 61, 150, 180, 223-4, 230, 244
Solicitor-General (Queensland) 60-1
Solomon, David 110
Somare, Michael 109
Special Branch of NSW Police Force 135
Spielberg, Steven 83
Spigelman, Chief Justice Jim 155
State Rail Authority (SRA) 219, 221-3
Staunton, Patricia 173
Steering Committee 151-4, 159, 163
Stephens, Tony 8
Stevens, Sir John 12
Stiles, Alan 48
Stone, Justice Harlan 184
Stone, Justice Margaret 123
Street, Sir Laurence 127
Sullivan, Greg, QC 125

Sumner, Chris 130
Sumption, Justice Jonathan 240
Supreme Court (NSW) 2-3, 10, 23, 55-7, 60, 65, 67, 123, 153, 171, 181, 192, 207, 212, 216, 246
Supreme Court (Victoria) 13, 181, 183, 232-4
Swancott, Neal 99
Sydney Morning Herald 5, 8, 63-4, 123, 127, 139, 144-5, 153, 173, 194, 196, 242
Sydney University Law Graduates' Association 127

Tange, Sir Arthur 100
Taronga Park Zoo 218
Taylor, Justice 55
Thatcher, Margaret 62
The Great Crash 95ff, 117-9
The Legal Mystique 24, 78, 180, 182, 194, 196, 216
Theophanous, Andrew 133
Thermoskin 187
Thompson, Peter 214
Thorins, Romanèche 179
Tickner, Robert 126
Times (The) 192, 245-6
Tobin, T.K. (Terry), QC 184-5, 188, 192, 194, 197, 212-3, 231-2
Toohey, Brian 236
Tunney, Senator John 87
Turkish Consul-General 63
Turnbull, Malcolm 127, 237

Uncertain Justice 7, 9
University of New South Wales 122, 149
University of Virginia 85-6
Unsworth, Barry 174, 176
Unwin, Rayner 135
US Environment Protection Agency 97
US Supreme Court 78, 88-9, 184

Victorian Law Institute 102
Vietnam war 50, 70-1, 135-6
Vincent, Justice Frank 234

Walker, Frank 125-6, 135
Walker, Judith 226
Waller, Sir Keith 142
Walsh, Eric 146
Walsh, Max 99
War for the Asking 139-40, 143-4, 146
Ward, Stephen 191-3
Watergate 88
Watson, John Christian 30
Weatherburn, Don 8-9
West, Morris 37
Whelan, Bernard 66-7
Whelan, Kerry 66-8
White City Club 131
Who Weekly 244-5
Whitlam, Gough 5, 43, 74, 91, 94ff, 124-5, 128, 131, 133-4, 139, 157, 161, 166, 223, 249

Wilkinson, Marian 232
Windsor, Gerard 49
Windsor Hotel 109-10
Windsors (The House of Windsor) 195, 236
Woods, Greg, QC 159
Work Choices 3

Wran, Neville 125, 135, 158, 168, 176, 237
Wriedt, Senator Ken 115
Wright, Robert 76

Young Lawyers (NSW) 10
Young, Mick 146-7

www.ingramcontent.com/pod-product-compliance
Lightning Source LLC
Chambersburg PA
CBHW071832230426
43671CB00012B/1944